Contents

ACKNOWLEDGEMENTS

Sincere thanks to the following people for their help with this book and their support while I was in India.

Firstly, the one and only Deepak Gautam and then, in no particular order: Javagal Srinath, Anil Kumble, Mohammed Kaif, S.S. Das, Akash Chopra, Ajay Ratra, Ajit Agarkar, Parthiv Patel, Andrew Leipus, Adrian le Roux, Greg King, John Gloster, Sriram Bhargav, S. Ramakishnan (a.k.a. Ramki), Nandan, Sanjay Manjrekar, Dr Omkar, Saba Karim, Bruce Reid, Murali, Sandy Gordon, R. Kaushik, Ram Sharma, Arun Kumar Gopalakrish, Ramesh Rao, Pintu (a.k.a. Raghunath Basak), Shiv Shankar, Amrit Mathur, Trevor Crouch, Rocky Harris, Sundra Reddy, Kapila and Arvid Hari, Jayesh Patel and his family and friends, Nagesh Sharma, Robin Lindsay, S.N. Onkar, Yousuf Arakkal, Dave Lambert, Graham Wardrop, Yashovardhan Azad, Masood ul Hasan, Sohail Khan, Joy Battacharjya, Andrew Hall, Bob Woolmer, Anand Vasu, Nishant Arora, Clayton Murzello, Siddhartha Vaidyanathan, Ed Smith, Geoff and Helen, Sue and Tim, Hamish and Nicky, Cathie, Annabel, Isla and Jack, Sue and Robyn, Sandy and Chet, Gundry, Ron, Karl and Amyla Dantas, Donowyn and staff at Bombay Travels, Bruce and Peg, Ant and Ruth, John and Christine, the staff at the C.C.I., the Taj, and Café Mondegar, 'Going Nowhere', 'Dad's Army', everyone at the B.C.C.I. Mumbai office, Ansar, Hassan for the rugs and Kashmiri tea ('I am a small man, I have a car my own size').

Thanks to the following players and support staff. It was a privilege to work with you all.

The players: Sourav Ganguly, Rahul Dravid, Sachin Tendulkar, V.V.S. Laxman, Anil Kumble, Javagal Srinath, Virender Sehwag, Harbhajan Singh, Mohammed Kaif, Yuvraj Singh, Ashish Nehra, Zaheer Khan, Shiv Sundar Das, Sadagopan Ramesh, Hemang Badani, S. Sriram, Venkatesh Prasad, Sarandeep Singh, Murali Kartik, Ramesh Powar, Lakshmipathy Balaji, Irfan Pathan, Dinesh Mongia, Parthiv Patel, Sanjay Bangar, Ajay Ratra, Vijay Dahiya, Dinesh Karthik, Nayan Mongia, Deep Dasgupta, Samir Dighe, Ajit Agarkar, Aakash Chopra, Sairaj Bahutule, Nilesh Kulkarni, Wasim Jaffer, M.S. Dhoni, Tinu Yohannan, Narendra Hirwani, Harvinder Singh, Rohan Gavaskar, Gagandeep Singh, Shib Sankar Paul, Debashis Mohanty, Jacob Martin, Avishkar Salvi, Rahul Sanghvi, Connor Williams, Reetinder Sodhi, Sunil Joshi, Gautam Gambhir, Venkatapathy Raju, Amit Bhandari, Amit Mishra, R. Vijay Bharadwaj, Jai Prakash Yadav, Iqbal Siddiqui, Robin Singh, Amay Khurasiya, Joginder Sharma, Rakesh Patel, Ashish Kapoor, Abhijit Kale, Nikhil Chopra.

The support staff: Andrew Leipus, Nandan, Sumeet Pai, Adrian le Roux, Sriram Bhargav, S. Ramakrishnan/Ramki, Greg King, John Gloster, Bruce Reid, Sandy Gordon.

JOHN WRIGHT'S
Indian Summers

JOHN WRIGHT'S
Indian Summers

With Sharda Ugra & Paul Thomas

Hodder Moa

National Library of New Zealand Cataloguing-in-Publication Data

Wright, John, 1954-
John Wright's Indian Summers / by John Wright ; with Sharda
Ugra and Paul Thomas.
ISBN-13: 978-1-86971-062-0
ISBN-10: 1-86971-062-2
1. Wright, John, 1954- 2. Cricket—India. l. Thomas, Paul, 1951-
II. Ugra, Sharda. III. Title.
796.358092—dc 22

A Hodder Moa Book
Published in 2006 by Hachette Livre NZ Ltd
4 Whetu Place, Mairangi Bay
Auckland, New Zealand

Designed and produced by Hachette Livre NZ Ltd
Printed by Tien Wah Press Ltd, Singapore

Front cover: Getty Images
Back cover: John Wright

Dedicated to Harry and Georgie

WELCOME TO THE REAL WORLD

At first it seemed as if cricket wouldn't let me go, rather than the other way around.

It was late 1992: I was 38 and noticing another grey hair every time I shaved. It felt like it was time to stop playing games. After 15 years of test cricket I'd made myself unavailable for the tour of Zimbabwe and Sri Lanka in order to prepare for life after cricket, i.e. getting a real job and rejoining the real world. I hadn't retired as such — there was a home series against Australia coming up and I wasn't far short of becoming the first Kiwi to make 5000 test runs — but in a career context, I was in injury time.

Then I got a call from Ross Dykes, one of the New Zealand selectors. A bomb had gone off in Sri Lanka. Some players and the coach were thinking of opting out of the tour, so Dykes was looking for volunteers. I told him it wouldn't come to that because the team would stick together; they'd either all stay or they'd all come home. That was the New Zealand way.

But not any more, apparently. When the volunteers got to Sri Lanka, we found a group of players who'd withdrawn into themselves, as if they were in a state of shock. And these were the guys who'd decided to stay. I'd had two innings on artificial wickets in club cricket, and because of the disruption our build-up to the first test amounted to two one-dayers, in which I scored 0 and 6.

The first test was at Moratuwa, on the outskirts of Colombo. The Sri Lankan opening bowler obviously thought there was a nip in the air because he kept his short-sleeved sweater on. It was bad enough being hopelessly out of touch, but somehow that really rammed home the fact that I was the wrong man in the wrong place. I'd flown in from a raw New Zealand spring to the hottest conditions I've ever played in, and here I was, sweating like a hog in a sauna, facing a bloke tearing in off a long run, and he was still wearing his sweater. A misnomer if there ever was one: he looked like he'd stepped out of an air conditioning advert; I, on the other hand, was gushing sweat from places I didn't think you could sweat from.

I scratched around for an hour. It wasn't one of my better 11s. While I'd been learning about the real world, I'd forgotten how to bat. I reached the 5000 runs milestone in the second test, but we lost the game, and the series, 1–0. The final match of the tour was my one-day international swan song. I was run out for 1, left stranded in the middle of the wicket, too hot, too tired, too slow, and perhaps too old to make it back to the crease.

Despite that experience, or perhaps because of it, I was keen for one last tilt at the Aussies. For me, test cricket against Australia was what it was all about. The thought of it had fired my ambition when I was a kid on a North Canterbury farm reading *Six and Out*, Jack Pollard's famous book on Australian cricket, and listening to the commentaries of Alan McGilvray and Lindsay Hassett: big crowds and famous grounds and flint-eyed men in baggy green caps, who played for keeps. There was no better way to finish.

I finished test cricket as I started it — slowly — occupying the crease for 19 and a half hours over the course of the three tests. In the second test at Wellington, which not surprisingly ended in a draw, I made 118 runs (once out) in 578 minutes. If Virender Sehwag batted for that long he'd get 800. Steve Waugh was moved to point out that we weren't playing seven-day tests. Even I found my second innings painful, as I'd rolled an ankle and was getting grief from my dodgy back. Allan Border showed his caring side by standing at slip and calling to his fast bowler, Craig 'Billy' McDermott: 'Come on, Billy, hit those old bones.'

For reasons that in hindsight seem absurd, I didn't announce my retirement before the third test. I didn't want it to cloud the occasion or get in the way of the team's performance. I wanted to go quietly and without embarrassing myself.

I got a couple of 33s, which certainly beat a pair. In the second innings we needed 201 to win and square the series. As I walked out for the last time, Mark 'Paddy' Greatbatch, my tenth opening partner, urged me to look for ones. It wasn't quite, 'We'll get 'em in singles', but the gist was that we should go about it in a sensible and controlled fashion. He took guard, then stormed down the wicket like a Viking in a batting helmet and slogged a perfectly good ball from McDermott high into the terraces. 'Come on, Billy,' yelled Steve Waugh from gully, 'let's hit the teddy bear.'

But it was the teddy bear who was doing the hitting. Merv Hughes also got the treatment, and after one extravagant Greatbatch air shot, the cultivator of cricket's best-known face fungus launched a spray of saliva in the batsman's general direction. The subsequent mid-wicket face-off looked like a territorial dispute between two bull walruses. On my way to Eden Park the next morning, I got a call from Paul Holmes. I assumed he wanted to do a 'John Wright: This Is Your Life' interview and was prepared to be suitably modest, but all he wanted to talk about was the spitting scandal.

I was feeling pretty good until I was run out by a direct throw. I thought I was okay, but had forgotten that we'd entered the age of the television replay and the third umpire. I didn't know where to look to find out my fate. After the game I received a form confirming that I'd been run out. It looked a bit like a speeding ticket.

We won the test. I had a few beers with the team, and ended up in the Australian dressing room watching Mark Taylor do a passable imitation of my stance and deliberately slow pre-delivery routine, which often involved a minute adjustment to the sightscreen. I liked to play the game at my pace, and the fact that it enraged opposition bowlers and captains was a bonus. It certainly brought out the 'Captain Grumpy' side of Border, who never seemed to take my apologies at face value.

And that was that. I packed up my cricket bag for the last time and went home. I was an ex-cricketer and tomorrow was the first day of the rest of my life.

I began the transition process at Fletcher Challenge, then New Zealand's largest company. My path had been smoothed by John Hart, the head of employee relations, who within a few years would be coaching the All Blacks. My final interview was with the head of the building industries sector, John Hood, who's now Vice-Chancellor of Oxford University.

I started at the head office in Penrose. On my first day I was so apprehensive that I drove past the Fletchers building twice before pulling into the car park to commence my climb to middle management. It felt like the first day at a new school: I didn't really want to be there, I had no idea what to expect, but I knew I didn't have much choice.

I had to get used to my new colleagues looking at me strangely, obviously thinking: 'What the hell's he doing here?' I had to absorb the implications of the fact that many of the guys on my level and who, therefore, I'd be competing with for promotion, were 10 years younger than me and had MBAs and a rather frightening appetite for work. The main thing I learned was that there's a quick way to tell if a building supplies branch is any good: check out the state of the men's toilet.

I spent three months in a Placemakers branch doing every job there was. I discovered I was good at two things: driving a forklift and hiding from customers. Serving in the retail section was a nightmare. There was a fundamental imbalance in my relationship with the customers: they knew or quickly established who I was ('Don't I know you? Your face looks familiar.') but I had no idea what they were asking for or where to find it.

The tradesmen would come in first thing to get what they needed for that day's job. They weren't inclined to muck around; time was money and all that. Listening to them spell out what they wanted was like reading a foreign language menu: it could be steak and chips but, on the other hand, it could be raw sea slug on a bed of seaweed. I took cover behind lines like, 'G'day, Jack, how can I hold you up this morning?'

It was impossible to shake off the sense of being out of place. The people I dealt with saw me as a cricketer, not someone who could take them by the hand and lead them through the hardware/building supplies maze. One day an elderly lady asked me for a dozen pozi screws. I didn't know what they were but led her to the most likely aisle with that familiar sense of being under close scrutiny.

'I know your face from somewhere,' she said.

I waited, certain that she'd work out who I was before I found her screws. Sure enough: 'You're John Wright the cricketer, aren't you?'

I nodded.

'What are you doing here? Are you running short of money?'

Looking back on it, working at Fletchers was a valuable experience. It brought me back down to earth and gave me a crash course in everyday reality, which for many people boils down to earning a living doing something they wouldn't necessarily choose to do. I'd spent my adult life to that point playing a game that I took too seriously. As John Arlott supposedly said to Mike Brearley: 'Mike, you're the only one who understands that it doesn't really matter.'

After a year or so, one of my bosses admitted that he still hadn't found the key to unlock within me the desire that would ignite my business career. In turn, I admitted that some of the products I was supposed to get excited about didn't get my pulse racing. 'It's not about the products,' he said, 'it's about the people.'

I tried to take this on board, along with all the other advice I was given. I tried to get fired up about it. But despite all the help I was given and my desire to make a go of it, nothing I did in my new career was remotely as satisfying as grafting 40-odd on a green wicket against a pace attack who'd sniffed blood.

I moved from building supplies into the bloodstock industry, saddled with the impressive title of Commercial Manager, Wrightson Bloodstock. The main thing I learned there was that you can tell a race horse owner or breeder many things — that his personal hygiene isn't up to scratch, that his face gives small children nightmares, that his wife's as much of a run-around girl as his mother was — but you can't tell him his horse is a dud.

My last hurrah business-wise was as National Sales Manager for Ernest Adams, a food company renowned for its cakes. My brother Hamish and former Canterbury and All Black fullback Robbie Deans ran the distribution side, and the main thing I learned there was that business, friends and family can be a difficult mix. It's probably no coincidence that for both Robbie and me Ernest Adams was our last stop before going back to our respective sports.

I also learned that supermarket owners are tough hombres. Some of them made Colin Croft seem like the Dalai Lama. As far as they were concerned, if you didn't show up with the right products and the right answers then you shouldn't have shown up at all.

Once I had to fly from Christchurch to Auckland to explain to the girl in charge of the cake stand at Henderson Pak'N Save, our largest customer, and her older and even less forgiving category manager, why we'd delivered pink meringues instead of white ones. Having my eyebrows singed by a fire-breathing supermarket manager over a couple of missing cakes gave me an insight into how sheepdogs are made to feel when they fail to follow instructions.

At Ernest Adams they probably remember me as the man who shot his company car. One night after work I borrowed a mate's 12-gauge shotgun and set off to rid the world of a couple of infuriatingly noisy birds that hung out at the end of my drive. As I was trying to get out of the car I somehow triggered a premature discharge that blew a sizeable hole in the driver's door. The noise inside the car was literally stunning. When the smoke cleared I found myself rocking back and forth in the driver's seat, shaken and disorientated, but relieved that I'd managed to pull off this difficult feat without losing any body parts.

By this stage, I recognised the fundamental truth that I hadn't changed jobs in the sense of going from doing something for $X a year to doing much the same thing somewhere else for $Y a year; I'd gone from doing something I had a passion for, to doing something completely different which, with the best will in the world, I wasn't passionate about.

Not that my passion for cricket was always evident to other people or, for that matter, myself. When you're caught up in the year-round professional grind it's easy to forget that, first and foremost, you do it because you love it; it's easy to lose sight of the fact that you're one of the lucky ones who get paid to do what they love.

Familiarity can breed contempt: you can slip into the pro's mindset of getting the job done rather than playing cricket, and lose some of the passion that propelled you into a county cricket contract and the New Zealand team. Peter McDermott, a former chairman of New Zealand Cricket, said the only thing I hated more than playing cricket was not playing cricket. He was certainly half right: I hated not playing cricket.

It's not until you have a real job and you're sitting in an office looking at the clock and realising only two minutes have passed since you last looked at it, that you really get it. That's when you realise you never really appreciated what you had, and you're forced to acknowledge that it left a hole in your life which you haven't been able to fill.

At the same time you're suffering the post-retirement blues or its advanced form, Limelight Deprivation Syndrome. You feel a sense of loss, bordering on resentment, that you're no longer involved. Cricket seems to be getting along just fine without you; in fact, it's almost as if your career never happened. One day you're having those last-minute chats with the selectors and tactical discussions with the captain, the next an old lady's asking you for a dozen pozi screws. One day you're deafened by the roar of the crowd, the next the only sound is the ticking of the clock.

What I really missed was competing. It's pure and basic out in the middle: they've got a ball, you've got a bat. You're the master of your own destiny.

You lose yourself, disappear into a zone that's impossible to replicate in everyday life. You strive to achieve a state of total concentration in which everything you know, and think you know, about the game is distilled into two or three key thoughts. Having got to that plane of intense focus, you then have to switch off at the last moment and let your instinct take over.

Ed Smith, a talented cricketer — Kent, Middlesex and England — and writer, gave me this quote from W.H. Auden: 'The one necessary prerequisite for all works of art and for scientific innovation, no matter how great or small, is an intensity of attention or, less pompously, love.'

I'd aspired to a successful second career. I wanted at all costs to avoid living in the past. In a sense, I failed. I thought I'd be like former All Black captain David Kirk and make a seamless transition to the business world, but I didn't enjoy it enough. To succeed at anything you have to work bloody hard, and if you don't love it, the chances are you'll struggle to do the work.

The call came in February 1997, in the middle of a management meeting. A year earlier, chatting to Graham Cowdrey, son of Colin and, like his father, a Kent player, I'd asked him to let me know if any interesting opportunities came up. He was ringing to say the coaching job at Kent was about to become vacant: did that qualify as an interesting opportunity?

I didn't have to think about it. Business, particularly the cake business, wasn't my thing; for better or for worse, cricket was. I couldn't wait to get back to it.

Back to the Future

Kent was where it all started. In 1976 I got the opportunity to play for their second team, which was a toe in the door of county cricket. I set off like Dick Whittington, leaving behind a girlfriend and a stereo, both in prime condition. The lanes of Kent weren't paved with gold but people who knew a thing or two murmured in the right ears and at the end of that season I was offered a contract by Derbyshire, despite having played only 11 first-class games.

And now I was back. It felt good to walk across the beautiful St Lawrence Ground, home of Kent cricket, and see the familiar faces: Brian Luckhurst, who ran the indoor centre; Alan Ealham, the second team coach; and Mike Denness and Derek Underwood, who were on the cricket committee. They'd all been around in 1976, which emphasised the continuity and tradition.

Tradition runs deep at Kent. It was the last county to accept coloured clothing. The St Lawrence Ground had a lime tree inside the boundary, in the field of play. In most parts of the world that tree would have been deemed an anachronism long ago but it was part of the fabric of Kent cricket. If you hit the tree, it was an automatic four. When the tree died recently, they didn't console themselves with the thought that, when all was said and done, it was a relic of a bygone era. They planted a new tree. Dave Gilbert, the former Australian fast bowler who became a coach and administrator, reckoned this was typical of English cricket: 'A tree gets in the way for 200 years and, when it falls down, instead of cheering, they plant a new one.'

The Kent cricket scene wasn't exactly blue collar. The cynics reckoned general committee members were elected on the basis of what sort of car they drove and what school they went to. If those were, respectively, a Toyota Starlet and Gravesend Comprehensive, you had a lot of ground to make up.

I played golf with E.W. Swanton, the doyen of English cricket writers and still a keen Kent supporter at the age of 90. E.W. was a member of Royal St George's at Sandwich which has hosted 12 British Open Championships. I've heard it said that the members there treat their dogs better than their wives.

Kent didn't have a chief executive, it had a secretary. He was an ex-brigadier who kept a tight hold of the purse strings and attached great importance to players looking the part. On the first morning of Canterbury Week, the annual cricket festival, he became greatly agitated when three players turned up unshaven. The committee would find this intolerable, he said, and there would be a flood of complaints. I was instructed to commence Operation Baby's Bum forthwith. It turned out that one of the players was growing a beard, which wasn't in breach of his contract, and another had six stitches in his face and couldn't shave.

The county game has its critics, but it's unique and provides the best cricketing education you can get. That's because you play a hell of a lot of cricket and playing is the best way to learn. Better than nets, better than academies, better even than being coached.

And as I was quickly reminded, it's full of characters. On the first morning of my first game in charge, I was walking through the car park in my tracksuit with my sawn-off fielding practice bat when I bumped into Peter Willey, the hard-bitten ex-England all-rounder turned umpire. I hadn't seen him for years, but nothing had changed. 'Come over here with your little bat to take our money, eh?' he said.

The lads up north like getting stuck in to teams from the soft and affluent south and at Derby the locals were particularly raucous in the field. Nigel Plews, one of the umpires, asked the Derbyshire captain, Dominic Cork, if their twelfth man was doing anything.

'Don't think so,' said Cork. 'Why?'

'Well then, send him down to Boots to get me some ear plugs.'

I often travelled with our scorer, Jack, either in his Jaguar or my sponsored car. Navigation wasn't our strong suit and we bickered over who was at fault like a husband and wife whose marriage has seen better days. Going around in circles somewhere near Gatwick one night, Jack advised me to 'stick your bloody head out the window and listen for the planes'.

I did a lot of preparation before leaving New Zealand, which included picking some good coaching brains. John Hart encouraged me to understand the culture and avoid going in with a head full of preconceived ideas.

I asked Glenn Turner how he coached batting. 'I tell them, always look to play with the full face of the bat,' he said, 'and if you're moving sideways when the ball's delivered, you'll struggle.'

This was promising; I was clearly on to a good thing. 'What else?' I asked eagerly.

'Nothing else,' he said. 'That's it.'

I was raw and keen and jumped right in, telling the players what I stood for and setting some pretty lofty goals. The players were enthusiastic, although there's always a honeymoon period as they respond to a new voice and a new way of doing things. To begin with anyway, everyone wants to get along.

My name and standing had changed overnight. I was now 'Coach' and judging by the way the players sought my advice and hung on my every word, it seemed as if I'd suddenly become the fount of all knowledge. I resisted the temptation to believe that.

I watched and listened very carefully, and took complaints and hard luck stories about the previous regime with a grain of salt: 'The trouble was I never got to bat at three — that's my best position by far' and 'He always bowled me from the wrong end at the wrong time to the wrong fields.' I was determined to make judgements at first hand, rather than based on spin, whether that was from the horse's mouth or behind his back.

Ed Smith, just down from Cambridge University — and like a breath of fresh air — laid his cards on the table: 'Hello Coach, I'm Ed. Some people say I'm arrogant and maybe I am, but I'm going to play for England and you're going to help me. Now here's a list of things I need to work on.'

Then there was Matthew Valentine Fleming, formerly of Eton and the British Army (he'd served in Northern Ireland), whose family owned a bank. He was a nephew of Ian Fleming, the creator of James Bond, and had a touch of Bond's reckless courage: no matter how many fielders the opposition put out for the hook shot, he'd still go for it.

After some pre-season nets, I suggested to Graham Cowdrey that he should change the position of his bottom hand. That night at the pub he reminded me that he'd been around for a while now, since my day in fact, and it was a little late to be changing his grip. Lesson Number One: If it ain't broke . . .

That first season was a bittersweet experience: we finished second in three of the four competitions, including the championship, in which we were pipped by four points by Glamorgan under current England coach Duncan Fletcher. The consensus seemed to be that we'd had a great season. When it was put to Fleming that we'd often been the bridesmaid but never the bride, he replied that 'at least we got to go to the wedding'.

I looked at it differently, believing that we'd keep coming second unless we got rid of more than a third of the 24 players on the staff. The cricket committee thought I'd gone mad. After that meeting I went through the exercise of separating the squad into three categories: those who were good enough and hungry for success; those who were good enough but not hungry enough; and those who were neither. There was roughly the same number of names in each category. Kent being Kent, and county cricket being county cricket, it was almost three years before the majority of the squad fell into the first category.

This episode summed it up: the secretary informed me that he'd signed a player for another three years. He obviously regarded this as a considerable coup, but if he'd bothered to run it past me, I would have told him that while the player concerned wasn't at the very top of my hit-list, he was up there.

The cricket committee chairman was Derek Ufton, a man of wisdom and integrity. He'd been a professional footballer with Charlton Athletic and played a lot of cricket for Kent, mostly for the Seconds because he overlapped with Hopper Levett and Godfrey Evans, two of the finest keepers from a county with a tradition of producing England glovemen.

He gave me a lot of good advice, notably that I should always bring the debate back to the question: what's best for Kent County Cricket Club? I asked that question and its Indian variation — 'what's the best for the team?' — many times. If everyone involved with a sports team, whether amateur or professional, was always honest enough to ask that question and brave enough to act on the answer, life would be less complicated and teams more successful.

There were too many people involved with Kent — and I found the same later for India — who avoided asking the question, let alone answering it and following through on the answer. They looked at things from a personal perspective, which seldom translated into decisions that helped to improve the team's performance. As coach, my sole focus was on winning cricket matches. The Kent County Cricket Club exists to win cricket matches, which pleases its fans and satisfies its sponsors. If it's a choice between a new car park and a quality fast bowler, the question should be: which of the two will win us more games? What's more important: performance or all the peripheral stuff?

Not that I got everything right. Sometimes I baffled the players. Sometimes I talked too much and smiled too little. In my second year I attached too much importance to nailing down our vision and values and put too much pressure on the young batsmen. I tended to live every ball, which isn't a recipe for serenity. Cricket starts in the morning and finishes in the evening, so it's like watching your rugby team play four games a day, every day.

I discovered that nothing turned players off like the word 'don't'. 'Don't' is a stark, blunt prohibition. Watch your audience closely when you say it and you'll see eyes tilt down and mouths twist into sour shapes. It activates that bloody-minded rebel within all of us who delights in doing exactly what we've just been told not to do. Far better to provide a positive alternative — 'play straight' instead of 'don't hook that quickie from the top end'.

I discovered that the simple act of saying 'good morning' can be very effective. It's not as easy as it sounds. Some mornings aren't that good: you didn't sleep a wink and the breakfast you ordered never arrived. The boys blew it and the bloke sauntering towards you grinning as if he hasn't got a care in the world is the idiot whose hare-brained dismissal was the turning point in the game. But it sets the tone: you're putting whatever happened yesterday behind you and showing a bit of humanity and respect and care.

A huge part of coaching and man-management is making players believe they're better than they are. The great soccer manager, Brian Clough, reckoned you could talk theory and tactics till you're blue in the face, but the most valuable thing you can do for a player is give him confidence. There's still a tendency in English cricket to get it the other way around — to go overboard on the technical stuff and neglect confidence building. Some of their players bat as if they've got four elbows and the price of failure is a date with a firing squad. One year we literally ran out of fit fast bowlers and ended up with a couple of absolute greenhorns who surpassed all our expectations. There seemed to be a simple formula: the more I encouraged them, the better they did.

I discovered that coaching is very different from playing. It's more difficult to turn off.

As a coach you sometimes have to look at the game through the players' eyes while avoiding the temptation to try to play the game for them. Body language is critical; the coach must have and maintain emotional control.

Our failure to win trophies made the natives restless. My new boss, now called a chief executive, instituted a monthly 'Meet the Coach' session for the members. The mood at these meetings fluctuated according to our results and they were always very well attended when we were struggling. Most of the questions came from the usual suspects, a small group of members who took the cup-half-empty view of Kent cricket and, I suspect, most other things, but whose research was frightening in its thoroughness.

'Coach, we've now played almost half the season. How many no-balls and wides have we bowled in one-day games?'

I gave what I thought was the safe answer: 'Too many.'

'Well actually, Coach, we've bowled 41 no-balls and 98 wides, which is 22 more than at the same stage last season.'

'Coach, in statistical terms, how are our opening bowlers performing compared to last season?'

Pause before replying to surreptitiously identify the nearest exit. 'Well, I don't have those figures in front of me . . .'

'Fortunately, I do: they're performing twenty three percent worse than last year and I'd like to know what you're doing about it.'

Then there were the letters. Some were congratulatory, some were full of well-meaning advice, many were neither:

Dear Sir,

Congratulations on beating Middlesex at Lord's but that was mainly due to some excellent bowling and fielding. Lord Cowdrey, Brian Luckhurst and other top batsmen of yesteryear must be appalled by the pathetic performances of our leading batsmen this season. Fortunately you as coach still have several days before our match against Worcestershire to get this problem sorted out.

To the Coach J. Wright and Captain M. Fleming:

So the circus has returned to HQ and the clowns — i.e. the players — are performing true to form, led by you two, the stars of the show. I have watched some awful cricket played by Kent teams in the last few years and it gets worse every season, without anything being done to stop the rot. And no doubt it will carry on next year unless you two do the honourable thing and resign. NOW.

These people thought that because they paid their annual membership fees, they owned the club; and to an extent they were right. I didn't particularly relish being the target of these diatribes, but I loved the attitude that generated them. Those members really cared; they desperately wanted Kent to succeed.

The Cowdrey connection was central to my relationship with Kent. When I went there in 1976, I met Colin and played with his son Chris in the Seconds for five quid a day. I stayed with them and met another son, Graham, whose phone-call almost 20 years later launched my coaching career. When the Seconds were playing in the vicinity, a few of us would stay at the Cowdreys' seaside home in Sandwich. These nights invariably degenerated into drawn-out Scotch and poker sessions, but if Colin was aware of it, he never let on.

There can be few more devoted Van Morrison fans on the planet than Graham Cowdrey. If you think that's a big statement, ask yourself how many of the great man's fans have seen him in concert 120 times. When we saw Van in Swindon, he actually asked if Graham was in the audience. After the show we had a few beers with Van and his group, and I urged him to tour New Zealand. His reply was swift, to the point, and in keeping with his reputation for prickliness: 'Kiss my arse.'

Apparently he's not terribly keen on flying.

Before a home game, a preoccupied Graham pulled me aside. 'I've got a steerer,' he muttered.

That was a new injury to me. He rolled his eyes. 'It's not an injury,' he said, 'it's a horse — a horse that all you have to do is sit on its back and steer it and it'll win by a mile.'

Now he was talking my language. Fifty quid was duly placed on the steerer's nose.

Graham looked a bit deflated when he came into the dressing room after listening to the race over the phone. The steerer's name hadn't been mentioned, which made him think it had been a late scratching. In fact our steerer, the surest of sure things, had point-blank refused to leave the stalls.

My most bizarre experience at Kent was sitting in a pavilion that was on the side of the ground, as opposed to behind the bowler's arm, and having Dean Headley, our England fast bowler, stare straight at me as he ran into bowl. This went on for two overs. The rest of the team were having trouble standing up, while I was on my feet demanding to know what the hell was going on. It transpired that Headley had been having no-ball trouble and Cowdrey, who was fielding at mid-on, persuaded him that the solution was to run in with his head turned sideways, so that he was looking over his left shoulder, as opposed to the time-honoured method of focusing on the spot on the pitch where you want to land the ball. In Cowdrey's defence, I don't suppose he seriously expected Headley to give this ludicrous suggestion a moment's consideration, let alone follow it to the letter.

Until his death Colin remained devoted to Kent cricket, and was a great source of wisdom and support. By 1997 he'd become Lord Cowdrey, and at the end of the season I'd put on my best suit, catch the train up to London, and go to see him at the House of Lords to review our performance over a cup of tea and anchovy toast. I'd never had anchovy toast before and I don't imagine I'll have it again.

I hadn't been impressed with the players' fitness and identified it as a priority for the coming season. Colin responded with an anecdote from his playing days: he had lunch with the then Prime Minister, Sir Alec Douglas-Home, who surprised him by having a glass of wine. When Colin commented on this, Douglas-Home said that as long as he drank three glasses of water for every glass of wine, it had no effect on his concentration or productivity. There was no harm in focusing on fitness, said Colin, as long as the players spent three hours on their cricket skills for every hour they spent in the gym.

The following year I asked him to talk to our batters. He spoke with great passion for an hour and a half. The key points (assuming the batsman is right-handed) were:

- Build a sound framework: stance, grip, head.
- The first key to batting is head position.
- The stance must be totally relaxed, a leopard waiting to pounce.
- The grip should be left hand tight, right hand light (fingers only).
- The head should be erect and still without being stiff and tense.
- The second key to batting is the left shoulder which must lead and take the head to the ball.
- The third key to batting is that the left forearm must control the stroke.
- The back-lift must be strictly controlled and grooved.
- The batsman should have strict rules for starting an innings which should be practised under pressure.
- The eyes must remain glued to the ball until the point of strike.
- Concentrate on two levels: the next ball and the bigger picture.
- Shot selection must be disciplined and based on pre-planning.
- The batsman must be immune to distractions, which requires a thick skin and the ability to neutralise the opposition either by freezing them out or with a smile.
- Build one brick at a time: take the singles.
- Bat in pairs.
- Keep it simple.

I had the strong impression that these rules had been handed down through the lineage of great English batsmen, from Hobbs to Hammond to Hutton to May to Cowdrey.

Just before I left for India I went to see Colin in hospital. He was born in India and knew it well. He told me to ring if I needed help, to pass on his regards to his old friend Raj Singh Dungarpur and not to forget that a nip of whisky in the evening would take care of any bugs.

Colin died soon afterwards. His advice was sound right to the very end.

Don't Call Us . . .

Kent hired me on the basis of a five-page submission, a few phone conversations and an exchange of faxes. I was to find out the hard way that this was the exception rather than the rule.

Early in 1999 I learned that the English Cricket Board (ECB) wanted to short-list me for the position of England coach, one of the bigger jobs in world cricket. The other contenders were Bob Woolmer, formerly of Warwickshire and South Africa and now of Pakistan; Dav Whatmore, who'd taken Sri Lanka to the 1996 World Cup; Jack Birkenshaw, who'd had success with Leicestershire; and Duncan Fletcher, who'd been similarly successful with Western Province and Glamorgan. On paper I was the least experienced and least credentialed candidate, so I was going to have to deliver a dazzling interview.

After a couple of weeks without any follow-up, I got home late one night from an away trip to find that the ECB had swung into action. There was a message from an ECB official saying terribly sorry, old boy, but you've been cut from the short list. He didn't say why; presumably he thought the thing spoke for itself or maybe he was pushed for time. It seemed a little unprofessional, not to mention discourteous, that I could be put on the list and then removed from it without a single conversation with anyone at the ECB.

But as the much-sacked soccer manager, Tommy Docherty, observed, as one door closes, another slams in your face. A few months later New Zealand Cricket (NZC) got in touch to ask me to apply for the position of national coach. This was tricky on several counts. I enjoyed being at Kent and didn't want them to think I was shopping around. The England job was different, in that Kent was a constituent member of the ECB; the initial contact, such as it was, had actually come via the county. That experience had left me a bit gun-shy, so I wanted reassurance that this was a genuine approach and I was a serious contender, before I allowed my name to go forward.

Perhaps my caution was viewed as diffidence and had a bearing on the outcome — although my conversations with various NZC officials were uniformly encouraging and left the impression that I was in with a very good chance.

John Bracewell had also been approached but decided not to apply. That left me, plus David Trist, a former Canterbury fast bowler who'd coached at provincial level in South Africa, the former Worcestershire and New Zealand all-rounder Dipak Patel, and John Stevenson, a Hampshire player who'd applied for the Wellington coaching role and somewhat to his surprise found himself on the New Zealand short list.

As I understood it, the first step in the process would be a satellite-link interview. We were playing Sussex at Hove and I had to go into a television studio in Brighton after a day's play, armed with a list of questions I'd been sent, and speak via satellite to a panel that included NZC chief executive Christopher Doig, cricket operations manager John Reid, former New Zealand players John Parker and Terry Jarvis and a representative from the New Zealand Sports Foundation.

The reception was blurred. It was like trying to talk to someone who's having a steaming hot shower. It was artificial and unsatisfactory, but

I didn't worry too much because it was just a warm-up for the real thing. New Zealand were touring England that summer; the big cheeses would be coming over and I'd be able to present to them in person.

The call I'd been waiting for came at the end of June. It was Doig to ask if I could get myself up to London within the next couple of days to talk to him and NZC chairman Sir John Anderson about the coaching job. Too right, mate. I put on my blazer and tie and sat on the train thinking about terms and conditions, going through my notes and trying to anticipate their questions.

They were staying at a posh hotel in Kensington. Doig came down to the foyer looking very relaxed in jeans and a polo shirt. That struck me as a bit odd, but then he was an ex-opera singer and I wasn't exactly Beau Brummel. In the lift, he said, 'Oh, by the way, I want you to know you've been unsuccessful in your application for the New Zealand coaching job.'

I was shocked and bewildered to the point of speechlessness. I'd been psyched up for a make-or-break interview and simply hadn't entertained the possibility that I'd be written off on the basis of a fuzzy teleconference interview and denied the opportunity to make my case through a written submission and a face-to-face discussion.

Anderson and Doig informed me that NZC was into 'Best Practice', one of those nifty corporate terms that on close examination are little more than a statement of the bleeding obvious. It was comforting to know they weren't into Mediocre Practice or Completely Shithouse Practice. I was angry, which probably wasn't very sensible, and the ensuing discussion wasn't constructive. As we parted, Anderson, who probably didn't know the history, asked me if I was happy with the process. It was a gobsmacking bookend to Doig's earlier bombshell and an appropriately surreal note on which to conclude my dealings with NZC.

At the time, the only explanation for this fiasco that made any sort of sense was that I'd been roped in to make up the numbers, and the decision to appoint Trist, a serious cricket coach, had already been made. A couple of friends advised me that since Anderson and Doig had sought my opinion of their process, I should give it in detail and in writing, which I did.

Doig's reply referred to what was deemed to be a poor showing on my part in the teleconference interview and stated that NZC's area of greatest concern was over my ability to apply my cricketing and people skills 'in the team environment over a period of time in order to enhance performance'. I was advised to 'work on strategies' to overcome the impression I gave of being 'indecisive and unspecific'. They would be 'reassured' to hear that I was attending courses to address this 'perceived weakness' and urged me to attend sports and sports science conferences to develop a 'philosophical approach to practice methods' and 'full familiarity with technology and its ability to support performance enhancement'. I was asked to consider getting involved with the national under-19 and A teams.

To this day, I have no idea why I was summoned to London. The charitable explanation would be that there were misunderstandings on both sides. At the time it was a shattering experience, but now it just seems like another eventful night out in London. Eventful, but perhaps not worth the twenty-odd quid I shelled out on the train fare. And as it turned out, of course, they did me a huge favour.

When the India job came up, I took comfort from the fact that my experiences with the ECB and NZC had prepared me for anything. Silly me.

In 2000, Rahul Dravid played for Kent. He'd batted superbly in New Zealand in 1996 and when the opportunity to sign him arose, we grabbed it. Kent has been trying to get him back ever since. That 1996 Indian team was an impressive outfit. Through my commentary work I met Dravid, Sourav Ganguly and Sachin Tendulkar, whom I'd actually played against. I was struck by their courtesy and humility.

I discovered from Dravid that the senior Indian players were pushing their board to consider bringing in a foreign coach. Ganguly was Lancashire's overseas player that year and we had a chat when we played them. Looking back on it, that chat was the first step in the process.

It was a hugely exciting prospect and I told them so, but any decision was months away and it was questionable, to say the least, whether the board would agree to a foreign coach. Even if they did, I'd be a long shot. India was the biggest and most passionate cricketing country, so there was bound to be a lot of interest.

These thoughts bubbled away as the season progressed. Towards the end of it, I got a call from J.Y. Lele, who'd been the liaison officer for the New Zealand tour of India which I'd captained in 1989. Now he was the Secretary of the Board of Control for Cricket in India (BCCI) — at the time I didn't appreciate just what a high-powered position that was — and we had a chuckle over our changed circumstances and the way fate had conspired to bring us back into contact. He was ringing to confirm that I was interested in the job and to ask me to come out to India for an interview.

This was more like it, being flown out business class for a face-to-face interview. It certainly beat the hell out of paying my own way up to London, to be told I wasn't worth listening to.

The BCCI's travel people had told me just to turn up at the Lufthansa check-in counter with my passport; everything would have been taken care of. The dragon behind the desk asked, 'Where's your visa? You can't travel without a visa.' My explanation didn't soften her demeanour one iota. Fighting off that terrible sinking feeling, I explained why I was going to India, emphasising that my career hung in the balance here. For all the good it did me, I could have produced a ukulele and serenaded her with 'Tiptoe Through The Tulips'. She was one of those implacable petty functionaries whose guiding principle is that there's no point in having the power to screw up people's lives unless you exercise it. I spoke to her supervisor, who'd obviously taught her everything she knew. There was no way they were going to let me on that plane.

I rang Colin Cowdrey's friend Raj Singh Dungarpur, a senior figure in the BCCI. He was having a massage at the Cricket Club of India. No problem, he said; the airline couldn't stop me going to Frankfurt, so they'd fax me some sort of authorisation there and have someone meet me off the plane in Chennai to tie up the loose ends. I got to Frankfurt: no fax. I had to start again, but now I was dealing with Germans, the most by-the-book people on earth and who didn't know cricket from spin-the-bottle. I worked my way up the chain of command, drawing increasingly direct comparisons between myself and Franz Beckenbauer, until I got to the flight controller, God bless her. I had to sign a sheaf of documents exposing me to financial liability and probably criminal charges if the Indian authorities didn't play ball, but I made the flight, albeit reduced to a quivering jelly. There were many times that morning when I was ready to accept that I was terminally jinxed, that a higher power had decreed that I should never coach at international level. During the flight they screened a commercial containing the line: 'The future belongs to those who dare to be first.' Not a great omen, given that I'd been the last passenger on board.

At Chennai I was met by K. Murali, a BCCI official. There was no problem with the visa, barring the fact that it had to be paid for and neither of us had any cash. Murali talked them around and I eventually made it to the Radisson Hotel at about 1 a.m. I've made it, I thought; it can only be downhill from here. I turned on the television and there was my old friend Lele saying it was extremely unlikely that the board would appoint a foreign coach and that if it did happen, it wouldn't be any time soon. It was like a recurring anxiety nightmare.

Speaking of anxiety, my state of mind wasn't helped by the fact that Kent had just informed me that my services were no longer required. Halfway through the season, I'd told the chairman that four years was a long time and coaches had use-by dates, so if there was a mood for change within the club, we should talk about it now. It was turning out to be a tough season; we had a lot of injuries and were in danger of relegation. I wasn't looking to bale out, but I wanted to give them the option and bring some clarity and certainty into the situation, for their benefit and mine.

No one came back to me and nothing was said. We avoided relegation. The day after the season ended, I was told the club felt it was time for a change, thank-you and goodbye. I'd been hung out to dry and left to confront the very real possibility that the coaching career I'd embarked on so enthusiastically was already over. This no-man's-land is the coach's natural habitat. You serve at other people's pleasure and sacking the coach is a quick and easy fix for administrators, who may themselves be under pressure and/or want to be seen as proactive, take-charge kind of guys. A player who's been dropped can go out and get 150 for the Seconds, but a sacked coach can't do a damn thing until someone else gives him a job.

I tried to put all that out of my mind and prepare for the interview. I bought Mihir Bose's *A History of Indian Cricket* but didn't get to the end of it. I did a lot of research on Indian domestic cricket; there seemed to be an extraordinary number of competitions. I knew quite a lot about the players and their ambitions from my discussions with Dravid and Ganguly and was aware that the 2003 World Cup loomed large in their thinking.

The word was that Geoff Marsh was the hot favourite. He had a World Cup in his CV and was known to the BCCI president, A.C. Muttiah. And then there was Greg Chappell, a genuinely great player and legend of the game. I was the outsider, but at least I had a chance to look them in the eye and make my case. The BCCI had given me a shot at it.

Before the interviews, Chappell and I had lunch with the panel — Muttiah, Raj Singh, Hanumant Singh, S. Venkataraghavan and Lele. Chappell must have seen the Lele interview too, because he asked me if I seriously thought they'd make an appointment. I wasn't sure. It was a strange situation, having lunch with a group of BCCI officials that I'd only just met, and a rival for the job I desperately wanted, whom I'd often played against. The atmosphere was polite and formal, but I didn't contribute much to the conversation.

Chappell went first, which meant more waiting. His interview seemed to last an eternity. I'd made up my mind to be completely upfront and honest, and the relaxed atmosphere encouraged that approach. I emphasised a few key points: that I loved being a coach and a teacher; that my approach was based on hard work and the primacy of the team; that as a New Zealander I'd been on the receiving end of the same sort of patronising attitudes the Indian players often encountered; that I was a self-made player who'd been learning my trade as a coach for four years; that I was sensitive to Indian culture.

There were two particularly pointed questions: would I drop Tendulkar? — without hesitation I said yes, if I had to — and what sort money was I expecting? I told them what I was getting at Kent; India was a much bigger job and I would expect a fair wage but money wasn't an issue for me. Some of the subsequent media coverage suggested that the remuneration issue had loomed a little larger in the other interviews. There was certainly a perception in some quarters that Indian cricket was a golden goose.

The panel was fair, inquisitive and knowledgeable. I sensed that they recognised that I really wanted the job. It's all very well saying the right things and having your spiel down pat, but you have to exhibit desire. When I'm on the other side of any kind of selection process, I look for individuals who are desperate for the opportunity. You know that if they don't succeed, it won't be for lack of trying.

Afterwards, Muttiah rang to say the interview had gone very well and they'd be in touch. I went back to England and waited. And waited. The only news came from Indian journalists who kept ringing to tell me I was still in the race. One morning I got a call on my mobile from a reporter from Calcutta with whom I'd never met or spoken. 'John,' he said, 'I want you to know that you're very well placed for the job.' I was so flabbergasted that all I could think of was how the hell did he get my number?

Then the 'noise' started in various media outlets and on Ceefax. 'John Wright' and 'Indian coach' were often appearing in the same sentence, but if it were true, it seemed I'd be the last to know. I started packing up because, whatever happened, I wasn't going back to Kent. Then at 10 a.m. on 2 November 2000 an item flashed up on Ceefax: the BCCI has confirmed that John Wright is the new coach of the Indian cricket team. By that stage my flat was empty, so I could dance around the living room without knocking anything over.

I didn't know how much I was being paid nor the length of the contract. In fact when I thought about it, I didn't know anything beyond the fact that I'd landed one of the biggest jobs in the game. I rang Muttiah and Raj Singh who confirmed that it was a one-year appointment; they'd like me to go through to the World Cup but there was some problem over a work permit. It sounded like I was on a year's trial, but that was fine with me.

From what I've been able to pick up since, it seems that Raj Singh, who was driving the process, had been in touch with his old friends Colin Cowdrey and Raman Subba Row, another ex-England player and an influential figure in the game. He'd also spoken to the former Australian coach, Bob Simpson, who'd done some coaching in India and had been a consultant to the Indian team at the 1999 World Cup. I knew Simpson well and had enormous regard for his coaching abilities, having seen at first hand what he'd done with Australia. He proved that cricket coaches could have an impact, and set up the great Australian dynasty which continues to this day. Perhaps he hasn't been given quite as much credit as he deserves because of the lingering animosity from the World Series split. Some Packer loyalists have never forgotten that Simpson, then in his 40s and playing Sydney club cricket, came out of retirement to captain the official Australian team.

I first met Simpson when New Zealand played Australia at Brisbane in 1988. He talked about things I'd never thought of, like keeping the hands and knees loose and taking the pace off the ball to create singles. He convinced me to change my stance, arguing that you needed to have the bat on the ground to get rhythm into your batting. On my last tour of England in 1990, I didn't have a productive first test. The next match was against Leicestershire, who were coached by Simpson. He wasn't really a success in county cricket — he was probably too tough for them and perhaps too used to dealing with international players — but I knew he'd work out what was wrong with my game. He told me I wasn't watching the ball out of the bowler's hand. In the next test at Lord's I got 98.

He was a canny operator too. At the 1987 World Cup we lost to Australia in a shortened game at Indore. At 8 a.m. the next morning, as we left the hotel, the Aussies were having fielding practice. Apparently, as soon as we'd gone, they went back to the hotel and had breakfast, but word spread that the Aussies were practising every hour of the day.

We'd kept in touch. I had him down to Kent to work with the players and we talked cricket till the cows came home.

I found out later, that after my interview Simpson wrote an article for the Indian magazine *Sportstar* saying I was the man for the job and Sunil Gavaskar told me that I wouldn't have got it without Simpson's backing. Having said that, Raj Singh was definitely in my camp. He flew to Nairobi where India was playing in the International Cricket Conference (ICC) Champions Trophy to get the players' views.

I wasn't sure what lay ahead and it looked like the Indians weren't either. The photos of the new coach that appeared in the papers were at least ten years old. Some Indian cricket followers must have looked at them and wondered if the BCCI had taken leave of its senses: they could have had anyone, but they'd gone for a little-known, wet-behind-the-ears foreigner.

WELCOME TO THE UNREAL WORLD

I'm sitting in my room at the Taj Palace in New Delhi. The good news is that I'm here and I'm definitely the Indian coach. The not-so-good news is that we've got a test against Zimbabwe in three days and I haven't seen or heard from my new employer or anyone in, or involved with, the Indian team since I've been in the country.

I've spent two days thinking about my first team meeting and first practice, but if the players don't turn up soon we won't have time for either. When I'm not doing that, I read the papers, watch TV, dodge reporters — they seem to be the only people who know or care that I'm in the country — and write in my diary. Things like: 'This isn't how I'd choose to prepare a team for my first test match as coach.'

It was a huge relief when the phone rang and I heard: 'Hi, I'm Andrew, your physio.' It's important that the coach and his support staff have a solid relationship; if they don't gell, it undermines the whole operation. Seeing Andrew Leipus *was* my support staff, it was doubly important that we hit it off — and, fortunately, we did immediately.

His good news was that the players were great to work with and eager to learn. His not-so-good news came in the form of an inventory of the team gear: three baseball mitts, 30 cones and three old and crooked blue plastic stumps. No drink bottles, no sports drinks, no electrotherapy unit, no heart rate monitors. He also gave me a two-page list of things that needed immediate attention, starting with players' clothing and ending with menu guidelines. He could have saved time by listing the things that didn't need attention.

The players began drifting in that evening. I held my first team meeting at 9 the next morning, 48 hours before the test started. I kept it simple and low-key to avoid cluttering their minds or causing them to dwell on their new foreign coach rather than concentrate on the game. I told them I was honoured to be their coach and that we'd set goals and team values that would apply to everyone, from the captain to the newest player. I laid out the non-negotiables: honesty, hard work, punctuality, dressing as a team so that we looked like a team. That must have confused them, because they hadn't been issued with travelling clothes.

Practice was an unforgettable experience; the first of many. At the training ground the players left their gear on the bus and ambled over to the nets on the other side of the field where they lounged in cane chairs while waiters served them tea and biscuits. Leipus had briefed me on what to expect, but there'd been no mention of tea and biscuits. Or waiters. Or the porters who were now lugging the players' cricket coffins across the field. While all this went on — it took about half an hour — I busied myself sorting through the team gear. I can't remember how I filled in the remaining 29 minutes. After the tea came the taping. A lot of the players taped their fingers for fielding practice, so before Leipus could take the warm-ups, he had to work his way through a queue of guys wanting their fingers taped. I filled in the time by starting a list of things that were going to change.

Finally, we were under way. The first batter, a skinny lad I didn't know, started with four magnificent shots, timed to perfection. Christ, I thought, this boy can bat; he must be the opening batsman, Shiv Sunder Das. When I sought confirmation I was told, no, that's Ajit Agarkar, our opening bowler.

'Oh yeah, of course,' I mumbled. 'He looks smaller in the flesh.'

The debutant off-spinner Sarandeep Singh wore a vivid purple turban and had a smile to match, but was absolutely smashed by the senior batsmen. It was an instant reminder of how well the Indians play spin. Perhaps they didn't rate him, but he was just the latest in a long line of spinners who've been taken apart in the Indian nets.

The cane chairs went the next day and the tea soon followed. The players weren't bothered; the resistance came from the people who lavished this care and attention on their beloved team. It took a while for word to get around that the new foreign coach didn't believe in tea and biscuits at practice. He didn't believe in taping fingers either. If you do enough catching practice, hands and fingers eventually harden up.

My first press conference was even more mind-blowing. After practice, Sourav Ganguly and I sat on white plastic chairs in the middle of the field while at least 60 media people swarmed all over us as if we were the story of the decade. It reminded me of my rugby days, getting caught at the bottom of an old-fashioned ruck. A couple of cameramen accused each other of getting in the way and traded punches. At Kent, I appeared on television once a year; I spoke to the bloke from Radio Kent and a couple of local reporters and that was it. The cricket writers on the national papers were as interested in talking to me as I was in talking to them.

By the end of that press conference, I had a clearer picture of just how big cricket is in India. It was an invaluable lesson: the cricket media was a many-headed monster and if I didn't handle it right, it would chew me up and spit me out.

Reporters had been after me from the day I arrived and my phone never stopped ringing. The last thing I wanted to do was give a raft of interviews full of big statements. I didn't want to be a high-profile coach; I wanted to get to know the players and work with them as unobtrusively as possible. So I put my phone in bar-all-calls mode — some journalists would probably say it stayed that way for the next four years — and released a statement saying I'd be available to answer questions immediately after practice the day before each match and at the end of each match. What I didn't spell out was that at all other times I'd go to great lengths to be unavailable. Those were my rules of engagement, or perhaps disengagement, with the media.

My first television interview was with Ian Chappell on the morning of the test. As I'd done many times in the previous 48 hours, I said it was an honour and a privilege to be the Indian coach. Most interviewers would have taken these fine — and genuine — sentiments at face value; perhaps only Chappell, whose bluntness is legendary, would have come straight back with, 'Why?'

I made a point of talking to the former Indian all-rounder Ravi Shastri, who was part of the commentary team. I'd played against him, in fact I hit him for six to bring up my first test century (he was 18 at the time). He was one of the few ex-players who'd been in favour of a foreign coach and I wanted to get his perspective. His view was that:

- The senior players had to make a bigger contribution and give the youngsters more help.
- We had to start winning away from home; the public would like to see us go for wins even if it meant losing a few.
- We needed to improve the running between the wickets and get the fielding right; part of that was having specialists in the close catching positions.
- The batters had to take more responsibility, to enable us to play five specialist bowlers, particularly in one-day cricket.
- As the coach I had to be either hard or soft; in between wouldn't work.

Shastri was to be a valuable supporter and a good sounding board; someone I could rely on to give an honest answer.

When play started, I realised that I was the new circus act everyone wanted to see — an oddity like the Bearded Lady or the Wolf Boy. Every time I checked a TV replay, there I was. I found it disconcerting having a camera trained on me, so I asked one of the cameramen, an Aussie, if he could point his camera somewhere else. 'Don't worry about us, mate,' he said. 'We'll be getting in the way like bottles of stale piss.' I thought of pointing out what sensible people do with bottles of stale piss but there wasn't much point. It went with the territory; I had to learn to live with it. There's a considerable mental strain attached to knowing that you have to keep yourself under control and refrain from picking your nose for six hours a day. I decided that safety lay in remaining deadpan whatever the situation, on the basis that the Indian fans wouldn't be impressed if the camera caught me smiling when we were six down for 60. I was probably being overcautious: I was as likely to crack a smile when we were in trouble as I was to strike oil weeding a flowerbed.

Watching our batters murder the Zimbabwe attack in the first innings, I made a mental note to avoid telling them how to bat. At Kent I'd put too much pressure on the batsmen and when you have world-class players the last thing you want to do is interfere with them. I learned that if something was amiss, it was better to wait to be asked or else to ask a simple question and listen to and observe the reaction carefully. Once he's out in the middle, a player should be putting his energy and concentration into the contest, not worrying about his technique because it's been questioned by an intrusive coach. Besides, changing your method is very difficult and takes an immense amount of practice. You do it over time and in the nets, not in the middle.

We declared 36 ahead, which seemed to surprise the Zimbabweans. That evening Javagal Srinath knocked over four of them and we took control. I have an abiding memory of Rahul Dravid, Sachin Tendulkar and Ganguly rattling off the 190 needed for victory on the last afternoon. I was now the coach of this team whose results meant so much to so many. Coaches sometimes talk about journeys, but the uncertain nature of sport means that you often don't know your final destination until you get there. But sitting in the afternoon sun amongst a joyful crowd, watching sublime batting in the great Indian tradition — effortless and unhurried, the ball being dispatched at exquisite angles, with a flick of the wrist — it was impossible not to be exhilarated at the prospect.

The performance wasn't without blemishes. The umpire John Hampshire, a former England player, didn't think our spinners bowled well and if that was a sign of things to come, I was going to have my work cut out. We dropped nine catches close in. Whenever it happened, the culprit was reassigned to a different position in the field. It was like a game of snakes and ladders: no one seemed to be in the same place from one over to the next.

It was obvious that the rumblings of discontent over the appointment of a foreign coach weren't going to die down quickly. Anshuman Gaekwad, who'd succeeded Kapil Dev on an interim basis when the latter quit in the middle of the match-fixing scandal, reckoned the team had been doing just fine under him. They'd got to the final of the ICC Champions Trophy in Nairobi; what more could a foreign coach do? And, anyway, when they'd had Bob Simpson as a consultant, he'd said the same things as the home-grown coaches. One ex-player chose the Delhi press box as the venue for his announcement that, come the second test, I'd be making tea for the team. Given that I'd knocked the tea ceremony on the head, that would've represented a swift fall from grace. I came to expect criticism from ex-Indian players and they never let me down.

During the test I had my first meeting with the selectors. We circled each other like boxers in the first round. I'd got the sense from the players that there was a feeling of them and us. I knew that feeling from other teams I'd been involved with, but Indian players had more reason than most to believe there was a political element in the selection process. Each of the BCCI's five geographical zones nominated a selector to serve a one-year term, so there wasn't much continuity. In my five seasons I worked with 14 selectors and four chairmen. The players felt that some of the selectors were unduly focused on getting players from their zones into the team, which led to chopping and changing. Over time it became apparent that there was some truth in that, but the selectors themselves were victims of the system with its politicking and lack of job security.

Because I didn't know how Indian cricket worked, I relied on the players, who'd come up through the system, to interpret the nuances for me.

I couldn't understand why the selectors picked 14 players for a home test; I like small, tight-knit squads. When I raised the issue at a selection meeting, I got blank stares. The players explained that the larger squads contained enough places to keep all the zones happy and therefore off their nominated selector's back.

Of that first committee, I'd played against Madan Lal and Ashok Malhotra, and as a boy had seen the chairman, Chandu Borde, at Lancaster Park. I didn't know T.A. Sekhar, who ran the fast bowling academy in Chennai with my old mate Dennis Lillee, or Sanjay Jagdale. I sat with them on the first morning drinking tea and talking cricket. They were just like me, cricket men who wanted the best for the team. Borde talked about wanting players who were tigers in the middle rather than tigers in the nets, a principle I wholeheartedly agreed with and a description I loved. Lal, who'd been a warrior, emphasised that it wasn't about individuals, it was about the country. Malhotra had an active sense of humour, while Jagdale, a huge man, said little and listened a lot. This isn't always a sign of wisdom — the person concerned may simply have nothing to contribute — but in his case it definitely was.

The first selection meeting I attended lasted two hours. That was one of the shorter ones. As with any selection process, the bulk of it is straightforward and the hard talking is done over the last few spots. Three-quarters of this meeting was devoted to the 14th place in the squad. The debate got very animated; I remember thinking a couple of the selectors might have to settle their differences outside. When things got particularly heated the participants tended to break into Hindi, which limited my contribution; not that I had much of one to make because I didn't know who they were talking about. The captain and two selectors wanted the off-spinner from the North Zone, the others wanted the off-spinner from the South. As in the American Civil War, the north prevailed. However, after the team was announced, the Man from the North was implicated, unjustly as it turned out, in the match-fixing scandal and temporarily banned, so the sound and fury had all been for nothing.

Another surprise was that I wasn't just the coach, I was also the team manager — by default, because the BCCI hadn't appointed one for that series. I relied heavily on Babu Meman, the Zimbabwe manager, for logistical information such as flight times. I had two jobs, which was one more than I really wanted, but no contract. It was a bit unsettling and when I wasn't in the brightest of moods, it was hard not to dwell on the fact that, in the event of a bad result or two, there was nothing to stop the BCCI having second thoughts. The ignorance and indignation of my diary entries from that period — 'It's not the way I'm used to doing business' — are, in hindsight, laughable. The reality was that I wasn't going to dig my heels in and have a scrap over a piece of paper.

The first version of the contract was actually two pieces of paper. The second draft was 12 pages long, very legalistic, and not quite what I thought we'd agreed on. I raised it with Raj Singh Dungarpur who was already keeping a paternal eye on me. He said this was the way things worked and I just had to go with the flow. 'Patience, John, patience. It takes time. This is how we've survived and outlasted the English and the Portuguese and everyone who came to colonise India.' If I was patient, he promised, India would be patient with me. It was great advice. The only problem was that the Indians did patience much better than I did. As Pradeep, who often collected me from the airport, once said, 'To lose patience is to lose the battle'.

I was to learn that there was absolutely no point in fretting because nothing seemed to be happening. This was India: it mightn't happen straight away, but it would happen. In the end, things just fell into place, often without you quite understanding how or why. I must have got used to it because over the time I was Indian coach, I was out of contract for almost as long as I was under contract.

Before the one-dayer in Jodhpur the BCCI treasurer Kishore Rungta, J.Y. Lele and I hammered out a formula that we could shake hands on. Rungta told me: 'We're expecting the sky.' When we lost the game I wondered if Rungta was familiar with the saying: 'We do the impossible every day; miracles take a little longer.'

Although I didn't want deference from the players, respect for one's elders is a big part of Indian culture. Once a man reaches a certain age, he gets called Uncle by all and sundry as a sign of respect. I told the boys they could call me anything they liked except Sir. It took a while for some of the younger ones to be comfortable with that, but once they were, I got called all sorts of things. It was already apparent that I was working with a group of fine young men who possessed humility and a distinctively Indian brand of charm.

The players found out a little more about their new coach during the drawn second test at Nagpur. I raised the intensity, gave a couple of blunt team talks and let fly with the odd bark at training. In India giving someone a verbal kick up the backside is known as 'firing' them. I 'fired' Srinath because I felt he'd put less energy into his opening spell in the second innings than the team deserved. It was a borderline call, especially in his mind. Srinath was what they called a senior, the most senior in fact, and it was his misfortune that I decided to start at the top, with someone I knew could take it. He was the heart and soul of the team, a leader who looked after the young fast bowlers and cheered us up if we'd had a rough day. He was a bit upset — it was clear that some of them, particularly the stars, weren't used to being told to pull finger — but it was nothing that couldn't be sorted out in a one-on-one chat. The point was that he and the rest of them now had a better idea of where I was coming from and what my expectations were. My next trick was a general blast following a sloppy session in the field. Up until then I'd been fairly easy-going, so they could've been excused for thinking the coach had an evil twin.

Yuvraj Singh had become a star almost overnight after wading into the Australians on debut in Nairobi. As tended to happen with young players whose lives changed out of all recognition on the basis of a couple of performances, he was struggling to cope with sudden success. I asked Yuvraj if he'd heard of the Bay City Rollers; he hadn't, amazingly enough. I could see what he was thinking as I proceeded to tell him about this Scottish pop group who'd been a big deal when I was growing up: what the hell has this got to do with anything? I explained that the Bay City Rollers were basically one-hit wonders whose fall had been as precipitous as their rise: did he want to go the same way? He got the message.

The players had grown up in a culture of seniors and juniors; it was a subject that came up time and again in newspaper articles and on television. Ganguly and I were as one on this: it had to change. He was determined to create a new culture and did an admirable job of making the younger players feel that they belonged.

My relationship with Ganguly was obviously going to be critical. I thought I could help him tactically, but I began with the basics, suggesting that he get a new watch as it was important the captain was on time. I talked about setting an example and the importance of body language and how those sorts of things were more pertinent to leadership on and off the field than what you said. We came from different backgrounds but had plenty in common. We were both ambitious and desperately keen to succeed in our respective roles; to do that we'd need each other's help. And our destinies were linked: we'd sink or swim together.

Running practices was easy in one respect because there was never a shortage of net bowlers dying to bowl at the Indian team. At the Kent nets I was always having to juggle limited human resources. The hard part was getting the batters out of the nets. Back in their home towns, they could have one- or two-hour bats at centre wicket practice or spend all day in the nets whenever they liked, but when we came together we had to practice as a team. Once I'd decided to put the emphasis at training on fielding, that meant 15 minutes' batting each. There are easier things in this world than telling Dravid or Tendulkar that their time's up but eventually they were able to take it with a smile. My stock line was that I enjoyed watching them bat in the middle more than in the nets. That wasn't entirely true: some of the batting I saw in the nets was out of this world.

When it came to batting practice, the challenge was getting them to stop; with physical fitness, it was getting them started. There were mitigating factors. Leipus explained to me that the players could only jog at the ground, which meant lunchtime or after play, because if they ran on the roads, they'd be mobbed. When they did go for a run, they set a pace that a tortoise with a double hip replacement would have found comfortable. I told them I had to rub my eyes to make sure they were moving. When I asked a player how come his shirt was dry after he'd been in the gym, he said the air-conditioning had been turned up so he couldn't raise a sweat. Basically, there was no fitness regime. Most of the players came from backgrounds and cricketing environments which didn't place a value on fitness and few of them had access to gyms and physios when they weren't on international duty. We badly needed a fitness trainer, but that would take 18 months and a changing of the guard at the BCCI.

Leipus had tried to change the attitude, but it was an impossible task given his physiotherapy workload. Without a fitness trainer, it was up to him and me. The players tried every excuse under the sun, so we trained with them in the hope that it would motivate or shame them into greater effort. After we'd done a bleep test, Leipus said, 'Wrighty, there's one thing about this set-up that worries me'.

'What's that?' I gasped.

'The possibility of you having a heart attack.'

During the one-day series, I began to understand just what it meant to be part of the Indian cricket team. Touring India as a player you cotton on to the fact that their cricketers are pretty popular, but now I started to get a sense of the dimensions of their popularity. In fact to call it popularity doesn't do this phenomenon justice: the players were adored. Everyone wanted a piece of them: to touch them, shake their hands, be seen with them, take a photo of them with their mobile phones, introduce their kids to them. If you were in the aisle seat next to Tendulkar, you spent the flight trying to avoid being elbowed in the face by autograph hounds. He never refused.

Although Kent got good crowds by county cricket standards, their supporters weren't all that vocal or, for that matter, positive. In India we sometimes had 4000 people watching us practise. A 3000-strong crowd turned out at Bhubaneswar Airport to greet local hero Das after his debut test hundred. The police had to form a cordon so that we could get to the bus. It reminded me of images of Beatlemania. In Rajkot there was a 200-plus crowd outside our hotel in the morning when we went to get on the bus, and they were still there last thing at night. If you pulled back the curtain, you got a cheer; the bigger the star, the bigger the cheer. That sea of upturned, smiling faces waiting for a glimpse of their heroes is an enduring image of Indian cricket. People would line the roads outside towns and villages waiting for our bus to go past, even though they couldn't see the players behind tinted windows and drawn curtains. As the first guy out onto the field for warm-ups, I'd get a bigger cheer than I ever got in my playing career, even though at that time of the morning the ground would be quarter full. In Jodhpur, I went with a few players (not the superstars) to a department store in the main street. When we came out after an hour there must have been 2000 people waiting for us. They'd spilled onto the road blocking the traffic and I counted 35 policemen struggling to restore normality. You couldn't witness such scenes without thinking that these people deserved a great cricket team.

Kanpur, the leather capital, generates huge crowds and an electric atmosphere. When the game started there were 60,000 in the ground and a few thousand outside wanting to get in. A ticketing mess-up prompted the stoning of Australian match referee Barry Jarman's car. There were people on rooftops and perched in trees trying to catch a glimpse of the action. The air of excitement and expectancy was such that you would have thought it was a World Cup final rather than part of a series against Zimbabwe.

For Indians a one-day international is an excuse to celebrate the game they love. Every ball is an event and the noise is unbelievable — a surge of anticipation followed by wild celebration and great roars of approval for Indian boundaries and wickets. When India loses a wicket, there's a stunned silence, the sound of people struggling to believe their eyes. When I finish with cricket in a professional capacity and get back to watching it purely for pleasure, I won't bother going to Lord's; I'll go back to India.

While I was easing into the job I embarked on what would turn out to be a never-ending, and ultimately unsuccessful, campaign to protect the team's space. It wasn't too much of a problem in the bigger centres like Kolkata, Mumbai or Bangalore, but in the smaller places it was an issue that never went away. In the blink of an eye our changing room or viewing area would take on the appearance of a café renowned as a celebrity hang-out and a place to be seen, a magnet for wannabes. Practice days weren't so bad, the biggest hassle being clearing away the local police who were supposed to be protecting the team but were more interested in meeting them. But come match day I'd arrive at the ground to find that our viewing area had been invaded by well-connected spectators, usually related to high-ranking local government or cricket officials. There were times when the team was forced out of their viewing area to make room for the state's chief minister and his entourage; even the padded-up batsman had to shift. As a coach who believed in the sanctity of team space, I found this intolerable and set out to put a stop to it. I'd begin with a polite request, which was really just for appearance's sake, since it seldom had the slightest effect. The next step was a not-so-polite instruction and the last resort a threat to ring the BCCI President.

But that was a breeze compared to emptying out the changing room. We usually had our meals there, which meant six or seven catering staff plus a similar number of supervisors. Then there were three or four security guys, both police and army, plus the local liaison man and his assistant. The iron law of liaison men was that the smarter they dressed, the more useless they were. Finally, there were the changing-room attendants and the masseur, who were the odd men out in that they actually did something useful. Driving people who didn't belong there out of our dressing room was just a skirmish in an ongoing guerrilla war. Like the Terminator, they'd be back.

The players were astonishingly tolerant of this chaos. I wasn't, and my methods became more direct and dictatorial. I evicted all sorts: BCCI bigwigs, chief inspectors of police, hotel banquet managers, army officers, people with titles that sounded mighty impressive and probably were.

I never stopped to think how important they might be. In Jodhpur, a guy with the biggest diamond ear-stud I'd ever seen wandered into our viewing area as if it was his private box. I went nuts demanding to know who the hell he was and, more to the point, who the hell he thought he was. The answer to both questions was that he was India's biggest beer baron. In Rajkot the boys looked on in horror as I gave the secretary of the host association a fearful bollocking. Fortunately Niranjan Shah has a sense of humour and we became good friends.

I'm sure many people who witnessed these eruptions thought I was mad, but I had an unshakeable belief that the team needed private space, in the form of a changing room that was a no-go zone, and an exclusive viewing area, so that they could concentrate on what they were there for. I never gave up the fight, but although I won some battles, I didn't win the war.

India had changed enormously since my last tour in 1989. It was more modern and in more of a hurry. Grounds which had held 10–15,000 spectators were now two or three times bigger and still packed. The hotels had been lavishly upgraded. In Jodhpur I found myself in the most opulent surroundings I'd come across in my travels: an all-marble suite with two rooms, two bathrooms, eight sofas and twelve paintings. Television was omnipresent and pervasive, coming at you from a hundred or so channels. The food was excellent and they'd stopped putting glycerine in the beer.

In those first few months I was wide-eyed, entranced by the vibrancy, the colour and the difference. I took more photographs in my first two months than in my last two years. I filled my diary with signs I saw from bus windows: 'Keep your nerve on the curve'; 'Boredom can be fatal — consult your doctor today'; 'Dazzling shine ahead'; and my all-time favourite, which hung outside a Mumbai funeral parlour: 'When you drop dead, drop in'.

I still didn't have a signed contract but was coming to the view that being the Indian cricket coach was no ordinary job, so the usual rules didn't apply. Going home for Christmas, I had 30 kg of excess baggage. It could've been 300 for all the check-in man cared. I was the coach; the usual rules didn't apply.

The Greatest Comeback Since Lazarus

In January 2001, Steve Waugh's Australian team rolled into Mumbai like a conquering army. They'd won 15 tests on the trot and some were saying they were unbeatable. Just as rock groups attach labels to their concert tours (usually the name of the album they're currently flogging), the Aussies were calling this their 'Final Frontier'. They hadn't won a series in India for 31 years and the implication was unmistakable: they were on the finishing straight to world domination and we were about to become road-kill.

They trained at the Cricket Club of India, where I based myself between tours. On the basis that you should seek to learn from the best, I watched their net sessions, making notes and timing everything they did. During a wind sprint one of them pulled up clutching his hamstring. Poor old Jason Gillespie, I thought, what frightfully bad luck. I found out later that it was actually the coach, John Buchanan. I suppose it proved the old adage that no team ever lost because their coach wasn't fit.

The Aussies generated enormous publicity, nearly all of it positive. Indians love their own team, but when a major side arrives they know how to make the tourists feel special. There's very little of the media mind games and psychological warfare you get touring some other countries, notably Australia, where the welcome usually takes the form of a dismissive spray from a famous ex-player. The media greeted the Australians as if they were cricketing royalty who'd deigned to grace India with their regal presence.

And to give the Aussies their due, they worked the media brilliantly, using every opportunity to build their mental edge and reinforce the perception of an irresistible force bearing down on a somewhat fragile object. A number of their players were writing syndicated columns that weren't short of sly, and not so sly, digs at the Indian team, while the papers were full of stories about the professionalism of their preparation and how no stone was being left unturned, right down to taking urine samples to guard against dehydration. Even after we'd trained really well, I'd have Indian journalists telling me how impressive their practices were and how ours seemed flat by comparison.

If you went by what was in the media, you'd think it was pre-ordained: they were about to make history and we were simply making up the numbers.

The PR offensive didn't stop when the cricket started. In the first test Michael Slater had a major meltdown when Rahul Dravid stood his ground after the Australians claimed a disputed catch. Even before sanity had been restored I noticed the Australian PR man slipping into the seat next to match referee Cammie Smith.

Chetan Chauhan, the former Indian opener, was appointed manager for the series. He was quoted as saying that one of his tasks would be to help the foreign coach overcome the language problems he was having. Talk about shooting yourself in the foot: the Australians had the media and public eating out of their hands while the hapless Indian team couldn't understand a word their coach was saying. It crossed my mind that another of Chauhan's tasks was to keep tabs on me, but we hit it off immediately. He gave the players good messages — 'bat like you're the last man' — and I wish his appointment had been permanent.

0We had a lengthy build-up which gave me the opportunity to put my stamp on the team and put in place routines and systems to get them to start thinking and behaving as a unit. I'd gathered that team meetings had previously tended to be lengthy, unstructured affairs where food was ordered from room service and the younger players handed out the snacks. That changed. As one player put it: 'Now there's no eating, only meeting.'

Regardless of the opposition, every contest starts with the question: how do you beat them? Geoff Marsh, the former Australian coach who was in India doing consultancy work for the BCCI, was a good source of information; he certainly thought the Aussies were beatable. I believed we had to play on slow, turning wickets that didn't break up, our spinners had to bowl a fourth stump (i.e. outside off stump) line at all times, our batsmen had to play straight against their quicks, and we had to set run-saving ring fields and catch everything.

Twenty-five players attended our camp, which went from 7 a.m. to 7 p.m. for 10 days. There were two three-hour sessions — one in the morning and one in the afternoon — and at night we planned.

The ground rules were that we had breakfast together, all taping was to be done in the players' own time, and there was to be no sitting down on the training ground. It was relentless — there was hardly a moment when someone wasn't hitting catches and the players moaned endlessly about the battering their hands were taking — and it was hot. They say Chennai has three seasons: hot, hotter and hottest. As we were about to start an afternoon session, Javagal Srinath fell to his knees and cried, 'Relent, John, relent.' The others laughed at his theatrics, but I suspect he wasn't speaking just for himself. At day's end the players would complain that they were 'leg and leg' — Indian cricketing slang for knackered — and fall asleep on the bus back to the hotel.

Spin bowling was obviously going to be the key. Even without Anil Kumble, who was recovering from shoulder surgery, I felt we could beat Australia if our spinners were patient and consistently put the ball in the right area. Not that Kumble's absence could be down-played: in real cricketing terms it was the main reason why Australia would go in as favourites. We brought the ten best spinners in the country to the camp and I had Kumble run the rule over them.

During my first test in charge, Sourav Ganguly had dragged me to the nets after play to have a look at a young off-spinner he was very keen on. I'd seen Harbhajan Singh bowl a bit in New Zealand, but what I saw that evening in Delhi left me stunned. Harbhajan was out of favour — Sarandeep Singh was the incumbent offie — and I'd heard the talk about him: his action had come under scrutiny and he'd had disciplinary problems at the National Cricket Academy, which added to the perception that he was a hothead. What I saw was a skinny, frisky character in a black turban who turned the ball a mile and got more bounce than any spinner I'd ever seen. Furthermore, everything about him — personality, body language, the glint in his eye — said he was a real competitor.

On the first day of the camp, I told him that while he'd been coached by some of India's greatest spinners — men like Erapalli Prasanna and Bishen Bedi, who'd forgotten more about spin bowling than I'd ever know — I knew a special bowler when I saw one. My question was: did he think he was bowling in the right place? Using chalk I drew a box about 20 cm wide and 60 cm long on a good length outside off stump. If he pitched his off spinner in that box, I said, the ball would hit or threaten the top of off stump. It was up to him how he got the ball down there but that was the target and if he hit it over and over again, things would happen for him.

If any of the spinners questioned the logic of being told how to bowl by a former New Zealand opening batsman, none of them were impolite enough to do so openly. It helped that I had Kumble, with his arm in a sling, acting as technical adviser; he proved to be an outstanding teacher. The box generated a fair bit of banter, along the lines of what happens to our precious box if a batter plants his front foot in it, but as long as they kept landing the ball in it, they could scoff as much as they liked.

I wanted to cut the team off from all the hype and impress on them that what made them special was the people they represented. So I invited the TV commentator Harsha Bhogle to address them on that theme, and he told them that although they were young men they had an enormous responsibility to their people, many of whom led desperately hard lives. If India played well, those people went to bed happy.

I was coming to realise just how strongly the players believed in their ability to beat anyone in Indian conditions. This conviction would prove the bedrock on which victory was based. And, as I was to discover, the downside was how much of that self-belief ebbed away the moment our plane left Indian airspace.

For security reasons the two teams stayed in the same hotel. I wandered into the gym to find Ricky Ponting, Matthew Hayden, Justin Langer and Buchanan engaged in an intense work-out under the supervision of their fitness trainer. On the other side of the gym one of the Indian players was pedalling away on an exercycle in a somewhat lackadaisical fashion. So lackadaisical, in fact, that he was wearing those chunky, hippie-style sandals and having a cup of tea. Before I could get my head around the implications of this scene, the door burst open and a waiter bustled in with a plate of sandwiches for him. I looked at Ponting and he gave me a quizzical look. I knew he was thinking, 'You've really got these guys fizzing'.

Before the start of play we got our first taste of Aussie bravado. As we were doing our stretches, their whole squad, led by the tall, barrel-chested Hayden, jogged around Mumbai's Wankhede Stadium flicking a football to and fro. The banter got louder and more confident the closer they came to our stretching circle — and if they'd come any closer, they'd have trampled us. We were under way.

The first test was hugely intense and closer than it looks on paper, but whichever way you cut it, we came second. We had a chance when the Aussies were 90 for 5, but Ganguly made a bizarre bowling change, replacing Rahul Sanghvi, who'd just dismissed Steve Waugh, with part-time bowler Sachin Tendulkar. It was like having Dean Headley stare into my eyes as he ran in to bowl, in the sense that I couldn't believe what I was seeing — only it was much more serious. Hayden and Adam Gilchrist then took the game away from us, scoring blazing hundreds and setting a frenetic tempo that persisted throughout the series.

Tendulkar matched them, taking on Glenn McGrath and Gillespie, who were both steaming in. This was a batting master class: still head, precise footwork, sharp and economical execution. Mumbai is Tendulkar's hometown, or more accurately, his kingdom. The noise starts when he comes out for warm-ups and never abates. Every act whether magnificent — a thunderous straight drive off the back foot — or mundane — a bread and butter single, a simple stop at cover — triggers a roar. When he walks out to bat, you can't hear yourself speak, and when the strokes unfold, the noise is disorienting. Shane Warne and Mark Waugh said afterwards that they'd never heard anything like the din when he hit McGrath for six and four off consecutive balls. But for every action there's an equal and opposite reaction, and when Tendulkar is dismissed, the noise ceases as abruptly as if the power source has been shut down — which, in a way, it has. A deep, despairing groan trails off into a throbbing silence as he leaves the stage.

We lost in less than three days. It was Australia's 16th consecutive victory, a record. As I trudged through the packed hotel foyer, people congratulated me on a wonderful victory, thinking I was part of the Australian coaching set-up. I don't think I could have looked any glummer, but maybe they thought I was homesick.

India is a country of one billion people, but on the second night of the second test in Kolkata I sat in room 214 of the Taj Bengal with what felt like my only friends: four cans of Heineken and five cigarettes. Australia had made 445, despite a Harbhajan hat-trick, the first by an Indian in a test, and we were 128 for 8.

The beers and the cigarettes and I contemplated what suddenly seemed a very bleak future. After the first test someone said that they hoped I had sharp ears so I'd hear the knives going into my back, and since then things had gone downhill. I'd been remarkably calm going into the game, but this was one of the loneliest, most desolate nights of my life. We'd said all the right things, done all the work, laid our plans, but everything had fallen in a heap. The Aussies were an exceptional team, but we were playing as if we didn't think we belonged on the same park.

There would be other bad nights, but I was more vulnerable in the early days and I took it hard. Later I came to realise that this was the job, this was the reality of being a foreigner coaching India: one day you were pinching yourself and wondering how you ever came to be in this privileged and exhilarating position; the next day you were bemoaning the fact that you had the toughest, loneliest job in the world, albeit probably not for much longer.

I hadn't lost my fight or self-belief, but it was a stark fact of life that if the batting continued to fail, and fail comprehensively, I was a goner. Some time during that dark night I picked up a message from the front desk. It was a note, marked for my attention and addressed to 'our cricket team', from three fans — Vinay, Mahmud and Sanchayita. 'You guys can still win this match,' it said. 'We believe in you.' If the players and I ever needed an example of the belief that refuses to countenance defeat when logic says otherwise, it was right there in my hand.

The next day V.V.S. Laxman harnessed his talent and self-belief, and turned the game and the series on its head.

It began with a cameo that barely hinted at what was to come. Watching Laxman make 59 while batting with the tail, I remembered Ian Chappell arguing that your number three batsman should be a stroke player, someone who took the attack to the opposition and put away the bad ball. Dravid was our regular first drop, but he hadn't hit his straps; his partnership with Tendulkar in Mumbai had been slow. We simply weren't taking the initiative. Dravid was also copping flak because he hadn't had much success against Australia and there was a perception that they were his bogey team.

I'd thought about suggesting to Dravid that he change his guard, but

Ganguly and I decided to shift him down the order instead. Laxman looked in the mood to dominate and that was what we needed, so when he came in at the change of innings, I said, 'Lax, keep your pads on. How'd you like to bat three?' He just beamed.

Most batsmen like to settle back into their rhythm after a lunch or tea break, take an over or two to loosen up, get their feet moving, and get back in the groove. Laxman walked out after lunch, took guard to McGrath, and cracked a good length ball to the boundary. He did the same to Gillespie first ball after tea.

At stumps we were 254 for 4, with Laxman on 109 and Dravid on 7. We were 20 runs behind, with six wickets left and two days to play. It hadn't gone entirely according to plan for the Aussies, but they were still in the box seat.

Watching Laxman knocking up before play the next day, the former Indian player, and now commentator, Sanjay Manjrekar observed that it was like he hadn't had a break; mentally he'd never left the crease. Coaches are always telling batsmen to 'bat all day', but Laxman and Dravid set themselves to do it. We just watched and kept telling them, 'See you after the next session'.

Dravid suffered from dehydration — we didn't have enough of those neckerchiefs batsmen wear to keep cool, so we cut towels into strips, dunked them in ice and sent them out — but his discipline and concentration were fierce. When he reached 100 he made a pointed gesture to the media box, his only shot in anger. Laxman, meanwhile, sailed on imperiously. The Indian batsmen had no fear of Warne, so I didn't contemplate telling them how they should and shouldn't play him. When Warne bowled around the wicket, pitching into the rough outside leg stump, Laxman would go down the wicket. If he didn't quite get to the pitch of the ball, he'd hit inside out through the covers. If he did, he'd flick the same delivery through midwicket. For hour after hour, under the pressure of knowing that if he got out, the series was lost, he produced batsmanship that was beyond the imagination, let alone the capability, of most players.

Quite simply, he played the greatest innings I've ever seen. After the first few sessions he'd come in smiling, looking as fresh as a daisy, while Dravid was struggling. But things got really tough after tea. They were both running on empty and it was all about survival, because if the Aussies broke through, it was still anyone's game. When they came in at stumps, there were about half a dozen doctors waiting to lay them out on the lunch table and put them on drips.

Laxman very nearly didn't play that game. On the eve of it he was 'listing', meaning his shoulders and hips weren't in line. Listing is the body's protective mechanism to relieve the load on a damaged part of the back. Andrew Leipus straightened him out, but in the morning the tilt was back and we had to make a decision on whether he could play. It was a gut call and once it was made I forgot about it, because I knew Leipus would keep him going. And he did, although not without a certain amount of edge-of-the-chair anxiety, because he could see the warning signs before the rest of us. At every break he'd work on the Leaning Tower of India until Laxman was more or less in alignment and send him back out again.

Every time Laxman passed a milestone, a message would flash up on the giant screen at Eden Gardens announcing another financial windfall. Until then, the highest test score by an Indian was 236 — surprisingly low, considering how many great batsmen they've produced — and there was great celebration when Laxman passed it. The Cricket Association of Bengal (CAB), the host body, announced that they would give him 200,000 rupees for his double century, 1000 rupees for every run beyond 200, and 2000 rupees for every run beyond 236. (The current exchange rate is 28 rupees to the NZ dollar.) Then the West Bengal state government got in on the act, extending its largesse to Harbhajan. It caused some amusement in the dressing room, and I couldn't help dwelling on the contradiction between our team-building efforts and the authorities' rush to reward individuals. The next newsflash was more palatable: if we won the test, the CAB would give the team 500,000 rupees.

By stumps on the fourth day we'd saved the game and it felt like victory. Australia's winning streak was over. That evening, Ganguly hosted the team at his home. I don't know of any other cricketer who lives like Ganguly: in a mansion, with his entire extended family and a fleet of cars. Somehow word got around and there were crowds along the route as we drove across Kolkata. A boy shoved his autograph book through the window, but I couldn't give it back to him because the sheer volume of people meant he couldn't keep up with the bus.

Over dinner, Ganguly and I discussed the declaration. I was strongly of the view that the Aussies didn't like being played out of a game to the point that all they could do was hang on for a draw, so we delayed the declaration until just before lunch. After the Laxman-Dravid epic there was light relief for everyone but the Aussies in the form of Zaheer Khan and Harbhajan, who together put on a madcap 30-odd, throwing the bat like axe murderers. For the Australians it must have been the last straw. We'd left ourselves only 75 overs to win the game. Pretty much to a man the punditry reckoned we'd got it wrong and said so ad nauseam.

I'd never been at Eden Gardens with a full house. There were 40,000 there when New Zealand played Zimbabwe at the 1987 World Cup, but, impressive as that sounds, the scene bore no resemblance to that fifth afternoon, with 100,000 fans baying for an Indian victory. The crowd and the Indian players feed off one another, and the atmosphere builds and builds, which is why wickets tend to fall in clusters. When that happens, delirium reigns and the stands literally shake.

I typed away on my laptop to keep myself occupied and to appear coolly professional: 'There is absolute bedlam. A wicket went down four minutes ago and the noise hasn't stopped. It's absolutely humming, like a low growl.'

There's no more intimidating environment than Eden Gardens with a full house and the Indian spinners weaving their magic and the close-in fielders diving — and appealing — for everything. The pressure mounts and the atmosphere envelops the ground like a thunderstorm about to break. Watching a new batsman making his way to the middle brings to mind the image of a lone swimmer walking out into a threatening sea. And when he gets out there, the new batsman must feel like a lone swimmer in a threatening sea, surrounded by a school of sharks.

Slater and Hayden put on 74 for the first wicket. After the breakthrough, we chipped away and the momentum built. Something had to give, and it was the Australian middle order. S.S. Das and Sadagopan Ramesh were brilliant at short leg and bat-pad respectively, and with overs running out Das took a stunning catch to remove Gillespie.

They were all out for 212 in 68 overs; having followed-on, we'd won the test by 171 runs. I remember embracing Leipus and dancing a jig with him, which isn't something I do every day, and Buchanan shouting over the din, 'Just enjoy it'. The stands seemed to be on fire. When India wins at Eden Gardens, the spectators light up their newspapers like torches. I hoped they were the editions in which we'd been written off.

It's easy to be wise after the event and say Steve Waugh shouldn't have enforced the follow-on. They'd won the first test inside three days, and led by 274 in the first innings one hour into the third day; most captains wouldn't have thought twice. We were down and out, and if Waugh had elected to bat again and we'd got out of jail, he would've been castigated for his un-Australian caution. Ever since that game, though, captains are a little less gung-ho about enforcing the follow-on. It's as if Laxman and Dravid are looking over their shoulders.

They turned the tide and gave us the confidence to go out and compete, but it shouldn't be forgotten that without Harbhajan landing it in his box, it would have been a draw. I'd played 80-odd tests and seen a lot of cricket, but nothing to compare with that game. It was a privilege to be in the Indian dressing room that evening.

On to Chennai. The Aussies had been in the field at Eden Gardens for a long time and now it was the end of March, full-on summer, the 'hottest' season in Chennai. (As an aside, India shouldn't give their toughest opponents a break by having them tour before Christmas when the weather's cooler and the wickets don't turn as much, as happened when Australia returned in 2004.) The dynamic had changed: the Australians had lost a little of their stature and we'd grown. They'd been made to think, and although they were still confident there was less of the swagger that had been so evident in Mumbai. A few cracks were starting to appear. Warne's fitness had become a hot topic, fuelled by statements from within the Australian camp. Nothing illustrated the shift better than the fact that in Chennai a lot of the verbal jousting was initiated by the Indians. Guys like Tendulkar and Dravid, not normally the most loquacious characters on the field, enjoyed asking Steve Waugh how the final frontier was looking now.

The selectors, Ganguly and I were criticised for chopping and changing the spinners who bowled alongside Harbhajan. (Our bowling statistics for that series bring to mind the English jibe about the New Zealand attack when Richard Hadlee was in his prime: like facing the World XI at one end and the Ilford Seconds at the other.) It was horses for courses; Sanghvi was unlucky to get dropped but we brought in Venkatapathy Raju for the second test to tie up one end. We wanted to play three spinners in Chennai and felt we needed variety, so we brought in the tall left-armer Nilesh Kulkarni, who'd troubled the Aussies in a warm-up game, and the leggie, Sairaj Bahutule. It meant the Australians kept coming up against different spinners who posed different problems.

We were also getting our specialist catchers sorted out. Ganguly fancied himself as a slipper but Dravid was our best catcher, so he was first slip, and Laxman was very good at second. In Das and Ramesh we had superb operators at short leg and bat-pad. Their contribution was overshadowed by the bowling and batting, but it was significant nevertheless.

Meanwhile behind the scenes . . . The BCCI had agreed that we could have a computer analyst, but he had to stay in another hotel because his allowance didn't stretch to five stars. By the time a player or coach gets back to the hotel after a day's play and has a shower and a meal, the last thing he wants to do is get in a taxi to go and look at footage. On the one hand, a mundane detail; on the other, an irritant and a hassle we could have done without while trying to beat the best team in the world.

Nayan Mongia, who was by far the best keeper in India, had broken his nose in Kolkata but had passed his fitness test and was told he was playing. An hour before play started the selection panel turned up; they held a meeting on the ground as we did our warm-ups and decided Mongia couldn't play with a broken nose. I curtly commented that these things were best sorted out a little earlier than 50 minutes before the first ball was to be bowled. I had to tell Mongia he was out and the standby keeper Samir Dighe that he was in. We lost the toss, Dighe missed a couple of chances in the first session, and the selectors' ears must have been burning.

After the drama of Kolkata, Chennai could have been a let-down, but in fact there was no let-up in either the quality of the cricket or the tension. The catching went to another level; Hayden got a double century, Tendulkar produced the hundred he'd been threatening, and Harbhajan took 15 wickets. The crowd got right into this game too. In Chennai the players' viewing areas are at ground level and are separated only by a metal railing, so you have both the opposition and the crowd right in your face. This game was a real rollercoaster and I'd occasionally glance over at my counterpart, Buchanan, wondering how he was enjoying the ride.

Batting last, we needed 155 to win. After Das went early, playing an awful shot, things progressed smoothly until Ramesh had a brainstorm: he pushed a ball gently to cover, advanced to the middle of the wicket, and stayed there. Then those small-target wobbles set in as the Australians lifted their intensity, and anxiety crept into the batsmen's minds. The tension was enormous. I tried to relieve it by cracking jokes; they got a few nervous laughs, which were probably more than they deserved. At tea I sneaked off for a cigarette. I realise that smoking's bad for you, but the alternative seemed worse.

Laxman had made 65 in the first innings and looked like bringing us home in the second. He'd reached 66 off 82 balls, with 12 fours, and was taking them apart with surgical precision when Colin Miller bowled him a juicy long-hop. It was begging to be hit and Laxman obliged, smashing it clean out of the screws. No one but Mark Waugh could have caught it. Unfortunately, that's who happened to be at mid-wicket.

I tapped away on my laptop, a study in composed professionalism. What I actually wrote was: 'That may be the Test match. Shit, shit, shit.'

135 for 6. Laxman stood rooted to the spot in utter disbelief, looking as if he was going to burst into tears. Bahutule went for a duck — 135 for 7. An awful lot rested on the shoulders of Dighe, who shouldn't even have been playing. His earlier lapses notwithstanding, he was a good man for the situation, a cheeky, street-smart operator who knew every trick in the book. When Zaheer got out to the middle, Dighe told him loudly and in English that Miller was bowling really well and turning it square. Who knows whether Steve Waugh paid any attention, but he gave Miller another over from which Dighe took 10 precious runs. Then Zaheer went — 151 for 8. Enter Harbhajan, who, over the series, had taken 32 of the 50 Australian wickets to fall — a fantastic contribution but now at risk of being all in vain. He has a great sense of occasion and is a genuinely unpredictable batsman, in the sense that he doesn't really know himself how he's going to play. But we had two fighters out there, which is what you want in these situations. Harbhajan speared one between third slip and gully and Tony Greig screamed, 'And that's it, India have won the series'.

Some of the Indian players had been in the team that beat Mark Taylor's outfit in 1998, but this was a stronger Australian side. They'd rolled into India like an unstoppable machine with their state-of-the-art technology and lateral thinking and hardball mental disintegration tactics. We lost all three tosses; we were without Kumble, a genuine match-winner; and Srinath, our new-ball spearhead, missed the second and third tests. The series showed what this team was capable of at home and what the Australians were made

The first TV interview: 'Why?' Ian Chappell wouldn't take my fine sentiments at face value!

The men in the hot (plastic) seats — Sourav Ganguly and I face the press.

Getting to know you, take one. In discussion with Sachin Tendulkar and Sourav Ganguly (right) during my first test in charge.

'Patience, John, patience.' Raj Singh Dungarpur, who kept a paternal eye on me early on, dispenses valuable advice.

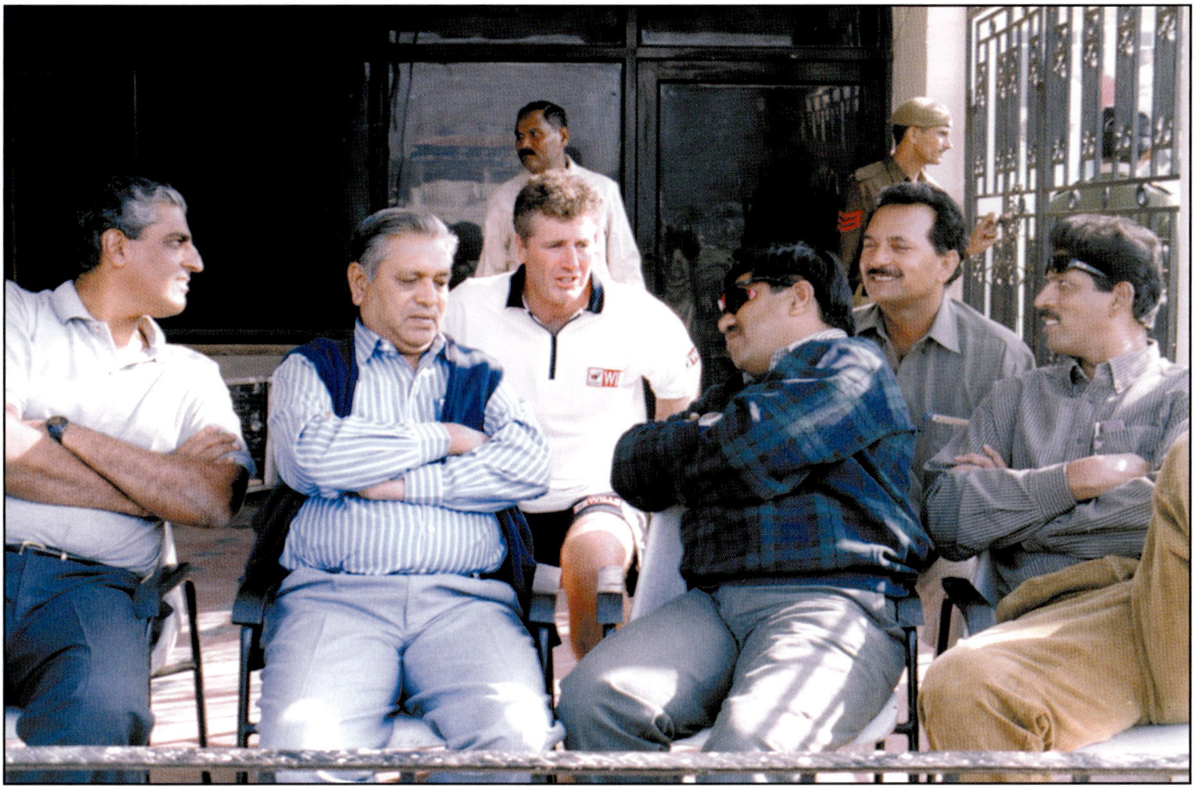

Pradeep Mandhani

Getting to know you, take two. My first meeting with the selection panel, from left to right: Sanjay Jagdale, Chandu Borde, Ashok Malhotra, Madan Lal and T.A. Sekhar.

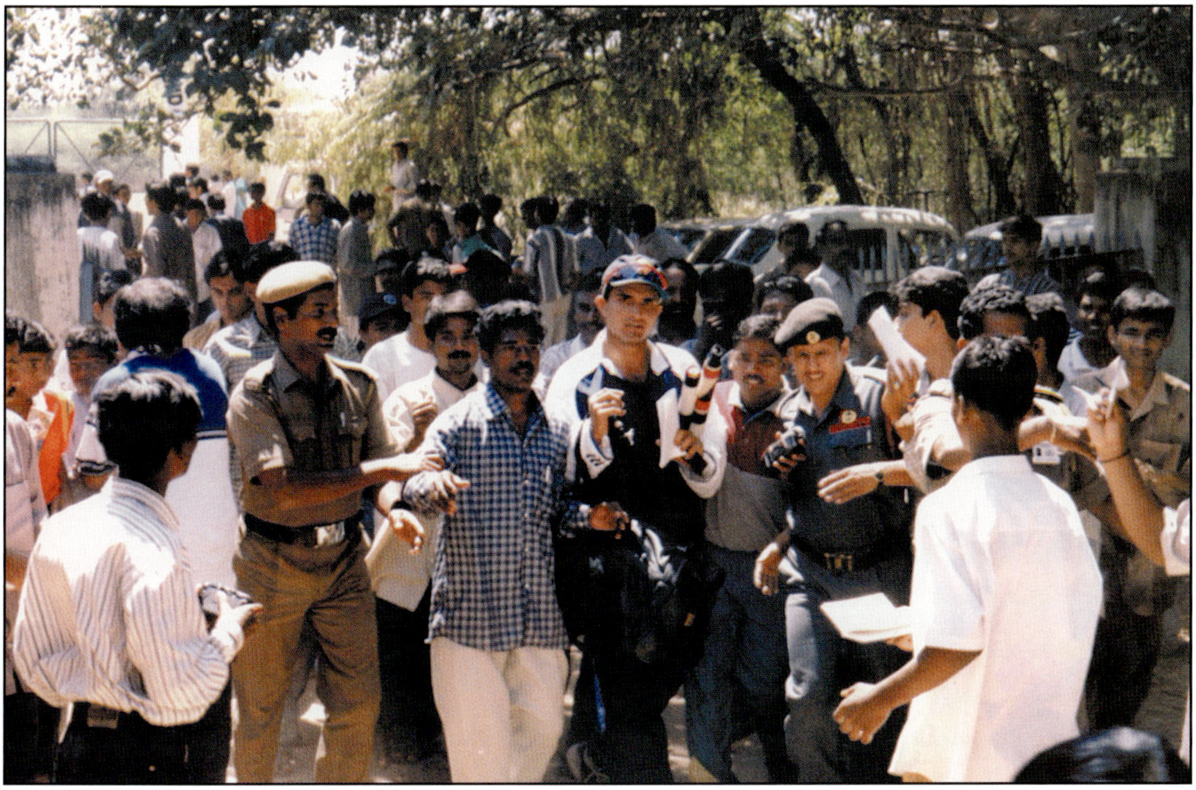

John Wright Collection

Indian cricket doesn't do low-key entrances. Sourav Ganguly and friends arrive at our training camp before the 2001 home series against Australia.

Pradeep Mandhani

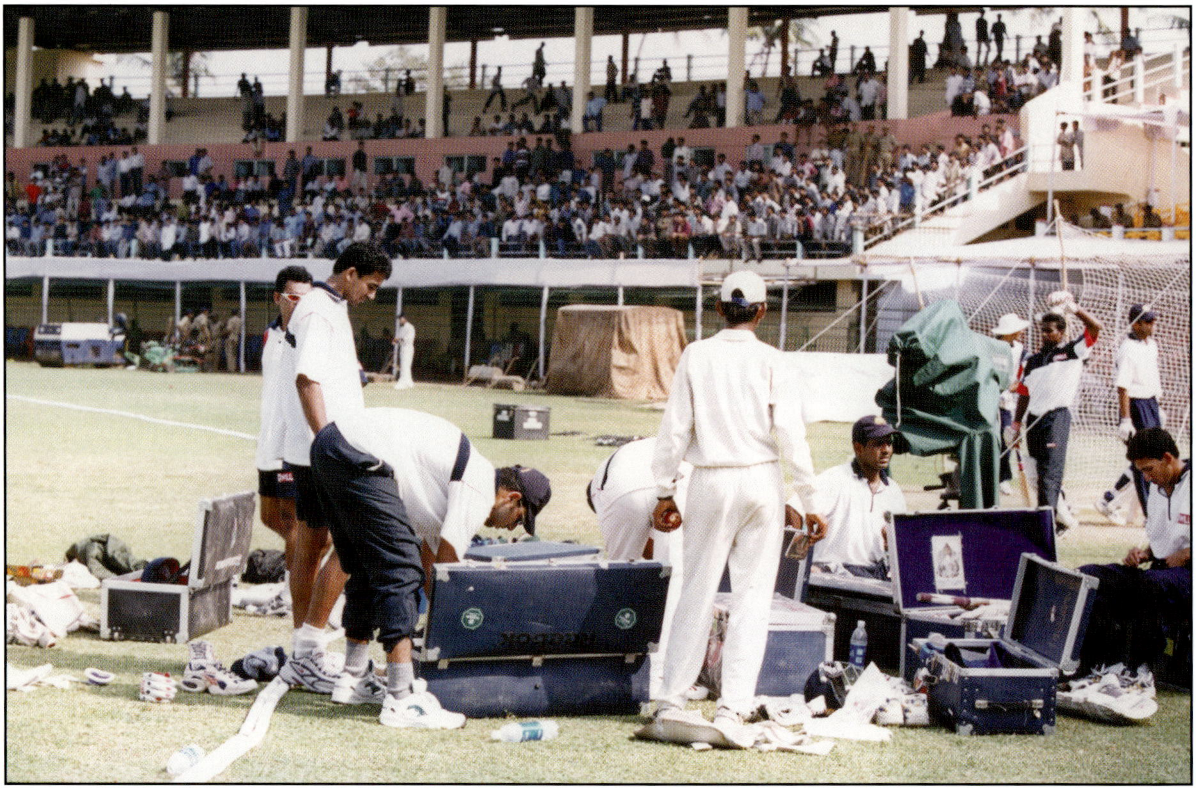

A reasonable turnout for net practice in Cuttack.

Pradeep Mandhani

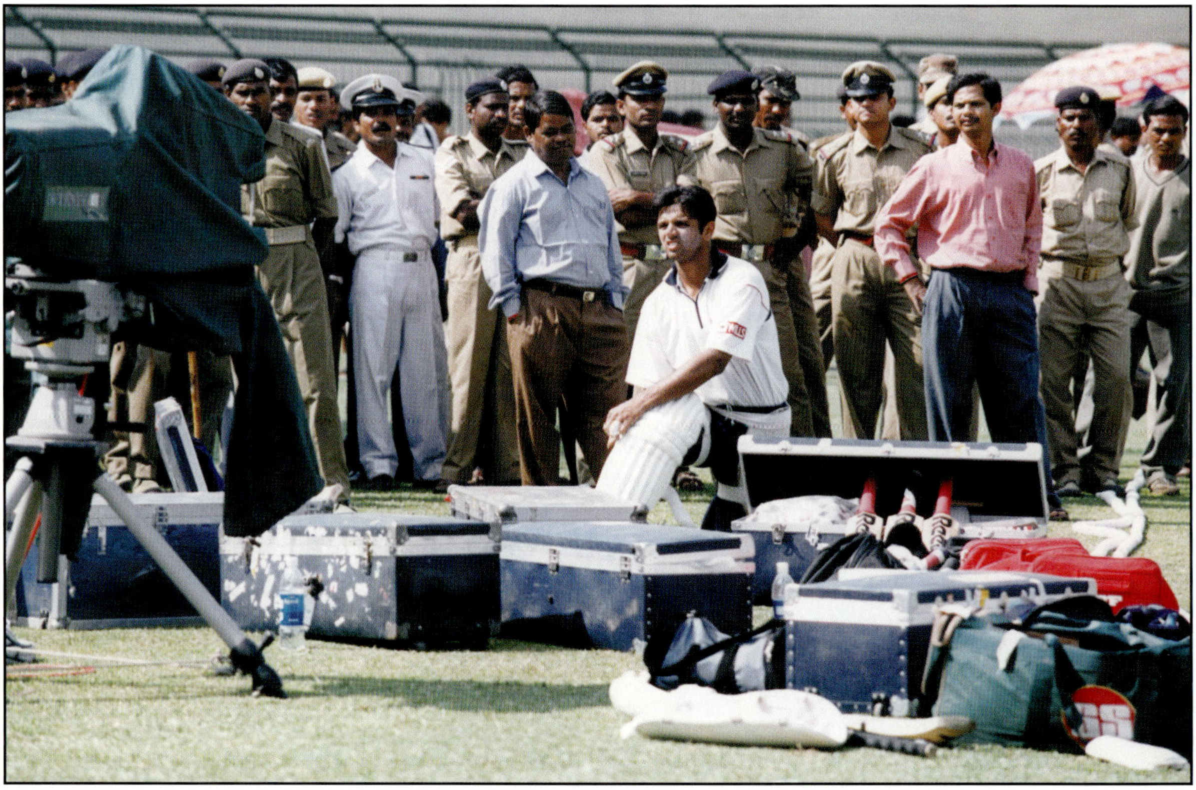

Rahul Dravid pads up, confident that his belongings will be safe while he's in the nets.

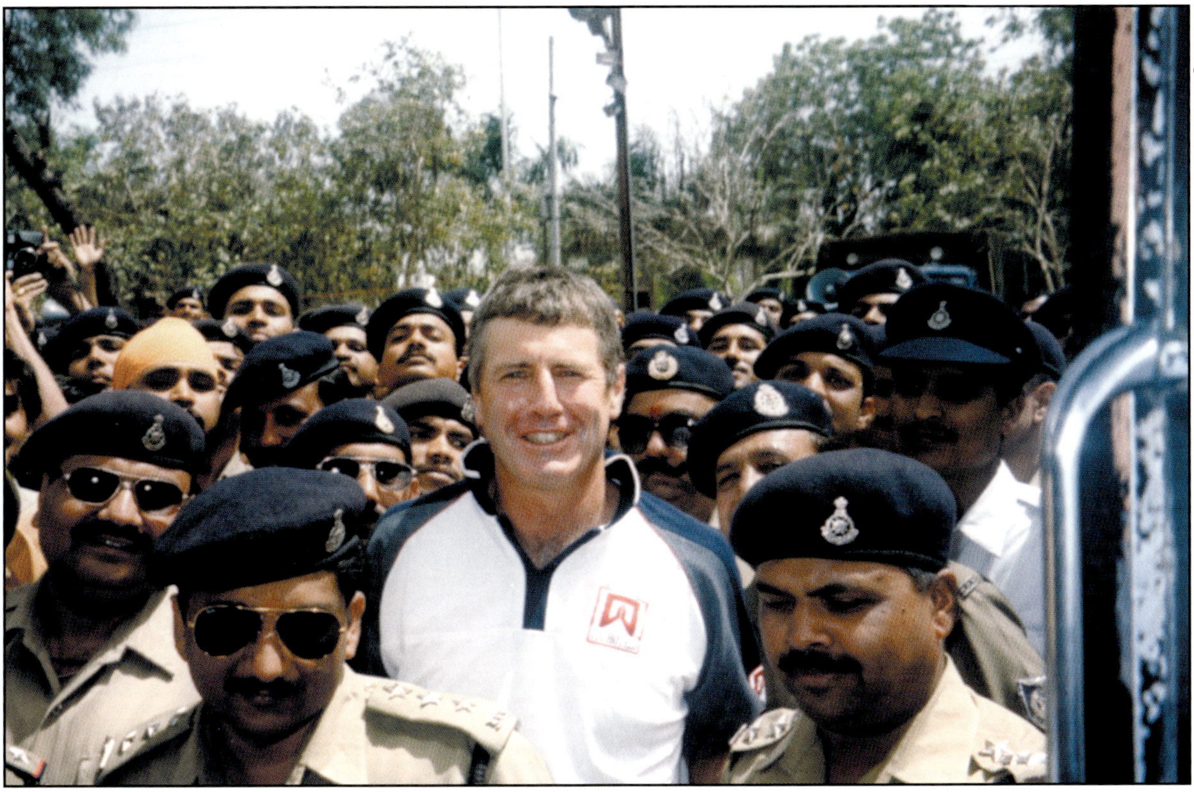

John Wright Collection

There's no such thing as too much security.

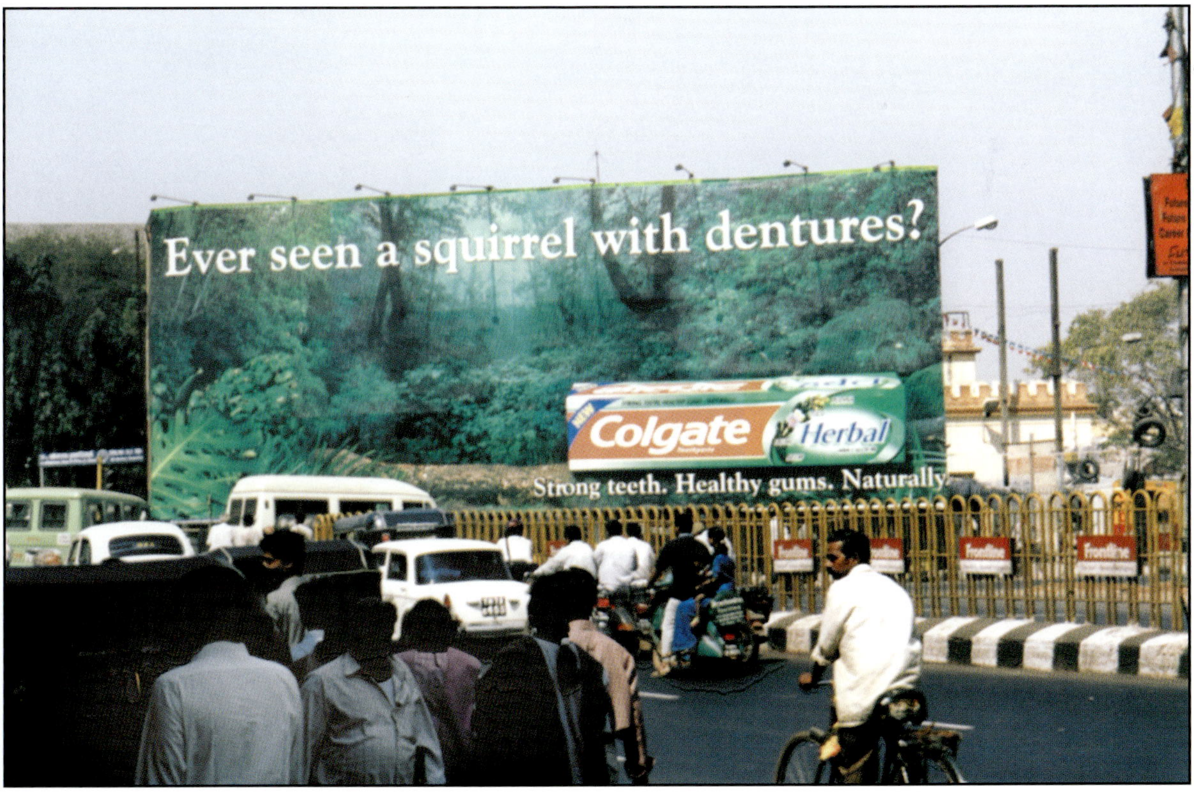

John Wright Collection

Well, since you ask . . . Indian billboards were a constant source of amusement.

Pradeep Mandhani

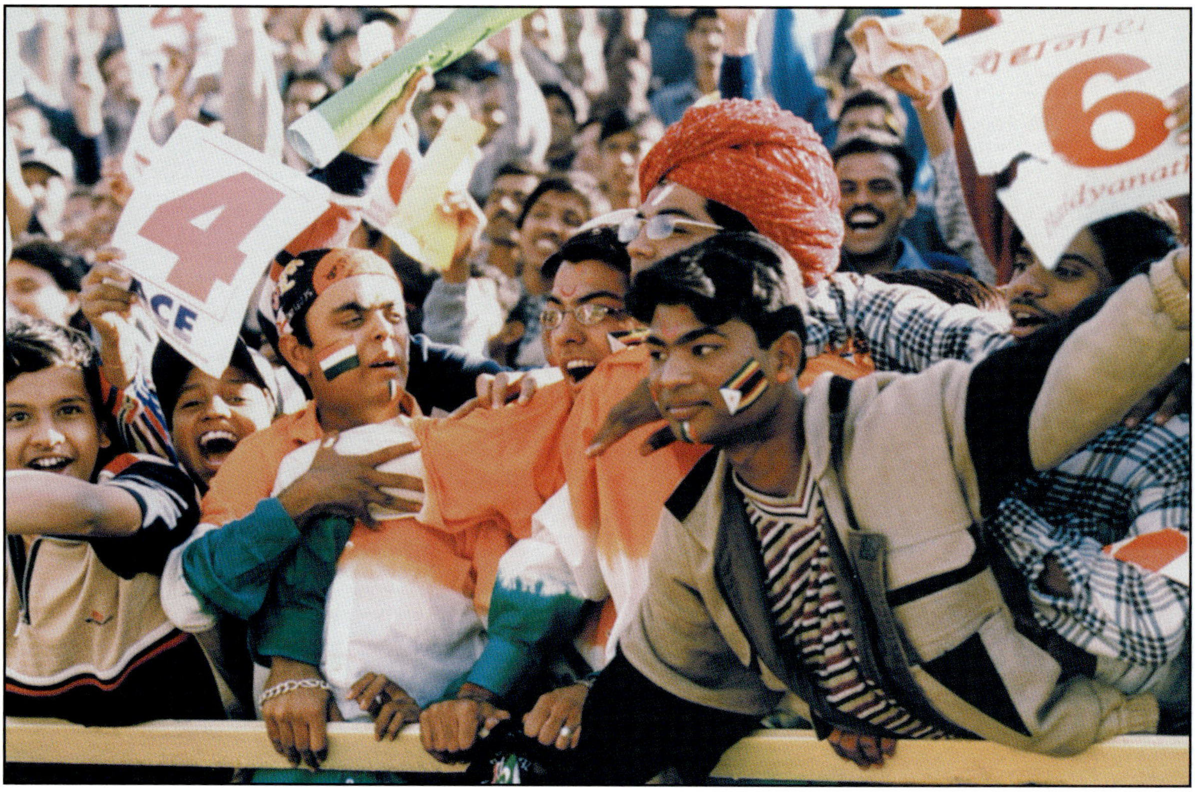

Indian fans . . . the colour and the passion.

John Wright Collection

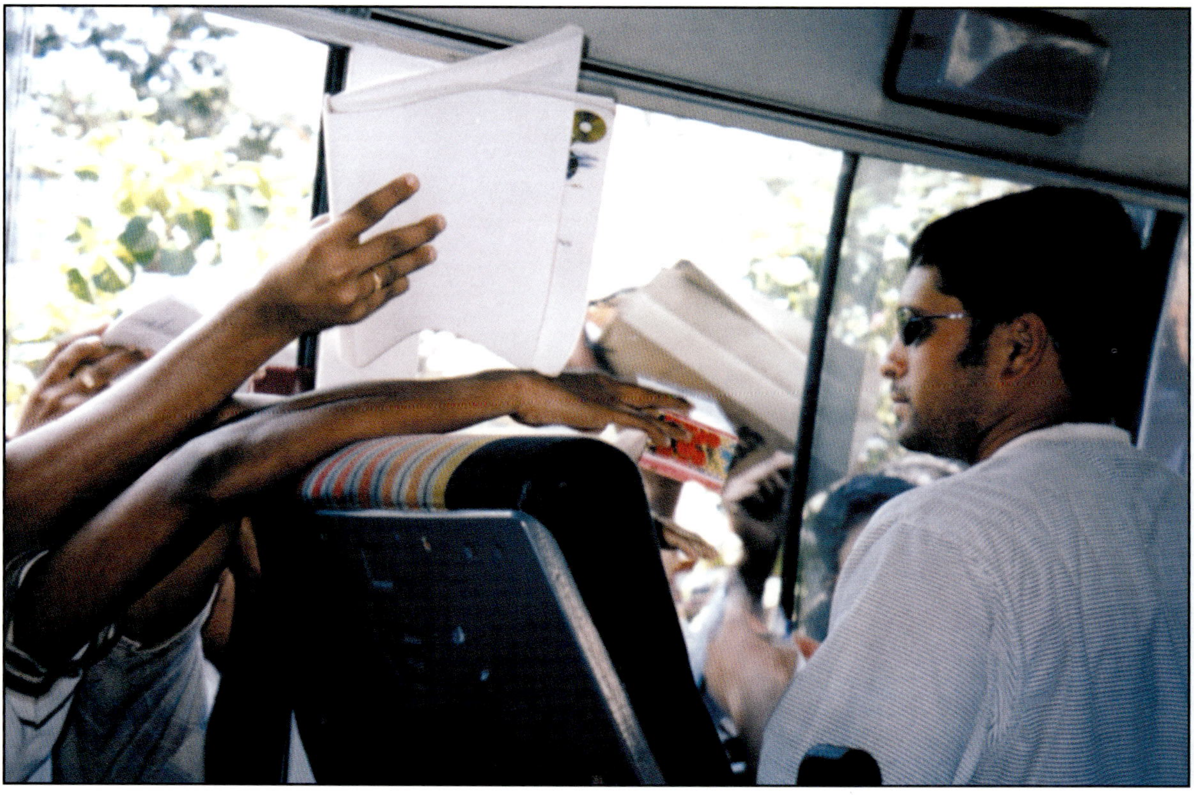

The everyday reality of being Sachin Tendulkar.

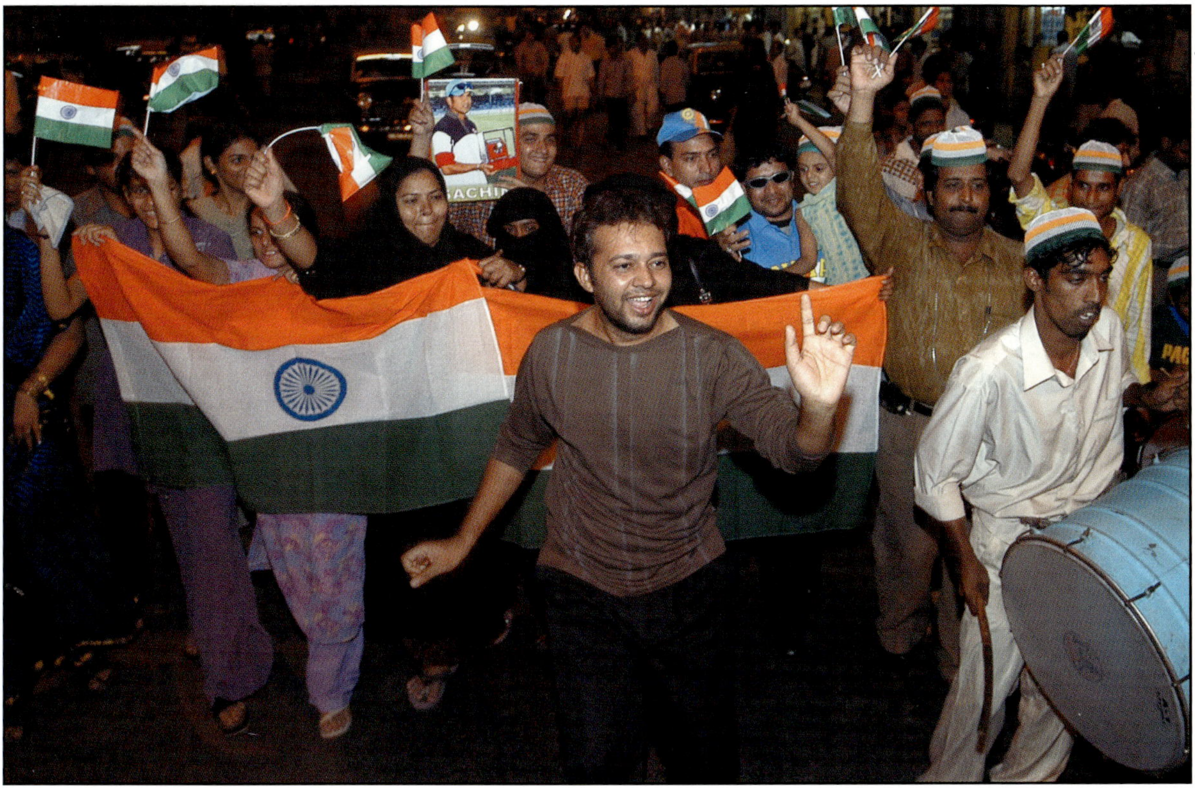

Mid-day, India

No matter how bad things are, you're always only one win away from glory. Fans take to the streets to celebrate our turnaround at the 2003 World Cup.

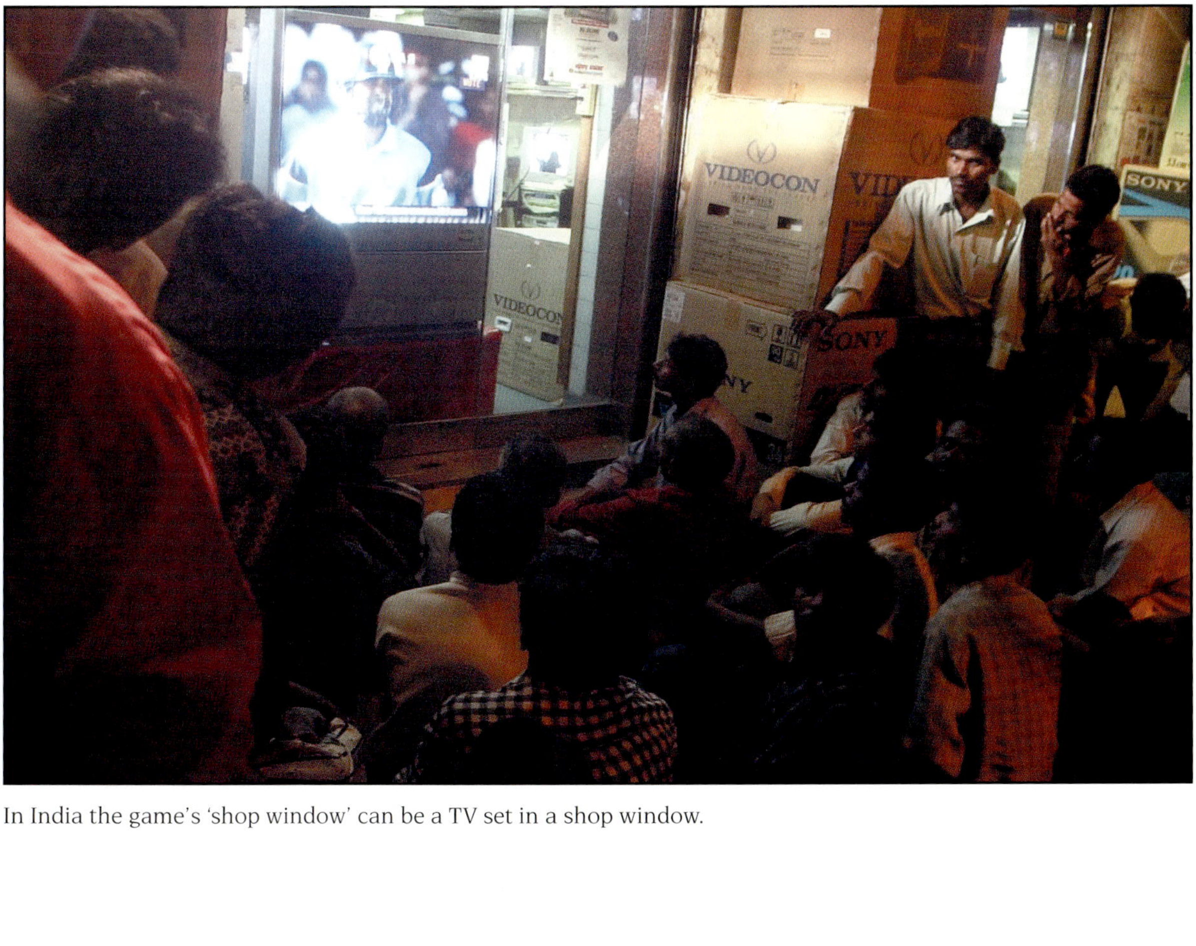

Mid-day, India

In India the game's 'shop window' can be a TV set in a shop window.

John Wright Collection

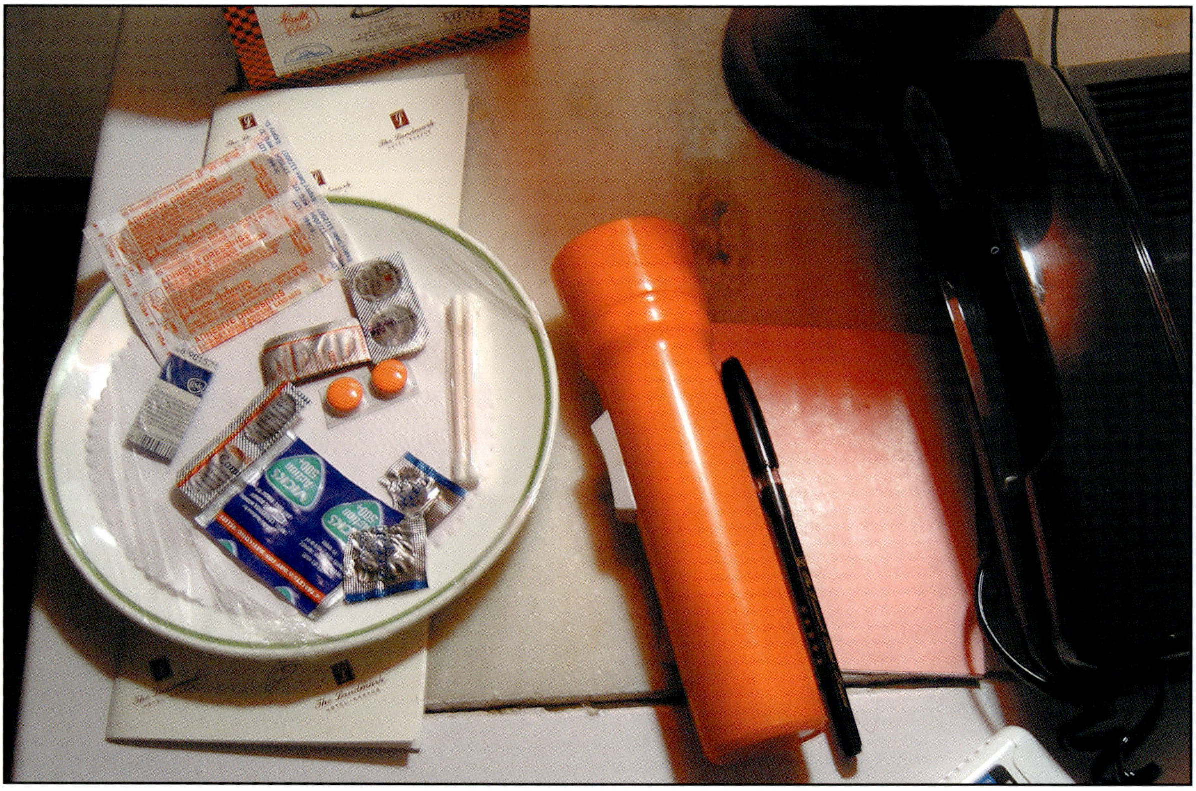

Prepared for any eventuality: the Landmark Hotel in Kanpur.

John Wright Collection

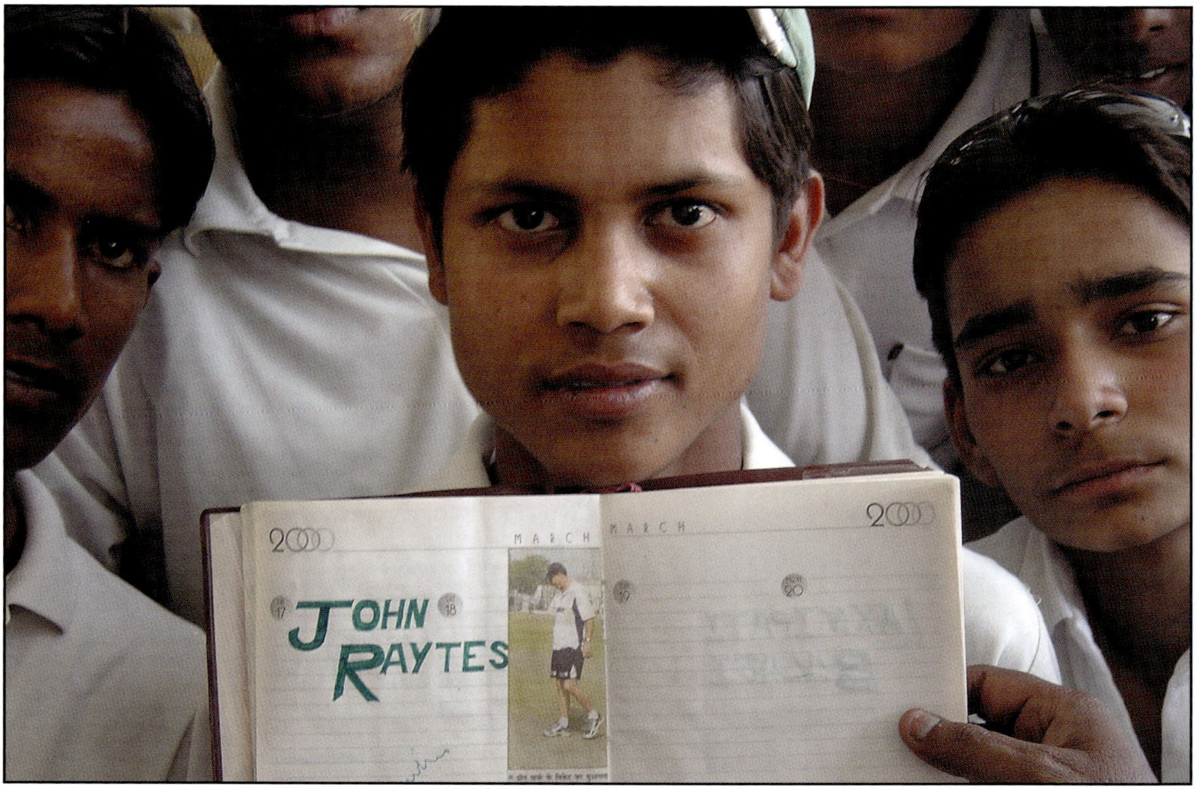

It's nice to be appreciated. Like any coach my ratings fluctuated according to results.

of. They fought to the end and left something of themselves in the Chepauk stadium. In their dressing room, Gillespie and McGrath lay on the treatment table, utterly exhausted. Some of them stared into space, others chatted quietly. It was Steve Waugh's last tour of India, their final frontier. And when they thought it was just a matter of snuffing out the last feeble pockets of resistance, they'd been hit by a counterattack from which they never quite recovered. But they took defeat like the champion side they were, making no excuses and acknowledging the Indian performance. No matter how good you are, there are no guarantees in sport, and the bigger the prize, the more devastating the disappointment if you fall short.

I was drained. All I wanted to do was unwind over a few quiet beers in a dark corner of a bar and start getting rid of the accumulated tension that had left me aching all over. Instead, we had to get on a bus and drive to an entertainment centre on the outskirts of Chennai to make a paid appearance at a corporate function that involved a question-and-answer session and playing ten-pin bowls in an indoor rink cheered on by a bunch of middle managers and their families. If you can think of a more bizarre way to celebrate winning one of the most memorable series in cricket history, you have a more creative imagination than I do.

That series was the making of Harbhajan. We started out in the same boat, both having to prove ourselves to the sceptics and detractors, who weren't exactly thin on the ground. He embraced the box theory and when he saw it working, his confidence grew. He also worked out a method of bowling to Gilchrist, bringing the ball in and keeping it up, denying him the opportunity to sweep without risk. Gilchrist didn't get many runs after Mumbai. It was the start of the Dravid-Laxman alliance. They've never forgotten how to create a partnership, no matter what the situation and what number they come in. They trust each other and bat accordingly: Dravid knows Laxman will cut loose when he can, and Laxman knows Dravid won't throw it away or fret about being overshadowed.

The series also set a benchmark for drama and excitement which, if it's maintained over the next two or three series, will surely see Australia versus India supplant the Ashes as the game's blue-ribbon rivalry.

For me personally, the series was a big step forward. I no longer felt like a punching bag for the ex-players-turned-critics brigade, and I'd become comfortable with the players and them with me. During the second test, I left my diary lying around. Before I could retrieve it, someone drew a couple of cartoons in it. The first showed a head hidden in wreaths of smoke, the second a stick figure en route to the gents. Below it the artist had scribbled, 'Coach, don't be in such a curry! I think we've got the Aussies on the run'.

We Don't Like Cricket, We Love It

In India's teeming cities the kids always find somewhere to play cricket: in narrow side streets, between buildings, beside railway tracks, in parking lots and, on Sundays, in the empty business districts. Legend has it that Sunil Gavaskar's technique was the result of playing in an alley where you had to play straight because hitting a wall or a window was out. In the countryside, they even play in paddy fields and in the sand on dunes. We once drove past a game going on around a dead horse. Andrew Leipus reckoned it must have dropped a catch.

The Azad Maidan is a Mumbai rarity: an open patch of clay and grass in the middle of a city. The Maidan is home to 20 cricket clubs, each with its own pitch and pavilion, which may be nothing more than a tent. You don't take your deck chair to the Maidan, because space is at a premium. There might be twenty games going on in an area ten times the size of a rugby field, so there's a lot of overlap: being at long on in one game could place you at bat-pad in another. It's non-stop action — bowlers charging in, batsmen throwing the bat, fielders throwing themselves, puffs of red dust raised by 40 batsmen pounding up and down 20 pitches, and a barrage of advice from the sidelines. In a corner of the ground, a mob of people mill around waiting their turn to have a hit or a bowl against a wall. At 6 a.m. that morning there would have been a queue of people, young and not-so-young, wanting a go in the practice nets run by the clubs.

In the — relatively speaking — smaller towns there might be one turf wicket or there might be none. During my first one-day series, we played in Bhubaneswar, a city of more than a million people. I got some odd looks when I told the team there'd be fielding practice the next morning; they said there was nowhere to do it. Our fielding had been awful, so I vowed to find a ground. I was up at the crack of dawn next day and set off with the liaison man to find a suitable venue. We went to the soccer ground, where the grass was too long; then to the athletics stadium, where there was no grass at all and the surface was like a gravel road. Our test opener, S.S. Das, was a local boy so I asked to be taken to his club ground. I'd been told it was unsuitable but figured it couldn't be any worse than what I'd seen. There was a concrete strip with a mud outfield that was so uneven you could get seasick walking out to bat. I couldn't comprehend how a product of that environment could develop into an international cricketer. No wonder some players, when venturing onto a test arena, would touch the ground, then place their hand on their heart and forehead. This very Indian gesture is a mark of respect for the place in which you practise your craft and earn your living. Many of India's classical musicians and dancers do the same when they go on stage.

Even though – or perhaps because – they start out playing the game in such insalubrious settings and straitened circumstances, India's best players possess great flair and, in some special cases, pure artistry. Rahul Dravid can appear unassertive, even passive, but looks are deceptive: the air of tranquillity is accompanied by a precision-tooled technique and an iron will that combine to blunt, then dismantle, bowling attacks. Sachin Tendulkar has the entire repertoire and can choose between subtlety and aggression, wrist and muscle, or touch and power, like a golfer selecting a club. V.V.S. Laxman is the cricketing equivalent of a faith-healer; his hands seem to possess magical properties enabling him to dispatch the ball in whichever direction takes his fancy. Sourav Ganguly strokes the ball as if not wanting to damage it and hits spinners for six down the ground with the nonchalance of a man tilting a top hat, as the great cricket writer Alan Ross wrote of Colin Cowdrey. And then there's Virender Sehwag, cricket's Jumping Jack Flash. When he goes off, you do not leave your seat, regardless of hunger, thirst or calls of nature.

India stops for cricket. When a team is announced, they break away from the news or current affairs programmes and cross live to their cricket reporter. Every news channel scrolls live cricket scores across the bottom of the screen along with the weather, the stock market and breaking news. When there was a terrorist attack on the Parliament in New Delhi during a test match in 2001, it took some channels a while to realise that it probably wasn't appropriate to keep running the cricket score.

When Harvinder Singh, a fast bowler from Punjab, made his debut in a one-day tournament in Toronto, the appliance shops in his hometown stayed open well past midnight so that people who didn't own a TV could watch the local hero. During the 2003 World Cup, the residents of a village in Northern India that didn't have cable TV chipped in 30,000 rupees (about NZ$1200; and to give that some context, the average annual wage is less than NZ$1000) to get a 6.5 km cable run in from the nearest town. They put TV sets on tractors in community areas and had generators and car batteries on standby in case they lost electricity. When that happened during one match, they restored the picture by connecting the TV to a high-voltage overhead wire.

During a test in Delhi, Sehwag dived for a catch at midwicket and stayed down. He thought he'd broken his shoulder, but it turned out to be a sprained AC joint. Rugby players suffering this injury have been known to get strapped up and sent back out to finish the game. However, Leipus decided on a precautionary X-ray to make sure nothing else had been damaged, so Sehwag was bunged into a standby ambulance that contained so many doctors that Leipus had to hitch a ride with the police escort, several jeeps full of heavily-armed cops. They barrelled over to the hospital, sirens blaring and lights flashing, as if they were rushing the President to the operating theatre after an assassination attempt. At the hospital, Leipus had to fight his way through a scrum of specialists to get to Sehwag. When the patient mentioned that he was feeling a bit faint, i.e. claustrophobic, the specialists insisted that he remain overnight for observation. As Leipus said, it was just India looking after one of its princes.

Not that long ago hockey was the sport in which India strutted on the global stage. But since India won the last of its eight Olympic gold medals in 1980, international success has been hard to come by and the sport has been in decline. India's cricketers won the World Cup in 1983 and the World Championship tournament in Australia two years later, and since then cricket has steadily cemented its position as India's No. 1 sport.

The potent combination of television and the one-day game has been a major factor in cricket's rise. TV has taken the game to far-flung corners of the country, where previously it was hardly played at all. The players now emerging from these regions have learned the game by watching and copying, which in some ways is preferable to being taught how to play by coaches. As a result, the likes of Sehwag or the wicketkeeper-batsman Mahendra Singh Dhoni can come out of nowhere with methods based on instinct and improvisation, and without the fear of failure that can be instilled by over-coaching and a conventional career path. In Dhoni's home town the batsmen apparently don't bother with ones and twos; they're only interested in fours and sixes. It's as if they've modelled their game on a one-day highlights package.

Indian cricket was far removed from the environment that I had played and coached in. It was involved and exciting. People would come to watch us practise in their thousands. On the drive to some grounds, I could see families gathered either at the side of the road or leaning over balconies or on other vantage points, just to see our bus go past. Mothers holding their babies, dads dressed in singlets, young kids smiling and waving. Brash young men on motorcycles would race right up alongside the bus, risking life and limb to wave frantically at their favourites. All the buses had curtains on them so the players could get some privacy.

There is no typical India or typical Indian. I've been a guest at the Maharajah of Gwalior's palace and at the ultra-modern headquarters of Infosys, the Bangalore-based software giant that earned NZ$2.2 billion in 2004–05. All of this is India, and the boys I worked with belonged to a country of a billion people where languages, customs and the landscape changed every few hundred kilometres.

I tried to understand the country through the Indian dressing room. It had Hindus, Muslims, Christians and Sikhs. Some were very religious, others less so. On checking into a hotel room, some players would put up pictures of their gods on the television or bedside table and pray at these mini-shrines every day. India has 22 official languages and, on a given day, there could be eight languages, other than English, spoken in our dressing room. Our run-outs sometimes suggested that the boys were perhaps not calling in the same tongue. Ganguly and Laxman, who weren't exactly greyhounds to start with, once managed to have a head-on collision. Unless they were talking to the opposition, the players generally swore in Hindi. Some boys were vegetarian, some weren't. Some ate rice, others ate wheat. From an outsider's point of view, you wondered what one corner of India had in common with the other. In our dressing room, it was cricket.

Historically, Indian cricket has had a heavy focus on the individual star but as public expectation grows there's an increasing emphasis on the result rather than individual performances. Getting them to play as a team was a priority. I used to tell them their fans deserved a fighting team rather than fighting individuals. The worst times for me were when team pride and a sense of obligation to the fans weren't in evidence; but when they went into battle together and fired up, the crowd's response was something to see.

Indian fans don't spend much time in a state of emotional equilibrium.

If they're not in ecstasy, they're in despair. If we'd won, the people at the airports we passed through en route to the next game were all smiles; if we'd lost, the atmosphere would be subdued but never, it must be said, hostile. Paradoxically perhaps, they have short memories and come the next game, they're once again full of hope and willing to invest the same amount of emotional energy.

It's actually not that easy to see big games live. Tickets are expensive, prohibitively so for the person in the street. In Chennai you paid 200 rupees (NZ$7) to 'squat', i.e. plonk your backside on a small area of concrete. For a seat, you'd pay three times as much. The cheapest seats for a one-dayer at Eden Gardens were about 700 rupees (NZ$25), although students and cricketers got them for as little as 150 rupees. That was all very well, but getting your hands on those tickets meant queuing up for hours, if not overnight, because there were never enough to go around. In the major centres, like Mumbai, only 10 per cent of the seats were available to the public, with the rest set aside for the host association's league or member clubs, donors, sponsors and other state associations. On top of that, thousands of complimentary tickets would be distributed to local government bigwigs and politicians, the police, the stadium's suppliers of commodities, such as electricity and water, and anyone else who had to be kept happy.

When India played South Africa in a one-dayer in late 2005, the queue began to form early on Friday, at a ticket outlet that opened on Saturday morning, for a game on Monday. By the time the outlet opened, the queue was a kilometre long. An 11-year-old boy and his father travelled 90 kms and spent the night on the street to give themselves a chance of getting 300-rupee (NZ$11) 'squat' seats. The police on duty were worried that the boy might get hurt if there was a rush when the booth opened, so they moved him to the head of the queue and gave him a chair to sit on. He got the first ticket and had his photo in the local paper. The father told the paper his son wanted to be a cricketer and the family was planning to move closer to Mumbai to give him a better chance.

Getting a ticket was only half the battle. If you wanted to see the first ball bowled, you had to be queuing to get into the ground at least two hours before the start of play. Often, when we played in the smaller centres, there were ticketing fiascos that led to angry ticket-holders clashing with police because the ground was full and they weren't allowed in. The president of one association was arrested for circulating 25,000 fake tickets, which led to 10,000 disgruntled ticket-holders protesting outside the stadium and getting a tickle-up from the police for their pains. One of those on the receiving end happened to be a lawyer who promptly sued.

To a Westerner, getting in to watch the game seems a mixed blessing. Ordinary spectators aren't allowed to take in bags or cameras, and often not even food or water. Alcohol is only available in the corporate boxes and special clubhouse areas. Buying something to eat and drink means queuing up — yet again. If the food is rubbish or costs too much or runs out, well, that's just too bad. These people put up with a lot to watch India play and I could understand their resentment when their support and stoicism were rewarded with an insipid performance.

The numbers are mind-boggling. They reckon the minimum TV audience for a big one-day international is 200 million, which works out at four people in front of every accounted-for TV set in the country. Occasionally, it hits 400 million which roughly equates to the combined populations of the United States, Britain and France. ESPN Star, the network that covered most of our overseas tours, created a fantasy league competition called Super Selector that you played via the internet. An hour after the first episode, they had 8000 registered players. By the next morning they had 30,000. The producers in India asked the UK company running Super Selector's computer servers to upgrade their systems because they anticipated a lot of traffic. They were told that the company had 15 years' experience of handling fantasy league traffic and knew what it was doing. Within two months the system crashed. By then Super Selector had 450,000 players, which was about 30 times as much traffic as the UK company had ever handled. During my last season, the same network created *The Search for Harsha*, a reality show to find the next Harsha Bhogle. They received 85,000 applications and gave the 45,000 lucky ones a one-minute audition.

Cricinfo, the game's biggest website, is also the largest single-sport website in the world, which is amazing given how few countries play cricket to a serious level. I'm sure a high proportion of their hits come from India and Indian expatriates. During the India-Pakistan tests in March 2005, the website was accessed by 4.6 million separate computers. When India played Sri Lanka six months later, the figure was up to 5.8 million.

I soon realised that India doesn't stop at its borders. There are one billion Indians in India and then there's the Indian diaspora, the many millions of Indians scattered around the world. Cricinfo's second biggest source of traffic is that well-known cricketing hotbed, the USA. Obviously, there are all sorts of expatriates in America, but I'd wager that a lot of those American residents logging on to Cricinfo are Indian. Indians living in the UK formed the Bharat Army (Bharat being another name for India) which descended on South Africa for the World Cup, and when we toured Australia in 2004 we had the Swami Army, made up of Indians studying at Australian institutions.

The Indians I met on tour welcomed me as one of their own. Arvind, an accountant, and his friend Kapila, a doctor, were from Johannesburg. They reckoned that since the end of 2003 they'd travelled 80,000 kms to watch the Indian team, giving up holidays and putting in long hours at work to be able to go to India's games in South Africa. There's a group of UK businessmen, led by Jayesh Patel, who started by following Indian touring teams around England and have now graduated to jetting in to wherever the action is. 'It's like India's calling us,' they say. On the spur of the moment they flew out to watch the Mumbai test against Australia in 2004. It was all over in three days, but India won, so they didn't feel short-changed. One of the group prides himself on watching every minute of every match India plays, either live or on TV, regardless of sleep deprivation or disruption to his body clock. I heard of Indian fans who by mid-2005 had already booked yachts so they can sail from island to island during the 2007 World Cup in the West Indies.

But the people who never cease to amaze you are the ordinary Indians whose love for the game and their team withstands pressures and circumstances that Westerners struggle to comprehend. Pintu, our masseur in Kolkata, supported his extended family of eight on about NZ$300 a month. Whenever we played at Eden Gardens, he'd be in the changing room doing what he called his 'national service'. In my last season, the local association wouldn't let us use him, so every night he'd come to the hotel and do three or four hours' massage for whatever the players tipped him.

Prasanna Raman, a software engineer in Bangalore, decided that the only way he could get involved in Indian cricket was to invent a video analysis system. For years he'd get home from his day job and work on it into the early hours. He used to catch trains all over India to update me on progress and lobby for us to trial his system. Or he'd e-mail me:

Dear Sir,

Trust this mail finds u in prime health and prosperity. Go thru the attachment which contains statistics and the graphics which might clearly tell the reason for India's loss against Sri Lanka. Tonight we r covering the match against Bangladesh and will give u the reports for that match as well soon. Wishing u all the very best. Do take care and give me the feedbacks. The attachment contains 6 pages.

Kind Regards,

Prasanna.

It paid off. Early in 2006 he became technical head of the National Cricket Academy and was computer analyst for the Indian under-19 team at the junior World Cup in Sri Lanka.

People would stop me in the street to thank me for being 'our' coach. It was humbling, but also guilt-inducing, because many of those who thanked me for doing a well-paid job that I loved led lives of desperate day-to-day struggle. The gratitude and support I received from ordinary Indians was the most positive force I've ever encountered, in that it simultaneously lifted me and kept my feet on the ground. More than anything else, that was what kept me going through the hard, lonely times.

I still find it hard to put India's passion for cricket into perspective. I've heard it compared to rugby in New Zealand. Others say that cricket and cinema are India's two great forms of popular entertainment, and many Indians respond to the cricket as they would to a colourful Bollywood melodrama. Then there's the big-picture view. In his address to the team in 2001, Bhogle told them that only two things united India: cricket and the army. Like Brazil and football, and New Zealand and rugby, cricket is intrinsic to how Indians see themselves and is, therefore, part of the image they present to the world.

Cricket is increasingly becoming an expression of national identity, an essential part of the new India. (There are certainly far more Indian flags being waved at cricket grounds these days than when I toured in 1989.) Just as India is flexing its muscles in regional and global affairs, those who run Indian cricket are determined to use their financial clout to make India a major — perhaps *the* major — player in the game. It mightn't be a case of No More Mr Nice Guy but the days when India could be condescended to and treated like a lightweight by the international cricket community are gone for good.

Homesick Blues

When we went into camp in Bangalore in May 2001, it was the start of 22 months of non-stop cricket going through to the World Cup. In that time we visited 11 countries, travelled more than 130,000 kms and stayed in 66 hotels. It did wonders for our frequent flyer points, if not much else.

The emphasis at the camp was on fielding, skill work and maintaining intensity. The players were right into batting and bowling, but couldn't summon the same intensity for the more mundane aspects of the game like ground-fielding, throwing and running between wickets. There was a good feeling in the squad, as there should have been given that we'd just beaten the best team in the world, and like all top athletes they enjoyed the challenge of competing against each other. For some of them, that meant gaining an edge by fair means or foul. The ultra-competitive Harbhajan Singh pushed the envelope once too often; I threw him out of the contest and sent him off to run laps on his own. Forty minutes later we were in the changing room packing up and getting ready to leave when someone asked, 'Where's Bhajju?' I'd completely forgotten about him. I went out onto the balcony and, sure enough, there he was, still plodding around the ground. 'Okay, that'll do,' I said, as if I was letting him off lightly.

I was aware that India didn't travel well, but was shocked to find out just how dire their away record was. During Anil Kumble's ten years in the team they'd won just one test overseas. In fact, India hadn't won a test outside the subcontinent for 15 years. I couldn't believe it. The way I looked at it, you'd have a better strike rate than that if you disregarded cricketing ability and just picked your fiercest, most dogged scrappers.

My first overseas assignment was to Zimbabwe. They were a reasonable side in those days, but hardly in the same league as the Aussies. We won the first test by eight wickets and the boys, who weren't drinkers, were so chuffed that they got stuck into the beer. Andrew Leipus said that, if nothing else, I'd be remembered for teaching them to drink.

The media posse were all smiles too. I didn't get it; I expected us to beat Zimbabwe, wherever we played them. But I certainly got it after the second test. The opener Sadagopan Ramesh was injured and the makeshift opening combinations got us off to starts of 7 and 8. The game turned when Rahul Dravid got out in the last over before stumps on the fourth evening. Another 100 or so the next morning would have given us a winning score, but we folded, losing six wickets for 37, and Zimbabwe scrambled to the target. Sourav Ganguly managed 14 runs in three innings and the Zimbabweans pioneered the tactic of trying to frustrate Sachin Tendulkar by bowling wide to him. It worked: they bowled way outside off and eventually he went for it and got caught at point.

With a tour of South Africa coming up, our batsmen had to work out how to play long innings on seaming wickets. My challenge was to learn not to take their failures personally. That meant finding a balance between being a demanding boss and a supportive mentor, pushing them to perform, but not so hard that they turned off.

During the Australian series I'd marvelled at the strength of the players' self-belief when playing at home. Now I had to deal with its infuriating flipside. There was almost an expectation that things would go wrong. If we lost a couple of quick wickets, the changing room would become what I called 'unrelaxed'; whereas in India, they wouldn't miss a beat.

There were two broad schools of thought about this inability to win away from home: the bowlers reckoned it was the batters' fault and the batters blamed the bowlers. The batters felt that it stemmed from our lack of a quality third seamer, which meant that we couldn't take advantage of the green wickets that were invariably prepared for us. We'd put the other side in, but they'd weather a brief storm and post a score. The bowlers' counter was that the batters freaked out as soon as they saw a blade of grass and couldn't wait to get home to do a repair job on their averages. A bit of this goes on in all teams; when things go wrong everyone looks at someone else, rather than in the mirror. As Wallaby great Mark Ella said of his time coaching rugby in Italy, 'I heard every conceivable explanation for failure, except, "It was my fault."' The bowlers also complained that we scored our runs too fast and consequently, no matter how many we got, there was still enough time for us to lose. I was inclined to put the heat on the batsmen. We had so much talent that it was reasonable to expect 350-plus on any wicket in any country.

The fact that we never got to play on turning wickets was undoubtedly a factor. Our hosts made sure that the wickets didn't turn and this, among other things, created a selection dilemma: was there any point playing two spinners, even if they were our best bowlers, when there was nothing in the wicket for them? Our young fast bowlers were improving, but their fitness didn't match their enthusiasm. They also would have benefited from having a specialist bowling coach. I know a bit about bowling, but I'm not a technical expert. I was to get my way over a fitness trainer, but to my lasting regret I wasn't able to convince the people who mattered that we needed a full-time bowling coach. Bruce Reid had a significant impact in Australia in 2004, but when the specialist coach only comes in now and again, guys slip back into their old habits when he's not there.

In Zimbabwe I got my first real experience of dealing with match referees.

Before drinks on the first morning of the first test, the late Dennis Lindsay summoned me to his room to tell me that we were appealing too much — 13 times in 35 minutes, he said, of which only two were upheld. I wondered why on earth he was counting. He followed this up by giving our wicketkeeper, Sammy Dighe, a talking-to at lunchtime. Our manager, Chetan Chauhan, asked, 'What is this? Are we playing backyard, friendly cricket?' Apparently, we were. Lindsay reminded me of my old housemaster ('Wright, I'll see you in my study'), but we ended up getting on well.

In the triangular one-day international (ODI) tournament that followed we won every game except the final, in which the West Indies made a big total and we fell just short. It meant that the tour would be seen as neither one thing — a success — nor the other — a failure — but I took a dimmer view, seeing it as two missed opportunities.

The team had another issue on tour — their diet. The boys missed their home-cooked Indian food. Ashish Nehra, after a poor spell one day, told us he'd been feeling weak and ill. Leipus asked him what he'd had for breakfast. He said, 'Three biscuits. There was nothing for me to eat.' When we found a good Indian restaurant in any town on tour they did a roaring trade, often running a delivery service from their kitchen to the players' rooms.

Off the field, I enjoyed my first experience of Africa. In Mutare, our driver took me to a bar where I was the only white person. There was no animosity, but no one wanted to talk politics.

Doug, our liaison man, was a chain smoker and proud of it, something you don't often come across these days. Like most liaison men he had an extraordinary ability to transform a glitch into a disaster. One day he announced that we had a major crisis with our laundry: some of the players had handed in their gear late and, according to Doug, getting it done on time would be 'nigh on impossible'. I suggested he might have to do it himself, and within half an hour a miracle had occurred. Doug was inordinately proud of his home town Bulawayo. On the bus trip from the airport to the hotel he subjected us to a hyperbolic rant, which climaxed with, 'We're now passing the oldest water fountain in Zimbabwe.' Let's just say that the Taj Mahal didn't suffer by comparison.

While we were in Zimbabwe, fuel prices went up 44 per cent and the signs were that things were only going to get worse. When we went back for the World Cup, the good restaurants in Harare had closed down, the local arts and crafts were much cheaper, and stall owners were accepting food in lieu of money.

A group of us visited Victoria Falls. There was a 100 m bungee jump off the bridge that spans the falls from Zimbabwe to Zambia. Dravid was dead keen to have a go, but Chauhan put his foot down. A sensible call: if serious harm had come to Dravid, Chauhan and I might as well have jumped off the bridge without a giant rubber-band attached to our ankles.

We went over to Zambia because we'd heard the view was even more spectacular. I was taking some snaps on the banks of the Zambesi when I noticed a sign saying 'Beware of the crocodiles'. I decided the view from Zimbabwe was quite spectacular enough, but they wouldn't let us back in because we didn't have our passports. There are influential Indians in Zambia, as there are in most countries, and the necessary strings were pulled. The BCCI wouldn't have been impressed by a coach who took half the team into a country that wasn't on the itinerary and couldn't get them out.

The subsequent tour of Sri Lanka didn't start well. Our point of assembly and departure was changed three times in 36 hours. When I got to Chennai, I tried to get hold of Chauhan only to be told he'd been replaced. I hadn't realised that having the same manager for consecutive series was the exception rather than the rule. It was a blow because we'd worked well together and he had the team's respect. His replacement, a Mr. Mhate, owned a trucking firm in Pune.

New Zealand was the other team in the ODI triangular tournament. Some people seemed to think I'd have divided loyalties when we played New Zealand, but in fact I wanted to win those games more than most; I wanted to be seen as doing a good job by New Zealanders. They say that prophets aren't honoured in their own countries, but I figured there had to be a first time.

As it happened we got cleaned up twice by the Kiwis en route to losing three of our first four matches. If there was a circuitous, convoluted route to a final, we'd take it. We then beat Sri Lanka twice and went into a play-off with New Zealand to decide who'd meet the host in the final.

We were without a few senior players, including Tendulkar, so we were casting around for someone to open with Ganguly. Eventually we decided to give Virender Sehwag a go. At that stage he batted five or six and bowled a bit of off spin. Batting in the middle order, he'd holed out in the deep a couple of times, but he was well-balanced, a sweet timer and played quick bowling well, so I thought it was worth seeing what he could do with the field up. And that was pretty much whatever he wanted, as it turned out. He got a century in 70 balls, with 19 fours and a six, reducing the New Zealand bowlers to helpless bemusement. They spent a lot of time standing in the middle of the wicket with their hands on their hips wondering how the hell he could hit that particular ball to that part of the field that hard. Sometimes a coach is like a prospector sifting through his diggings, discarding the rubble and trying not to get taken in by fool's gold. That day, India and I struck pay dirt.

In the final, we lost the toss and Sri Lanka made 295. We managed 174, with a top score of 37. It's hard enough batting second at the Premadasa Stadium in Colombo because the wicket changes character, and it is made doubly hard when Murali and his mates are on song. It was India's eighth consecutive loss in an ODI final.

Ganguly had started what was to become a habit — or perhaps trademark — of getting offside with match referees. He and I have probably spent more time in disciplinary hearings than any other captain and coach. It must have been a combination of my flawed messages and Ganguly's blithe refusal to take the slightest notice of what anyone told him to do. His high-handedness often annoyed me, but I secretly admired his rebellious streak because it gave the team some pepper and it got up opposition noses, most famously Steve Waugh's.

The match referee was Cammie Smith, the same who'd let Michael Slater off scot-free when he lost his rag with Dravid in Mumbai. He accused Ganguly of abusing a Sri Lankan on the evidence of what he'd seen on TV. After the apparently damning visual evidence had been replayed ad nauseam, it all seemed to hinge on Smith's lip-reading skills as no one would admit to having heard Ganguly say a bad word to anyone: not the umpires, nor the alleged victim, nor his batting partner. If the Sri Lankans had wanted to put Ganguly away, they could have, as it was their word against ours. But it would have soured relations between the teams. Instead, they played the game and pulled the rug out from beneath Smith's feet. But like the Mounties, Cammie got his man. Given out leg before in the next game, Ganguly examined his bat and looked heavenwards before wending his way off the field like a man searching for his lost car keys. Smith banned him for dissent.

During that tour I renewed my acquaintance with Percy, the famous Sri Lankan flag-man.

('I'm Percy; I'm cricket crazy; I have no mercy for cricket spectators and commentators who are lazy.') I'd first encountered him in 1984 when he'd chant, 'Bowl the ball to bowl John Wright'. We didn't draw big crowds on that tour so I could hear every word he said. David Boon was another of his targets: when Boon walked out to open at 11 a.m., Percy would chant, 'David Boon, come back soon, before noon'.

Mhate was new to management, so Leipus and I showed him the ropes on rooming lists, travel logistics, sourcing cricket balls and organising team rooms, while assuring him that we didn't mind if he didn't come to practice. He was a quiet fellow, but had a way of getting his message across: in the middle of one of my team talks he suddenly stood up and began handing out match tickets.

We had very little communication with the selectors on tour, but the BCCI secretary J.Y. Lele was an invisible presence. Lele carried two mobile phones and had mastered the art of using them both at once. I began to suspect that one of them was exclusively for badgering the coach. After a loss he told me, 'John, you must take the hunter in the hand and the stick.' Something definitely got lost in translation, but I presume he was telling me to crack the whip. I was always getting the message from administrators that the lash was the only treatment the players responded to.

My friend and mentor Raj Singh Dungarpur came over for a flying visit. He tends to shoot from the hip and doesn't mind who's in the firing line. With his disciplinary wrangles and lack of form, Ganguly was having an unhappy time of it and his state of mind wouldn't have been improved when Raj Singh strode into the changing room and told Dravid to get ready to take over the captaincy.

With Laxman added to the injury list, we went into the test series short on experience. In Galle they prepared a seaming wicket that later turned square, and the plan worked a treat: we were bowled out for 180 and 187 and lost by ten wickets. Our batting finally fired in the second innings at Kandy: we needed 264 to win and got them in a canter. Ganguly, whose previous six test innings had netted a grand total of 48 runs, stepped up with an unbeaten 98. Relief all round.

Speaking of relief, one of the first things I do at every ground is find a chair. I have a dodgy back and given that I have to sit for five or six hours at a stretch, for five days in a row, the wrong sort of chair means a date with the physio. The right sort of chair is absolutely flat, preferably wooden and harder to find than you'd think. By my last season in India most venues had one seat set aside for me.

Before play started in Kandy I lodged my request with the dressing room attendant, who assured me it wouldn't be a problem. Play got under way; no chair. I asked again and was told, 'It's coming, sir, it's coming.' Like Christmas. An hour went by. The drinks break arrived, but the chair didn't. I was slouched in one of those moulded plastic chairs. My back was starting to hurt, my fuse was getting shorter, and my manner and language were becoming more forceful, but whatever I said and however I said it the response was the same: 'It's coming, sir; it'll be here any minute.' Five minutes before lunch a waiter, resplendent in a white waistcoat and black bow tie, entered the dressing room carrying a silver tray which he placed in front of me. He removed the lid with a flourish to reveal a plate of cheese sliced horizontally like ultra-thin pizza bases. 'The flat cheese you requested, sir,' he said. He was half-right: it was the flattest cheese I'd ever seen. No wonder it had taken so long.

Boon tells a similar story. Right at the end of a tour of India he and his roommate Geoff Marsh came down with savage cases of Delhi belly. Gushing at both ends, they quickly ran out of toilet paper and put an urgent call through to room service. The same carry-on ensued: increasingly querulous demands countered with assurances that the desired items were on the way. Finally, the knock at the door; a waiter entered bearing a covered tray. They might be slow, thought Boon, but they've certainly got style, bringing bog rolls on a silver platter. The waiter whipped off the lid to reveal a bowl of spaghetti bolognese and a chocolate milkshake. Work that one out if you can.

I really wanted an overseas series win as an indicator that we were progressing and I was making a difference, but our batting let us down again in the third test. We won the toss and got 234. Sri Lanka replied with 610 for 6 and we lost by an innings and 77 runs.

Because of the injuries, that tour was a big opportunity for youngsters like the leggie Sairaj Bahutule. During the third test he came to see me, pretty upset that he hadn't got any wickets and fearing it would be the end of his test career. What do you say to guys like him, who perhaps won't quite make it at the very highest level but who'd run through a brick wall for you? Sometimes it's the ones you most enjoy coaching and having around who aren't blessed with that extra ability that you need to succeed consistently in test cricket. You work with them and encourage them and hope like hell they'll get there and you bleed for them if they don't quite make it. Sport's a cruel business in that sense. You fail in public, and there's very little comfort or reward in being a nearly man. Perhaps it's only at the end of their careers that they can take satisfaction from having got as far as they did and from knowing that, like the greats, they gave it everything and made the most of their ability.

I returned to India with the weight of the world on my shoulders.

Another one-day final lost, another chance to win an away test series blown. I didn't have a fitness trainer or a bowling coach and didn't seem likely to get either. Next stop was South Africa, where I'd have a new manager and the same old problems.

I got into a taxi in Bangalore. The cab driver said, 'Good to see you again.' As I mumbled unconvincingly he reminded me that he'd driven me to the airport three months earlier. It came back to me. We'd chatted about his working routine: he got up at 5 a.m., washed his taxi, said his prayers, and drove from six in the morning till midnight. I'd said he must look forward to the weekend and that had made him laugh; he got one day off a month. He earned 4000 rupees (NZ$140) a month. Our daily meal allowance was 2000 rupees.

'By the way,' he said, 'you left some money in the back of my car.' I told him that was his tip, but he insisted it wasn't because I hadn't given it to him. He got his diary out of the glove box and it was all there: the date, the time, my name and the 120 rupees I'd left, and which he now insisted I take. When he dropped me off, I tipped him properly. It was another encounter with the Indian public that left me humbled yet uplifted and that rekindled my enthusiasm.

Before the South African tour I snuck home to see my children. They were asleep when I left, so I rang them from Sydney Airport. My daughter Georgie tearfully suggested that I get on a plane back to New Zealand rather than one heading across the Indian Ocean, and that rubbed in the fact that I wouldn't be seeing them for months. The 9/11 attacks had just taken place and when I went through security they confiscated a pair of nail-scissors I'd had for 20 years.

Power Plays

Long before I met or spoke to him, I'd heard all about Jagmohan Dalmiya. An English county chairman called him 'that awful man from India'. Another administrator described him as 'a cricket terrorist'. Sandeep Patil, the ex-India batsman who coached Kenya, took the opposite tack: he reckoned I couldn't hope to work with a better man.

Who was he and why did he matter? Well, on the first morning of my first test match as Indian coach, Tony Greig took me aside. 'Never forget one thing, John,' he said. 'Jagmohan Dalmiya is the most powerful man in Indian cricket.'

It was a big statement given that the man in question hadn't held any position in the BCCI for three years, but Greig wasn't the only person who portrayed him in that light. Some people talked about him as if he was a master puppeteer, the man behind the scenes pulling the strings. Others portrayed him as a monarch in exile, biding his time until he was ready to reclaim his throne.

I steered well clear of Indian cricket politics, but it was useful to have some idea of how things worked. Essentially, at the time I worked in India, there were two factions, one headed by A.C. Muttiah, the BCCI president on whose watch I'd been appointed, and the other by Dalmiya, a former BCCI powerbroker who'd also had a stint as President of the ICC. Think of the mistrust and acrimony between rival political parties — Labour and National, Democrats and Republicans — and multiply it. Then multiply it again.

The board elections were taking place as the tour of South Africa began. According to the rumour mill, Dalmiya was poised to sweep back into power, and if that happened, anyone with links to the previous regime could start polishing their CV because he wouldn't be taking prisoners. Supposedly, at or near the top of his hit-list were the foreign coach and the foreign physiotherapist. The buzz was so persistent that Andrew Leipus and I concluded that if Dalmiya won, we were history. The timing wasn't propitious either, as my one-year contract was about to expire.

I've always been a bit of a worrier, but India made me fatalistic. It wouldn't have surprised me if I'd answered the phone when I was back in New Zealand on a break and someone from the BCCI had informed that I wasn't the Indian coach any more, that I'd been deposed like some self-appointed president-for-life who'd made the classic mistake of popping over to Switzerland for a chat with his bank manager. I'd come to realise that there was no point in fretting about things that were out of my control, and what Dalmiya thought of the 'goras' (whiteys) certainly fell into that category. All I could do was keep doing my job to the best of my ability and get some results.

Having said that, I followed the pre-election manoeuvring closely via the internet — it was all about 31 votes. The tour manager Dr Bhargava was from an association that was in the Dalmiya camp, so his appointment was seen as a sign that the tide was moving in Dalmiya's favour. I read stories that claimed the delegates would be quarantined to prevent them from being lobbied or heavied, and a claim that the leaders of 18 state associations had pledged support for Muttiah at a dinner. Dalmiya shrugged this off with words to the effect that attending a dinner wasn't quite the same as casting a vote. The most pertinent information I came across was that Dalmiya hadn't lost an election for a decade.

As we trooped into the dressing room after a tough fielding practice in Johannesburg, Dr Bhargava gave us the news: Dalmiya by 17 votes to 13. The players shrugged and went on with what they were doing. Leipus and I looked at each other and said, 'Oh, shit.'

I was out of contract and the bitter rival of the man who'd employed me was now calling the shots. The media guys started treating me as if I'd been diagnosed with a terminal illness. Six days after the election I got a fax from Dalmiya who wanted to know why the team was inconsistent, why our batsmen couldn't turn ones into twos, and why they lost their wickets by getting 'caught in the dilemmas of yes and no'. Then he got to the point: 'Are these a result of natural disability or a lack of proper training programmes?' He went on to talk about India's passion for the game, the BCCI's moral responsibility to the public and the fact that, despite cricket being a game of 'glorious uncertainties', India needed professionalism 'instead of always putting the onus on the whims of uncertainties'. He wanted Leipus and I to spell out the factors that were hindering the team's performance and the problems we faced and put forward suggestions for addressing them.

It may or may not have been an ultimatum, but it was certainly an opportunity for me to put my manifesto in front of the man who mattered most. I'd got on well with Muttiah, but we rarely discussed my role or what was happening with the team because he preferred to use Raj Singh Dungarpur as his point man on cricket matters. Dalmiya was obviously the opposite — completely hands-on. Over the next week I prepared a presentation covering all aspects of the job: fitness, selection, tour management, computer analysis, the India A concept, development of fast bowlers, pre-tour medical and fitness assessments, itineraries, and skill-training priorities at the academies. I put a lot of thought and effort into it and it was pretty thorough. Then my computer hiccupped and it vanished, so I had to do it all over again.

Any cautious optimism generated by that exercise evaporated when the cricket started. The third team in the triangular ODI series was Kenya and, yes, we somehow managed to lose to them. We got through to the final against the hosts but lost tamely, yet another one-day final in which India came second. On the first day of the first test in Bloemfontein we racked up 372 for 7, with Sachin Tendulkar and Virender Sehwag blazing centuries but then the tail folding. South Africa got 563, and Shaun Pollock ran through us in the second innings. Defeat by nine wickets; the murmurs got a little louder.

Our hopes of winning the second test in Port Elizabeth and my hopes of hanging on to my job were severely reduced by a balls-up for which I blame, er, the coach. We picked two spinners, then sent South Africa in to bat because it was overcast. If I'd been trying to impress my new boss with a tactical masterstroke — which I was — I'd managed instead to shoot myself in the foot. To make matters worse, this bungle was witnessed by a number of ex-Indian players in the commentary box, some of whom were founder-members of the We Don't Want A Foreign Coach brigade, some of whom were advisors to Dalmiya, and some of whom were both. Going by the expressions on the faces of the media contingent, it was time to check into a hospice.

Two days later I spoke to Dalmiya for the first time, but not about my future. The ICC match referee Mike Denness had pinged Tendulkar for ball-tampering and half the team for excessive appealing, coming down particularly hard on Sehwag. Dalmiya rang me at about 11 in the evening. He had three questions: was Tendulkar spoken to by the umpires? Was Ganguly asked to control his players? Was Sehwag spoken to by the umpires? Then he asked me to fax him my version of events immediately and said he'd leave his mobile on all night if we wanted to ring him.

The way Dalmiya handled this row sent out a very clear signal to the rest of the cricket world that from here on India wasn't going to take any crap from any quarter. His critics accused him of inflaming public opinion and turning a cricketing issue into a post-colonial 'us versus them' confrontation, but from the team's point of view it felt as if our integrity was being defended and our interests protected. I certainly sensed a difference in the way we were treated by match referees after Dalmiya took over.

He replied to my report by asking for my ideas for Indian cricket 'from cradle to maturity', and my plan for the 2003 World Cup. The tone was slightly warmer, but he noted that we'd been bowled out in four hours in the second innings at Bloemfontein. 'What's going wrong?' he asked. 'Is it that we have a misconception about our talent? Is there any problem of communication owing to diversities in language that prevent cricketers from discussing problems openly in team meetings?' He was also interested to know how I intended 'filling the missing links'. He indicated that we'd discuss these matters face-to-face when I got back to India, as he didn't expect me to write lengthy reports while on tour.

Within three days of getting back we were playing a test against England in Mohali, which we won by ten wickets. I was still picking up the buzz that I was on the way out and I'm not sure there would have been much point in me making the trip to Delhi to meet Dalmiya if we'd lost.

Within minutes of walking into his suite at the Taj Palace, I knew I was dealing with a pro. Dalmiya was immaculately dressed, thoroughly briefed, and all business. There was no false bonhomie or any attempt to put me at ease; the opposite in fact. He was quite a cold fish, with a piercing gaze, but I quickly found that I could speak bluntly to him. He grasped the issues and his questions cut right to the core of the matter.

I elaborated on the urgent action points in my paper, particularly fitness, the A-team and the selection system, although I wasn't silly enough to advocate scrapping the latter altogether. He wanted to know how the new players had handled touring, what their fitness levels were when they came into the team and why they dropped when they went out of the side. (We'd done some testing in South Africa which showed that virtually every player had an unsatisfactory weight-strength ratio.)

I'd made up my mind in advance that I wasn't going to be tentative or deferential. I told Dalmiya that if he wanted to get Indian cricket right, there were issues that had to be tackled whether I remained the coach or not. I suggested he should give me some of the things I was asking for and if he was still unhappy in six months, show me the door.

At the end of the meeting he said that a lot of what he'd heard about me on the grapevine seemed to be off the mark. 'You're quite tough,' he said, 'and I think perhaps we may be able to work together.' I could have said exactly the same. One thing I'd learned as a coach is not to judge players on what other people tell you about them. You have to sit down with them, look them in the eye, talk to them and then make up your mind. That's what the meeting was about.

The public speculation continued unabated. England were no pushovers; they'd recently won series in Pakistan and Sri Lanka. In Ahmedabad, we trailed by 116 on the first innings but hung on easily for a draw. In Bangalore, we got behind again, but rain washed out the last two days. England played some pretty negative cricket, putting sweepers out and bowling a leg-stump line, but the media, particularly the ex-players, slammed us for being boring. It was striking how high they set the bar for the Indian team now that they were safely retired. Leipus was being targeted as well: the former coach, Anshuman Gaekwad, said he'd seen him giving the players a white powder mixed with milk and speculated that it could have been steroids or illegal drugs. It was Myoplex, the protein shake.

Not surprisingly, others in the media followed their lead. The national news agency ran a report headed, 'Wright, Leipus on their way out'. An unnamed ex-coach described me as 'a diplomat who understood the Indian system of survival very well'. And here was me thinking I was simply keeping my head down and getting on with the job.

Various people were being touted as replacements for the inept foreigner, notably the ex-India player Mohinder 'Jimmy' Amarnath. And who should have suddenly turned up at the pre-match nets in Ahmedabad and had a long chat with Ganguly, but Armarnath? He didn't speak to me, but maybe there were too many cameras around.

The one thing I had going for me was that whenever the players were asked for an opinion they were supportive, so much so that one journalist referred to my 'fan club within the team'. After Dalmiya had held a meeting with the players, he informed me and Leipus that our contracts would be extended for another year, taking us through to November 2002; he also gave me the go-ahead to hire a fitness trainer. It meant I could start planning for the World Cup with some confidence that, unless things went terribly wrong, I'd probably still be the coach.

When Muttiah was the boss, I'd have informal chats on cricket issues with Raj Singh about team issues and hope that my message floated upstairs. With Dalmiya, I'd get a call from his right-hand man, Kunal, to say the President wants to see you, get yourself to Kolkata, but don't tell anyone you're coming. Then I'd get there and most of the Kolkata media would be waiting for me.

Interestingly, Dalmiya never let slip an opinion about a third party, not even when the third party was running around taking pot-shots at him. Raj Singh, for instance, was an implacable foe. He accused Dalmiya of not knowing a thing about the game, adding, 'No wonder he pronounces it as "kirkit" or "krikate". Fortunately he doesn't have to spell it.' Everyone knew what his adversaries thought of him, but Dalmiya was a sphinx.

As I tried to be. The late Jimmy Diwadkar, who ran the BCCI's Mumbai office, had warned me to be very careful what I said and who I said it to, and I was acutely conscious of the implications that could be drawn from the fact that I'd based myself at the Cricket Club of India in Mumbai, whose president happened to be none other than Raj Singh.

That first meeting with Dalmiya set the tone for our relationship. I found I could do business with him. I always told him what I thought and I knew where I stood. We didn't always agree and I didn't always get what I asked for — for instance, a full-time bowling coach. From time to time former Indian players would turn up at our training camps without being invited — by me. They were there because Dalmiya wanted them there.

Looking back on it, I tend to think we were all prisoners of the system, even Dalmiya. I'm sure there were things he wanted to change. I know for a fact that many coaches and former and current players want to do things differently, but they too are prisoners of the system and don't know where to begin.

Why did we have a new manager for every tour? So that the people in power could reward an association that had voted for them by putting one of its representatives in charge of the team for a couple of months. There are jobs for the boys everywhere, but this job was too important to keep shuffling around on the Buggin's Turn principle. But then patronage is as old as Indian cricket. The first regional teams depended on the patronage of princes or wealthy businessmen and later the big industrial concerns got in on the act. With cricket becoming a multi-million-dollar industry, a variety of powerbrokers have gravitated to the BCCI. Many state associations install leading politicians as their presidents in the belief that it gives them extra clout during elections, and it's not unusual for the central Government in Delhi to have a say in how the BCCI's government associations — the Services, the Railways and the Universities — vote.

Every time a new manager was appointed, I had to develop a working relationship from nothing and do it quickly. They came from a variety of backgrounds and professions — there was a Member of Parliament, a bank employee, a doctor, the owner of a trucking firm, another who owned a printing business, a civil servant with the railways, a professor of chemistry, and a fighter pilot — with varying levels of competence and efficiency. Some did everything, others did nothing. Some knew a lot about cricket, others didn't. Some smoked and drank, others frowned on both. As a rule of thumb, the good ones had a strong cricket background that included playing for India, but then administrators like Professor Shetty and Wing Commander Baladitya — who flew Mirage jets for the Indian Air Force — were excellent. I liked sitting next to Baladitya on planes, because if you hit turbulence, he could tell you exactly what was happening and why there was no need to worry.

In one sense, the ideal manager was a relaxed individual who viewed the whole exercise as a junket; at least that meant I could get on with my job without interference. The worst was the bloke who had a misguided confidence in his understanding of the game and was itching to get involved in the coaching. There was Colonel Sharma, who waved his handkerchief every time we got a wicket and considered himself a yoga expert, so much so that we once had to let him take the warm-up. There was a gentleman who handed out the meal allowance money in the dark so that it was hard to count, and another who nicked the players' official shirts. There was the manager who unilaterally changed the departure time for what would be a full day's travelling, with the upshot that half the team was on the bus and the rest were still in bed. When Leipus and I passed adverse comment on his organisational skills, he reported us to the BCCI, and at the end of the series he made me return all the white practice balls. One guy used to slip a sheet listing the scores of players from his region under my door and another managed to lose the entire party's meal allowance money for the last two days of a tour. Just as well aircraft meals are free.

The saving grace of this revolving-door arrangement was that I made some friends for life.

Another by-product of BCCI politics was euphemistically called 'rotation'. Rotation was the system for devising schedules and venues for home series, and was also a means of driving a bunch of more-or-less sane cricketers around the bend. Since 2001 the BCCI has followed a policy of allocating tests and ODIs among the nine test and 24 ODI venues in a fixed order. The idea was to ensure an even spread; in practice it locked the BCCI into a rigid programme, because no one wanted to give up their turn, and resulted in some of the most lunatic travel schedules imaginable. Rotation paid no heed to geography, airline route networks and schedules, or common sense.

The bizarre itineraries were compounded by baffling travel arrangements. It took three flights and a bus trip to cover the 750 kms between Jamshedpur and Nagpur. We could have done it on an overnight train and saved an entire day's travel, but that was ruled out for 'security reasons'. It wasn't quite so bad for the players because they had the happy knack, one I never acquired, of being able to fall asleep anywhere, anytime.

The season after I left, Dalmiya lost the BCCI election to a powerful cabinet minister, Sharad Pawar, and, as if to prove nothing was forgiven, the new regime attempted to take him to court on a charge of misappropriation of BCCI funds.

The BCCI is an extraordinary organisation. It's run by a handful of people who often make bewildering decisions and don't give a hoot what the outside world thinks of them. The staff are delightful and amazingly loyal — one of them told a local paper he hadn't had a raise for 35 years. Although the BCCI generates a major proportion of cricket's total revenues, its office in Mumbai has concrete floors and a toilet that requires key access. I reckon those ramshackle surroundings are the greatest feat of camouflage since a wolf put on sheep's clothing.

Rum Punch

In May 2002 I sat in my hotel room in Jamaica watching the rain come down, thinking it can't get any worse than this. I was wrong, of course. It did get worse and, to add insult to injury, it happened in New Zealand, but my imagination didn't stretch that far, thank goodness.

Half an hour after the Windies wrapped up our second innings and the series, the rain arrived and settled in for a long stay. Those few minutes were the difference between drawing and losing a five-test series. Drawing would have represented progress towards our goal of winning a series away from home; losing meant we were running on the spot, getting tired but going nowhere. A couple of batsmen had got out playing shots late the previous afternoon; I took them outside to watch the rain pelting down and asked them what was the big hurry.

As I was drowning my sorrows after the game, an Australian TV cameraman said, 'Wrighty, this foreign coach thing never works. That's just the way it is.' At the time I didn't feel like arguing the toss. We'd prepared thoroughly, we'd planned, we'd trained hard; the West Indies bowling attack wasn't exactly lethal and Brian Lara never really got going, averaging just 29. We'd lost a series we should have won, and it felt like an utter calamity. With the benefit of hindsight, however, and notwithstanding what was to happen in New Zealand, we turned the corner in the West Indies.

Before the tour I'd asked the Perth-based sports psychologist Sandy Gordon to create a touring plan to replace the good intentions and fighting talk. *India Touring 2002* led to the formation of a senior players group, whose job it was to ensure that the team stayed focused on the tour theme and maintained standards. My job as coach was to facilitate and look after training and pre-game planning. It wasn't rocket science, but in cricket, and particularly on tour, it's one thing to have a plan and another to execute it. We didn't quite manage it in the West Indies.

I quickly discovered that out of sight didn't mean out of mind: Big Brother was watching. On the second day of the first test in Guyana we were on the ropes. Carl Hooper and local hero Shivnarine Chanderpaul were well into a 293-run fifth-wicket partnership, and a happy crowd was chanting, 'Bat on, Chandi, bat on, bat on, bat on all day'. The manager, Goutam Dasgupta, handed me a phone: Jagmohan Dalmiya was on the line from Kolkata and he wasn't ringing to dispense bouquets. 'What's going on?' he demanded. 'The team appears to have given up.' I slunk back to my laptop. 'God help us,' I wrote in my diary, 'and God help me.'

In fact we helped ourselves. The West Indies got 501 and had us 21 for 2, before Rahul Dravid led the salvage operation; he scored 144 not out, despite a blow on the jaw that put him on a liquid diet for two days. The rain did the rest. In Trinidad, India won a test in the Caribbean for the first time in 26 years, on the back of a Sachin Tendulkar century and vital runs in both innings from V.V.S. Laxman. But we lost in Barbados and drew in Antigua, so it all came down to the fifth test in Jamaica.

The batting was still the problem. Our big guns were tending to get 70s and 80s rather than 150-plus and we weren't getting good starts. Opening partnerships set an innings up; you need to get to lunch on the first day with one or, at the most, two wickets down. We tried every conceivable combination, without finding the answer. For India, the key to succeeding overseas is getting a settled, high-quality opening pair.

It didn't help that our star-studded middle order was followed by a long tail without much wag in it. The Caribbean echoed to the sound of our lower-order collapses: in four innings, including the two in Jamaica, our last four or five wickets put on an average of 25. A fighting team will always strive to extend the game — into the next session, the next day, as long as they can — because you never know what might happen. What made the loss in Jamaica so galling was that we knew what would happen: we knew it was going to rain and we would have got out of jail. That's why I kept harping on about the importance of picking fighters who'd hang in there to the last minute of the last hour.

Guys like Anil Kumble: he broke his jaw in Antigua, but still wanted to bowl. After his jaw had been inspected by a couple of Indian dentists who were at the ground, and had been strapped up by Andrew Leipus, and after listening to their unanimous advice — 'don't do it' — Kumble went out to bowl. Leipus told him not to open his mouth, but telling Kumble not to appeal is like telling the tide not to come in. Leipus patrolled the boundary to adjust the strapping between overs and Kumble kept bouncing in. He got Lara and had Hooper off a no-ball, but eventually it became impossible to continue. The reason he did it, he said later, was that he so rarely got a chance to bowl in an overseas test after India had made 400 in the first innings.

It was a tough tour for Kumble because Sourav Ganguly always wanted to play three seamers and a spinner, and preferred Harbhajan Singh, whom he regarded as his match-winner. This scenario played out so often that Kumble eventually opted out of selection meetings — which he usually would have attended as one of the most senior players.

I'd toured the West Indies in 1985, opening in every game. That involved facing Joel Garner, Michael Holding, Malcolm Marshall, Winston Davis and Courtney Walsh in the tests and ODIs, and a line-up of their clones in the first-class games. There were no restrictions on bouncers then and you routinely got three or four an over; judging by the way the crowds reacted, they would have preferred more. I did so much ducking and weaving that I felt like Joe Frazier trying to avoid Muhammad Ali's left jab.

It had been a matter of survival in 1985, but on this tour I was able to appreciate the unique atmosphere of West Indian cricket. If cricket in India is a celebration, in the Caribbean it's an excuse for a party. The spectators are knowledgeable, and live and breathe the game, but in a more relaxed fashion than in India. In the West Indies the music never stops and the rum never runs out. The best disco in Antigua is the one in the stand next to the pavilion during a test match.

And close of play doesn't mean the party's over. Fuelled by rum, barbecues and music, it carries on till late. After our win in Trinidad, the spectators relocated to the bar across the road. By the time we left the ground, they'd spilled out onto the road, the reggae was booming and some serious partying was under way. 'Wait for Barbados, man,' they yelled. 'We'll get you in Barbados.' And they did.

West Indians have an appetite for life and a wonderful way with words. Smokey, our Antiguan liaison man, greeted a fat lady walking up a steep hill with, 'How ya doin, darlin? You walk like you don't wanna go.' The ground announcements tend to be a bit more colourful than 'A set of car keys have been handed in to the secretary's office'. When Tendulkar was performing twelfth-man duties during a warm-up match, the ground announcer said, 'And there's Sachin Tendulkar out in the middle, giving drinks to the batsmen and getting a feel of the local soil.' As Dravid approached his century in Guyana, there was an urgent request for Harry the carpenter to report to the secretary's office, and when the press box sprang a leak the call went out for Omar the plumber.

Cricket needs a strong West Indies. They're beset by structural, administrative and financial problems, and would seem to be in crying need of assistance from the International Cricket Council. If the ICC can't act to ensure that the West Indies, with their fantastic heritage and pool of natural talent, remain afloat and competitive, one would have to ask what is the point of having an international governing body. As the World Cup host in 2007, the West Indies won't suffer for lack of enthusiasm or support. The challenge will be getting the organisational and logistical side of things right. Teams and their gear are often sent in different directions, and you can't train without your gear.

Speaking of gear, the thief who nicked some of our kit certainly struck pay dirt. Two of the 12 bats in his haul belonged to Ashish Nehra, who'd come in at number 11 in most teams. They must have been as good as new. 'I scored three runs in two months,' he said mournfully, 'and now my bats have been stolen.'

But for all the doom and gloom, and suggestions that cricket is being abandoned in favour of American sports, there are still plenty of West Indians who are passionate about the game. When I arrived at the Police Club in Georgetown, an hour before training, the grass was still wet from overnight rain. A man wearing a singlet and tracksuit trousers was mowing the outfield. I assumed he was the groundsman and hassled him to get the nets up ASAP. At the next day's practice one of the spectators was a police inspector in dress uniform, shiny shoes and a peaked hat. He looked familiar and I realised, with some embarrassment, that the guy I'd given the hurry-up to wasn't the groundsman after all.

The following day he was back in his trackpants, putting up the nets. He came over to me: 'Coach, I feel like bowling today. I got five for last week.' I asked how he'd got them. 'When I bowl,' he said, 'I give you a straight one, turn one big, turn one small, then I give you my drifter.'

Net bowlers the world over want to bowl to Tendulkar. The difference in the West Indies is that they commentate as they bowl, with an aplomb Tony Cozier would admire: 'Overpitched, square driven, that's four, beautiful player.' 'Free runs,' said one guy when he bowled a bad ball. 'You don't have to pay, just collect.' I commented to Dennis, a strapping lad and still growing, that Dravid was looking pretty solid. 'More than a rock, coach,' he replied.

The caravan moved on to England, who'd been making steady progress under Nasser Hussain. We went into the four-test series with some confidence, having won the one-dayers in the West Indies (the trophy was left on the luggage belt at Heathrow Airport) and had a great run in the NatWest Trophy ODIs. I was in familiar territory, wanting to do well in the series to demonstrate that progress was being made and avoid further testing the BCCI's patience.

In the first test at Lord's, we unveiled Virender Sehwag as a test opener. This was part of our continuing search for a quality opening pair, but also a matter of fitting in our best batsmen. Sehwag saw himself as a middle-order player, but with Dravid, Tendulkar, Ganguly and Laxman there was no room there. None of them wanted to open, but he'd made a reasonable fist of it in one-dayers and he was dead keen to play.

People go on about his technical shortcomings and lack of foot movement, but his technique is actually remarkably good. He's beautifully balanced, with a very still head and no sideways movement. That minimal movement gives him extra time to play his shots, which he does with the full face of the bat, and his balance and hand speed enables him to hit the ball incredibly hard.

Sehwag has an uncluttered approach to batting: 'If the ball's there for hitting, I hit it. That's it; nothing else.' You can stack the point-gully region and feed him short stuff outside off stump and he'll still go for it. And if he catches up with it, good luck to those fielders. He doesn't beat himself up if he gets out trying to whack a loose ball because, as he says, whacking loose balls is the object of the exercise. Critics tend to be more forgiving of batters who get out playing defensively, but getting out bowled or lbw trying to block a straight one is nothing to write home about. Sehwag's a special player and the way he made the transition from the middle order to opening is nothing short of genius in my book.

The other notable feature of that game was that Ajit Agarkar did what neither Tendulkar nor Dravid have yet managed to do: score a test century at Lord's. But when you've said that, you've said it all. We were crushed.

At Nottingham, Sehwag got a hundred (with 18 fours) on a greenish wicket. England rattled up 617 to lead by 260, but we hung tough and batted our way out of trouble in the second innings. Ajay Ratra, our wicketkeeper and a hard-working young guy, got hit on the foot the day before the game. He was limping at the warm-up but desperate to play because he could see what was coming. He knew his place was under threat: he was struggling with the bat, part of our six down, lights out lower order. I felt for the kid, but we had to pull him out of the game. He was only 21 and a quality keeper, but hasn't played international cricket since.

His replacement, Parthiv Patel, was 16, but looked younger. When Trevor Crouch, our baggage-man and Mr Fix-It, saw Patel for the first time he assumed he was an autograph-hunter and was about to tell the stewards to move him on. Patel had captained India Under-19 and Dilip Vengsarkar, the former Indian batsman who was chairman of the age-group selectors, had assured us he was ready. He got a duck in the first innings, but hung around for an hour and a half on the last afternoon to help secure the draw.

I accompanied Patel to a post-match TV interview. He's missing part of a finger as a result of a childhood accident and, as the interview began, the floor manager asked me what happened to his finger. Thinking she was referring to his taped index finger, I said casually, 'Oh, it's just a bruise.' She gave me an incredulous look and wailed, 'But it's missing!'

Our batting was coming together and the tail had shown some fight, but off the field a storm was brewing over World Cup contracts. The ICC was insisting that all players had to sign contracts that would prevent them from having individual endorsement deals with companies that were competitors of the official sponsors. There was an obvious problem, as most of the Indian players had major deals with companies who fell into the banned category. They were effectively being ordered to turn their backs on lucrative deals with supportive corporations; who wouldn't have been up in arms?

I tried to stay out of it, but when it got to the stage where it looked as if the BCCI was lining up against the players, I warned them that it was one thing to take on the ICC but quite another to take on their own board. They were adamant though, and had high-powered legal advice backing their stance.

The pressure intensified in the run-up to the third test at Headingley. The BCCI announced a deadline and named an alternative team to contest the upcoming ICC Champions Trophy in the event that the contracts weren't signed. The inclusion of Javagal Srinath in this phantom team was one of the few light moments in the stand-off. Some of the youngsters were worried that they were putting their careers in jeopardy and the manager, Ranga Reddy, became the meat in the sandwich, having the BCCI constantly on his back to get the players signed up by one means or another. As the row threatened to disrupt our preparation for a crucial test, I stressed to the players that performing on the field could only strengthen their hand, whereas a poor performance would leave them more vulnerable.

The game began in damp, overcast conditions. We picked two spinners, won the toss and batted on a wicket with uneven bounce. Trying to plant a positive thought, I told Dravid at lunchtime that a hundred in those conditions would probably be his best. He and Sanjay Bangar showed great character, taking blows on the fingers as they blunted the attack. Dravid got a hundred (which I'm sure he rates up with his best) as did Ganguly and Tendulkar, who turned down the offer of bad light after tea on the second day and went after the bowling instead. We had successive partnerships of 170, 150 and 249 on the way to 628 for 8 declared.

Our batting had delivered, and having Bangar as an opening bat/third seamer all-rounder enabled us to play both Kumble and Harbhajan. Dravid had made the point that he was sick of us putting teams in on green wickets and not being able to roll them; he argued that with our spin attack, we'd always have a chance if we could make the other side chase 200 in the fourth innings. In other words, don't take the soft option just because there's a tinge of green in the track.

It was slow going as England followed on. They started the last day four down with Hussain and Alec Stewart still there, having put on 91 the previous afternoon. Before play we talked about body language and aggression. I asked who'd be the first to tell Hussain to 'piss off' or Stewart that he was too old to be out there. Not exactly Churchillian, I know. Then I sat down and waited for wickets to fall. Hussain got to a hundred but then he, Andrew Flintoff and Stewart went in successive overs and it was all wrapped up before lunch. Victory by an innings and 46 runs. It was India's first test win in England for 16 years, and maybe their best overseas win ever. If it couldn't get much worse than Jamaica, it couldn't get much better than flogging the Poms on their own patch.

In the decider at the Oval, England got 515, but we came right back at them with 508; 217 of them from Dravid. He was already a fantastic player, but in that series he went to another level and has stayed there ever since. It rained on the final day, snuffing out the very faint possibility of a result. In the West Indies we'd been one up and lost; here we'd been one down and had come back to draw. It was progress, albeit slow. Having learned the game in England as both a player and a coach, it was satisfying to go there with a team that played fighting and entertaining cricket.

One of the best things about touring England are the bus trips, a pleasant change from getting on and off planes three or four times a week. I could have done without the Hindi music and Hindi movies, but that worked both ways: whenever I pulled out my guitar, Harbhajan bolted to the back of the bus.

The charm of English cricket is undiminished: beautiful county grounds in the shadow of cathedrals; tiny changing rooms that are quite inadequate for a touring party and its gear; obliging dressing room attendants who dry the towels and serve cups of tea and fruit cake; indoor practice sessions because it's raining again; autograph hounds who wait for hours with books thicker than telephone directories and outdated photos. Away from the cricket I enjoyed reacquainting myself with old mates — particularly at my former county, Derbyshire, where Sehwag bombarded the pavilion scoring a run-a-ball century — and the unique pub culture.

All this and progress too. Life wasn't so bad after all.

One Fine Day at Lord's

If a week is a long time in politics, a few months can be an eternity in sport. Early in 2002 we were trailing Zimbabwe 1–2 in a best of five home ODI series. I was so concerned that I told Sourav Ganguly and the selectors that if we lost the series either the captain or the coach would have to go.

Later that year we went into a home series against the West Indies having won ten of our last 12 completed one-day games (including winning the series against Zimbabwe, 3–2) and picked up a couple of trophies in the process. The media and the Indian public were already making confident noises about the World Cup, now less than 100 days away. There was an air of excitement building in India.

The turning point was the rain-shortened series in the West Indies. After the deflation of losing a test series we should have won, the young Turks, Virender Sehwag, Yuvraj Singh and Mohammad Kaif, jetted in for the one-dayers and injected some energy and purpose into the team. We also made a couple of changes. The search for an all-rounder who could balance the side by being the sixth batsman and fifth bowler had proved fruitless, so we tried manufacturing a solution by having Rahul Dravid keep wickets. Ganguly, who knew that Dravid had kept at school, was very keen on the idea. Although the fact that Dravid didn't have any gloves might have indicated that he was somewhat less keen.

Having a dedicated fitness trainer in Adrian le Roux helped Dravid prepare for his demanding new role. Le Roux was in charge of getting the players fit, running warm-ups and working one-on-one with the boys in the gym. This enabled Andrew Leipus and me to focus on our jobs instead of being physio-cum-trainer and coach-cum-trainer. Le Roux, who took a fitness session when we were in South Africa in late 2001, emerged from the interview process as clearly the man for the job. Before I could tell him, however, he saw Jagmohan Dalmiya announce on TV that the Indian cricket team was hiring a South African fitness trainer.

Among the things he brought to the set-up was his dreaded vernier caliper which was used for fortnightly skinfold tests to measure body fat. That information, and the various fitness test results, were faxed to Dalmiya. Le Roux didn't arrive a moment too soon, as evidenced by the fact that after the first skinfold tests only two players — Kaif and Ajit Agarkar — were encouraged to put on weight.

Rather than rush in and try to change everything, le Roux took the time to get to know the players as individuals and understand their injury histories and playing roles. He assured them he wasn't there to overturn their traditional diet, but to ensure that their intake was appropriate for elite athletes and to help them get the best out of themselves.

By and large the players bought in to the plan, although they weren't above popping a sweet or two behind his back. It was almost as if they didn't want to upset him by getting caught; but they couldn't fool the caliper. The older guys could see the benefit of being fitter, whereas the younger ones were keen to get even quicker in the field, thereby enhancing their run-saving skills and making themselves more valuable to the team. On a good day, Kaif and Yuvraj would save us 20 runs in the field.

Kaif was the centre of much debate in selection meetings. He often came in to bat with either five overs left, in which case he had to go for it from the first ball, or with 25 overs left, but after the top order had failed and there was pressure on him. As a result he didn't have a great average, and that led some people to question his place in the team. But he did the tough jobs: he saved runs, he ran more singles than anyone, he batted at the death. He was a player Ganguly and I always wanted in the side, and when the captain made up his mind on a selection issue, he was a very hard man to shift. While we fought for guys whose contribution wasn't always appreciated outside the dressing room, the players understood that the only way to ensure the team remained intact was to keep winning.

Another step forward was the growing appreciation of the importance of singles. Our top-order batsmen were great strikers of the ball, but we were losing games because we weren't getting enough singles or saving enough singles in the field. Sometimes our fielding was simply substandard. Before going to the West Indies, we played a six-match ODI series against England that we drew, after being 3–1 up, as a result of some very casual cricket. After England squared the series in Mumbai, Andrew Flintoff ripped off his shirt and did a victory dance on the Wankhede Stadium pitch, whirling his shirt around his head. It wasn't a sight you'd forget in a hurry, and we didn't.

Over the course of that series we scored more runs, had a higher run rate and hit more boundaries than England. We lost the fifth game by two runs chasing 271, and the sixth by five runs chasing 255, and it was all about the singles. The TV commentators would say that a four or six 'relieved the pressure' on our batsmen, but I didn't agree. What relieves pressure is scoring off every ball.

After that series I spent a week reviewing the statistics, an exercise which showed quite clearly that our Achilles heel was failing to take and save enough singles. I produced a paper summarising my findings for the selectors. It contained some pretty blunt conclusions, beginning with the overview that the team had 'lost the ability to think through the basics of cricket'. I named the players who were getting out trying to play cute shots and those who weren't looking for singles or running aggressively between wickets. A lot of this sloppy cricket was coming from our celebrated batsmen, and some of our best cricketers were our worst fielders, which set a poor example for the younger players.

There was nothing there that I hadn't talked about, forcefully and at length, in team meetings. My intention in putting it down on paper was to provide a guide for the selectors: to underline what we needed to do to become a consistently competitive one-day team and identify the key skills that the established players need to work much harder on, and which the selectors needed to look for in up-and-coming players. A few days later I picked up the *Times of India* and, to my horror, my paper was plastered all over the back page. They'd hardly bothered to change a word of it. It was the only time anything I said or wrote was leaked to the media, and that could be regarded as quite an achievement given the way the floodgates opened shortly after my successor booted up his laptop. It didn't provoke much of a reaction, so I can only assume most of India agreed with me.

The upshot was that we went to the West Indies knowing that we had to change our approach to the one-day game. We tinkered with the batting order, moving Ganguly up to open with Sehwag, and dropping Tendulkar to four to give us more experience in the middle. We won the rain-shortened ODI series 2–1, with the reshuffled batting order working well and running significantly more singles and twos in our chases. Winning the series reinforced our belief in the new approach.

We went on to England to contest the NatWest Trophy with the hosts and Sri Lanka. England might have thought they had our number after drawing the series in India; certainly Nasser Hussain had seen enough to persuade him that we couldn't chase. Shortly after he went public with this theory, we chased down 271 against England at Lord's.

At the Oval, we bundled Sri Lanka out for 202 on a very flat wicket. I'd been trying to get Sehwag to temper his boldness, which too often of late had crossed the line into recklessness. I'd always encouraged batsmen to

Sport not only builds character, but also reveals it

TIMES SPORT

The Times of India, New Delhi, Monday, March 4, 2002

Wright report: Singles hurt the most

By Dinesh Chopra
Times News Network

NEW DELHI: Still wondering why India 'gifted' away a 3-1 advantage to finish 3-each against England in the recent One-day series? Or, why critics have ordered for a "Chokers" nameplate for the Indians after they lost nine consecutive One-day finals?

May be John Wright's analytical report submitted to the national selectors can help.

The coach blames the much touted Indian batting in his report, stressing on their poor running between wickets.

"Single is the most important reason for our inconsistent form. If we improve this, the team's performance will improve by at least 25% WHETHER we are setting a target or chasing."

Wright also explains how singles are paramount. "We need to understand and accept that time after time we got off to a frantic start and then there is a collapse."

"Where does the pressure comes from? Loss of wickets. Why? (Be- cause) Most of our wickets come from the BIG SHOT OPTIONS. Why do we need the BIG SHOT OPTIONS? Because we have failed to rotate the strike and get singles."

Wright maintains 4-5 singles and not boundaries relieve pressure in the middle overs. "Fours and sixes don't really relieve the pressure in middle overs. What really gets the momentum going is 4-5 singles an over mixed with the inevitable boundary."

He illustrates this by performances in the One-day series. First the losing encounters. About the Cuttack ODI where India lost merely by 16 runs, he says: "Sachin scores 45 off 60 balls, (with) six fours, 24 off six balls and 21 off the remaining 54 deliveries.

"India scores 234 off the 292 deliveries (we didn't manage to bat the overs out). There are 23 fours that makes it 92 runs off 23 balls. Taking away these boundaries we've managed to score 131 runs off 271 balls!"

Wright attributes the 'two-run loss in Delhi to lack of "Good strike rotation".

"We start with 53/1 off six overs. After 15 overs we are 76/2. That means in nine overs or 54 balls we scored 23 runs for loss of a further wicket. Good strike rotation could have helped maintain the momentum.

"We make 269 off 300 balls with 13 extras which is 256 runs off 300 balls including 25 fours and three sixes or 118 off 28 balls. The rest of the time, the team has managed 138 runs off 272 balls that is 45.2 overs!"

Even the winning encounters, like the fourth ODI at Kanpur, haven't been quite as satisfying for Wright. "We win easily due to good bowling performance...both openers (Tendulkar and Virender Sehwag) play brilliantly.

"Importantly, one of them is there at the end to finish the job. In this match we batted with what could be termed individual brilliance of Sachin and Sehwag."

Supporting his claim Wright gives a scoring breakdown of the One-day series. According to that India have taken 509 singles while England 590. Indians play 884 dot balls while England, relatively inexperienced One-day side, 842.

Wright suggests that improvement in singles will also elevate the performance in Test matches. "It (taking singles) will help put pressure back on the fielding side and the bowler not allowing them to pin us down and work at getting us out." *

The former New Zealand captain is worried that the opposition teams can take advantage of this weakness.

"Our inability to take singles with any consistency is no secret to international sides. With their computer analysis they will have highlighted exactly that. Particularly, since we have people like Veru (Sehwag), Sourav, Sachin who in first 15 overs fielders tend to stand as deep as they can to prevent boundaries, there are plenty of opportunities to take ones," the report says.

May be the players and the Indian think tank will pay heed to these suggestions sooner than later.

The contents of my confidential report splashed over the back page of the *Times of India*.

play their natural games, but with the proviso that they couldn't simply ignore the team's requirements given the state of the game or our strategy of building consistency and ingraining the winning habit. Shortly after Ganguly got out in the second over, Sehwag holed out trying to blast one back over the bowler's head. That left us 26 for 2, and a stroll in the park was turning into a hike across rugged terrain.

I'd had enough of players trotting out the 'natural game' line as an excuse for failing to take responsibility and disregarding the match situation. When Sehwag wandered in, I decided it was time for a sort-out. Not realising that my exasperation levels had soared into the red zone, I went up to him, grabbed him by the collar and barked, 'What the hell's going on? How can you come back in here after playing a shot like that and unbuckle your pads as if nothing's happened?' Everyone froze — it was like someone had pulled out a gun — and I turned on my heel and stomped out.

It was the closest that I ever came to losing it completely. I knew straight away that rather than ripping into Sehwag, I should have walked away, gone for a stroll around the ground or ducked into the nearest pub. Tendulkar got us home, although he killed a pigeon that was minding its own business at backward point, so there was blood on the outfield as well as on the dressing room floor.

At the subsequent team meeting it was put to me that I'd been a bit rough. I accepted that I'd gone overboard, but made it clear that I wasn't prepared to just sit there and say 'bad luck' when we threw away games because players were too self-indulgent to temper their individual approach for the greater good. I'd seen it happen against England at home, and it was a bad habit we had to get out of. 'I'll be your coach and I'll be your friend,' I said, 'but first and foremost we're here to win cricket matches. That's what I'm about, boys.'

Back at the hotel I had a face-to-face with Sehwag, who told me bluntly that he didn't like what I'd done. I acknowledged that he was entitled to feel aggrieved, but added that I didn't give a damn if he poured his heart out to every newspaper in India. Something had to be done, because the players hadn't got to the point where their single-minded commitment to winning overrode all other considerations, particularly this tendency to treat batting as if it was an individual Olympic sport in which you were marked out of ten for style. The volcano had been rumbling for a while, and it just happened to be Sehwag who triggered the eruption. He took it better than some of the others would have and we remained mates. I wouldn't necessarily say it was the moment the penny dropped, but on the other hand I'm pretty sure the boys didn't forget it.

The story didn't do the rounds by word of mouth or find its way into the press, which showed we were a pretty tight team. After I'd stepped down, Sunil Gavaskar, who'd spent some time in our changing room as a 'consultant', claimed in a column that I'd been abused by the players. If it happened, it was done in Hindi and behind my back, which is exactly what I would have expected. When they trooped in after a sloppy session, I didn't pat them on the back and say 'well done, lads', I asked them where the bloody effort was. If some of them called me a grumpy old bastard when I left them to think about it, so what? It wasn't beach cricket, and dressing rooms aren't churches.

I encouraged the boys to be honest and upfront. If a player thought I was stuffing up, he had every right to say so, either in private or in front of the team. I wasn't backward in letting them know what I thought of their performances, and I had no problem with them doing the same to me. Most disagreements tended to be one-on-one behind closed doors, but if hard things had to be said in front of the entire group, so be it. We wanted an honest and open environment, and you only get that if everyone feels they can speak their mind without being jumped on and without people getting precious and taking offence.

One of the reasons I wanted to control access to the dressing room was to restrict the number of shoulders to cry on; when players get a bollocking, they tend to look around for a sympathetic ear and usually choose the most recent arrival. I used Leipus and le Roux to keep track of the temperature and the mood. Sometimes when I asked them if I'd got it right, they'd tell me, 'No, you cocked it up, and they're pissed off with you.' From time to time outsiders who read too much into my public persona suggested that maybe I was too soft for the job, but I don't think that view held sway on the other side of the dressing room door.

Communication gets tricky when the players don't want to hear what the coach, if he's doing his job properly, has to tell them. When players perform poorly, they expect the coach to have something to say about it; but because the truth can be unpalatable, they don't necessarily want to hear it. No one enjoys being forced to face up to their failings. But there's a fine line between being frank and being brutal, and when players think you've crossed it, their response is usually to give you the cold shoulder: when you say 'good morning', they look right through you and keep walking. When that happened to me I'd answer for them — 'Good morning, John' — and take on board the message that there was a bit of bridge-building to be done. Sometimes it would come out of the blue and I'd wonder what's up with him, but usually the player was reacting to a verbal rocket or being dropped.

These freeze-outs weren't always 24-hour wonders. Some players would take a long time to get over it, and then all you could do was to be patient and persevere. Call it an ego massage if you like, but it's part of coaching. There were also times when I had to accept that maybe I'd got it wrong and there was some justification for the sulk. The core message that I wanted to come through in everything I did and said was that I cared; I cared for them as people, and as cricketers, and I cared for our team.

The Sehwag episode didn't derail us. We kept winning, and the support from the Indian community kept growing. Edgbaston, in particular, was like a home game, with Indian flags everywhere and deafening crowd support. We met England in the final at Lord's, in a game that marked the arrival of the new generation of Indian cricketers, who played with no fear and no baggage.

The dressing room wasn't exactly buoyant after England posted 325; since 1999, India had made ten ODI finals and lost the lot. Ganguly and Sehwag got us to 106 in less than 15 overs, but at the halfway stage we were 146 for 5, with Yuvraj and Kaif, the last and least experienced of our recognised batsmen, at the crease. Some Indian supporters headed for the exits, and they weren't the only ones who thought it was all over bar the shouting. Shoulders were drooping in the dressing room, and the English players might have figured it was in the bag and switched off ever so slightly.

Yuvraj and Kaif were very different characters, but had played a lot of junior cricket together. Rather than be panicked by our predicament or overawed by the occasion, they assessed the situation and concluded, after a couple of overs, that if you watched the ball, it was a good batting wicket. Then they settled into their games — Yuvraj the aggressor, Kaif the collector — and focused on the next ball and the next over. Adding some spice to it was the fact that Kaif had managed to get under Hussain's skin. Kaif is very active and vocal in the field; buzzing around, clapping his hands, shouting and geeing the others up. He'd clearly bugged Hussain when England were in India, and during the game at Durham he had had a real go at Kaif, telling him to shut up and calling him a 'bus driver'. It made Kaif laugh, and that day at Lord's the bus driver put his foot down and whistled right past Hussain's stop.

As the score mounted, dressing room superstition kicked in. Dinesh Mongia was on the physio's table and the boys made him stay there. Leipus developed a ritual of getting a drink of water between overs; by the end of the game he must have been experiencing serious bladder pressure. Dravid and Tendulkar watched from the side window, and now whenever le Roux is in the visitors' changing room at Lord's with the South African team, he always sits in the seat he sat in that day.

When Yuvraj got out for 69, we were still 58 short. Enter Harbhajan Singh, who strode out like a Sikh warrior going into battle. The crowd went nuts when he hit a six — there was supposedly a ban on bugles, whistles and flags, but many spectators seemed to have smuggled in the full set — and we were carried home on a wave of emotion. Kaif was almost run out going for the winning run, but it was his day — he got 87 off 75 balls — and ours. On the balcony, Ganguly took off his shirt and whirled it over his head, reminding Flintoff that what goes around, comes around. Harbhajan wanted the whole team to do it, but discretion, in the form of Dravid, prevailed. As hard as le Roux was working, they weren't exactly the Chippendale Male Revue. So instead they took off like a bunch of excited schoolboys, clattering through the Long Room and onto the field to get to Kaif, a pitch invasion with a difference.

My son Harry was there, and he joined us in the dressing room afterwards. From a personal perspective, it was nice that he could get a real sense of this job that kept me away from home and meet the people I worked with. I took photos of him with the team, but to our lasting regret the camera was stolen with the film still in it. My daughter Georgie, who's as interested in cricket as I am in taxidermy, was back at our hotel being looked after by Ganguly's wife, Donna.

Five days after we finished a four-test series in England, we were playing an ODI in the ICC Champions Trophy in Sri Lanka. The resolution of the World Cup contracts row involved changing the sponsors' logos on our gear, but the new kit wasn't ready, so the players had only one shirt for that first game, which was played in 30-degree temperatures and 75 per cent humidity. Kaif and Dravid scored 111 and 71 respectively, then had to field in the same shirts.

No one had ever successfully chased over 250 at the Premadasa Stadium. England put up 269 which we got for the loss of two wickets in 39 overs, not a bad effort for a team that couldn't chase. In the semi-final against South Africa we were gone for all money; they needed 69 off 78 balls with nine wickets standing. Then Herschelle Gibbs came off with dehydration, Yuvraj took two blinding catches, and we strangled them, winning by ten runs. We celebrated long and hard that night, because it was what we'd talked about so often: winning by fielding as if our lives depended on it and fighting to the very last ball.

The final against Sri Lanka was rained off twice, which was a damning comment on the stupidity and inflexibility of the organisers. It was scheduled as a day-night game, even though in Sri Lanka in September you can practically set your watch by the nightly downpour. Sure enough we were rained off after the first 50 overs, but apparently it was out of the question to finish the game the next day or, if we had to start again, to make it a day game. So we spent a beautiful morning twiddling our thumbs, played the first 50 overs and then at exactly the same time as the previous evening, thunder boomed, the sky turned an angry purple and it started hosing down. Dumb and dumber. We were declared joint winners, which struck me as utterly meaningless. The lesson wasn't learned: the 2004 Champions Trophy was held in England in September, just as the soccer season was getting under way. No one seemed very interested.

But our one-day game was developing. It had previously been built on making huge scores by hitting lots of boundaries. It had taken about a year to get through the message that running between wickets and fielding was just as important. The emergence of the young players, notably Yuvraj and Kaif, who understood the physical side of the game, accelerated the process. Early on, I'd got the players to fill in performance sheets and their responses showed they understood the game plan and their individual roles within it. Now, that theoretical understanding was being translated into performance on the field.

India's other historical shortcoming — fast bowling — is also being addressed. Ever since Kapil Dev, there have been plenty of young boys in India wanting to be fast bowlers. Javagal Srinath took up the baton, and as cricket tightens its grip on the Indian consciousness and the gospel spreads to all corners of the country, more and more fast bowlers are being unearthed. The key is not to overload them before their bodies can handle the stress.

In the one-day context the development of fast bowlers is doubly important, because the shortened game is increasingly stacked against India's traditional strength, spin bowling. The old maestros lament the lack of flight, but the game has changed: in the course of a year, someone like Harbhajan bowls more spells in one-day cricket than in test matches and if you keep floating it up to today's batters, you're going to get a sore neck watching it disappear. It's not just bat technology and flat wickets, it's the fact that boundaries are getting shorter. The TV companies know the public wants to see fours and sixes, so the ropes are coming in all over the world.

I had many deep and meaningful pre-game discussions with Indian groundsmen, pointing out that we had two spinners, so would they please push the ropes back? Then the TV company would demand more space for the advertising hoardings, and when we arrived at the ground on match day the ropes would have come in again and I'd get dark looks from the spinners.

Money talked a lot louder than I did.

THE YELLOW BRICK ROAD

His name was Avnish and he was about 15 years old. He came up to me in his school uniform to ask, 'How do I get better at cricket, sir?' I asked him how much he practised; an hour and a half a day, he said. 'Double it,' I said glibly. That wasn't what Avnish wanted to hear: first of all, his mother wouldn't let him and, secondly, there simply weren't enough hours in the day.

This was Avnish's routine, six days a week: up at 6 a.m.; off to school at 7; in class by 8, after half an hour of assembly and prayers; home for lunch at around 2.30, after six 55-minute classes; more study from 3 to 5; cricket between 5 and 6.30, then special tuition until 8; an hour off for dinner, then school-work till midnight. It was the same for many Indian kids aged between 13 and 16. Competition was fierce; everyone was putting in the hard yards, so you either kept up or fell behind.

Then there's the routine Sachin Tendulkar kept as a teenager: as a 13-year-old he played cricket for 55 days in a row during his summer holidays. After a couple of hours in the Shivaji Park nets in central Mumbai, he was ready to bat. He'd have an innings at Shivaji Park, then jump on the back of his coach's scooter for a thirty-minute ride to the Azad Maidan in south

Mumbai, where he'd bat for another team in another game. Then it was back to Shivaji Park for a two-and-a-half-hour net, finishing at 7 p.m. When he started to flag, his coach would put a one rupee coin on the middle stump. If he was dismissed, the bowler got the coin; if no one could get him out, Tendulkar kept it.

He'd moved in with his uncle and aunt because they lived close to Shivaji Park and the nearby school had a strong cricket team. From an early age he was called a prodigy, even a genius, as if it was just a matter of giving his natural talent free rein. But as the old saying goes, genius is one per cent inspiration and 99 per cent perspiration.

No matter how good you were, to play for India you had to be driven. These boys get very little handed to them on a plate, and there aren't many second chances. There's a perception that most of India's leading cricketers come from privileged backgrounds, but the stories the players told me on bus trips and flights and over dinners painted a very different picture. Most of them had done it the hard way; they'd got where they were through single-minded determination, tenacity and stoicism, not because Daddy was Mr Moneybags.

Most of them began by playing tennis-ball matches in the street or the local maidan (open ground) with friends. The ones who made it were the ones who had a dream of playing for India, and who were prepared to drive themselves in pursuit of it. As a kid, Harbhajan Singh would wear out a ball in two hours, bowling on the terrace at home. When it got dark, he'd go down to the narrow lane outside his home and carry on bowling by using the headlights of a friend's scooter to light up his pitch.

In the big cities, like Mumbai, Bangalore, Hyderabad and Kolkata, cricket is long-established and the road to the top relatively well signposted. But more and more quality players are emerging from small towns in far-flung regions that aren't traditional cricket strongholds and that don't have much in the way of facilities and support structures. Some of these guys make their mark without the benefit of formal coaching or facilities that young cricketers elsewhere take for granted. Like a ground.

Zaheer Khan is from Srirampur in central Maharashtra, a town no one had heard of. It had no coaches, no nets, no proper ground. For Zaheer, cricket meant watching it on TV and bowling to his mates. Until he was 17, he'd never bowled with a leather ball or played competitive cricket. After he missed an under-19 district trial because a friend forgot to tell him about it, his father took him to Mumbai. They went to the main maidans, traipsing from club to club looking for someone who'd give the small-town kid a chance. Sudhir Naik, a former India player, was impressed by Zaheer's pace and took him on. He was taught to bowl in stages: first with an old ball, then with a new one and finally with the balls used in first-class cricket. His father agreed to give him a year of full-on cricket to see what he could make of himself. Within five years of coming to Mumbai, he was playing for India.

Mohammad Kaif left his home town, Allahabad, at 12 to live in a sports hostel in Kanpur because it enabled him to play a lot of organised cricket. That involved getting himself enrolled at the local school, doing his own chores, hand-washing his clothes and going without his mother's cooking. He was one of the youngest boys in the hostel, and when there were practice wickets to be prepared, the juniors got the short straw: they had to fill buckets of water from a hand-pump and lug them out to the pitch. Kaif said that those early years made him tougher, and being around older boys helped him learn the game.

Every day after school, Virender Sehwag travelled 40-odd kms by bus to a Delhi college that had a comprehensive cricket programme. His first coach made him lift and swing a bat in a bat case filled with sand, using just his left hand, over and over, to strengthen the arm. To groove his backlift and make him play straight, the coach stuck a piece of bamboo in the ground just wide of the off stump, the idea being that going up and coming down the bat had to pass between the stumps and the bamboo. If he hit the bamboo, he wasn't playing straight enough.

As a boy growing up in Bhubaneswar in eastern India, S.S. Das would race to his club nets after school on his bicycle, only to find that by the time he got to the ground the sun had set. His school was eventually persuaded to give him permission to miss the last two classes of the day so that he could leave early and get a good net before it became too dark.

Yuvraj Singh's father, Yograj Singh, was a medium pacer who took one test wicket in his single test. Here's a clue: his sole scalp was a dashing left-hand opening bat from New Zealand who thrilled crowds the world over and later went into coaching. Yograj was hellbent on his son going one better; a situation that doesn't always work for either party, but did in this case. Yuvraj was good at tennis and had won a national roller-skating championship, but his father threw away his roller-skates, built a net with a concrete wicket in the backyard, and installed lights so Yuvraj could practise at night. Not that he didn't practise during the day: even in the dead of a north Indian winter, he was often woken up at 5 a.m. with a glass of water in the face. Yograj once gave an interview in which he said he trained his son for six hours a day and four at night. Compared to his father, I must've seemed like a teddy bear.

I loved going to the Challenger one-day tournaments, because every year players would turn up out of nowhere with astonishing ability based on hand-eye coordination, timing and minds that were uncluttered by doctrinaire coaching. The wicketkeeper-batsman Mahendra Singh Dhoni is an example. His school team didn't have a keeper, so a teacher hauled him out of the soccer goal and gave him the gloves. Once he started playing cricket, Dhoni discovered that he had a knack for hitting the ball out of sight. He put one onto the balcony of a teacher's flat overlooking the ground and another through a window next to where a selector was sitting. The selector hadn't picked him for a junior world cup, so perhaps his aim was off. Asked how he could hit the ball so far, Dhoni put it down to all the buffalo milk he drank when he was growing up. The story snowballed, as they tend to do, and soon one litre a day had become six. By the time I came across him, he'd traded up to milkshakes. Dhoni was the first cricketer from Ranchi to play for India. After he'd hammered a couple of ODI centuries, to avoid being overrun by local TV crews wanting to film them watching their son, his parents took to locking up their little flat and going elsewhere on match days.

Javagal Srinath hailed from Mysore, 130 kms from Bangalore. At 10, he started bowling in tennis-ball tournaments, but the teacher in charge of sport at his school limited her involvement in cricket to handing out the equipment. The only formal coaching he got was at summer camps. The city slickers in Bangalore would look down on the small-town boys, and it wasn't until Mysore won a state-level tournament, beating city and company teams containing professionals, that it really dawned on Srinath that he was quicker and better than he thought, and quicker and better than the guys he was playing against. On the field, he felt equal to anyone, but as his career progressed he had to overcome self-doubt, the legacy of his modest, provincial background. The gap between the small towns and the metropolitan centres has closed, to the extent that now the kids from the sticks reckon they're tougher than the city boys and carry that attitude on to the field.

Indians get more live cricket on TV than anyone else, and whether they'd been coached or not, the players had picked up a lot from TV. Zaheer would watch left-arm quicks, then work on his action in front of a full-length mirror. Kaif followed Australia, getting up at four or five in the morning or staying up late if they were in the West Indies, trying to work out what made them so successful. He concluded that it was their fielding. Having watched the Aussies dive and slide, he virtually taught himself to field in that style, starting during the monsoons when the ground was wet and soft.

Ajay Ratra, the youngest keeper to score a test century, grew up in Faridabad, outside Delhi. He learnt a lot about the art of keeping by watching his hero, Ian Healy, on TV.

After years of observing and imitating and asking questions of anyone who might know anything about keeping, Ratra found himself at the National Cricket Academy (NCA) with two high-powered wicketkeeping coaches — Rod Marsh and Syed Kirmani. They didn't always say the same thing, because the very different conditions in Australia and India require different techniques. To avoid offending either of his famous mentors, Ratra listened to them with equal attentiveness, nodding in all the right places, and took the best of both.

According to Kaif, if you come from an out-of-the-way place and have ambition, it's a matter of hitting the road and finding a way into the system at the under-16 level, and then working your butt off. (He saw himself as paving the way for players from his home state of Uttar Pradesh; the season after I left, he captained UP to its first-ever Ranji Trophy.) Indian junior cricket isn't for the diffident, and not just because of the intensity of the competition.

Anil Kumble remembered travelling for 38 hours to play in a zonal under-17 game. If you want to travel in comfort on a long-distance train trip in India, you need to book a seat well in advance, otherwise you have to take your chances in the dreaded 'unreserved' carriage, where there are four claimants for every available space. Kumble and his mate squeezed into the unreserved carriage and parked themselves on their kitbags near the toilet, before positioning themselves within striking distance of the ultimate prize — a wooden berth. Arriving exhausted and sleep-deprived, they then had to find their way to the stadium and, when they got there, locate and introduce themselves to their team. At the time he didn't think anything of it — if you wanted to play cricket, you did what you had to do, which might include wading to practice because a lake had overflowed or sharing a single seat with a team-mate for a 12-hour journey. 'Maybe you value the game more,' he says now. Kumble wasn't coached, although his brother advised him to switch from quick bowling to leg-spin. Within a year of playing first-class cricket, he was picked for India.

Indian Railways, the world's second largest employer (1.5 million employees) behind the Chinese Army, have a first-class cricket team. They hire athletes, including cricketers, from different states to play in their various teams, but if you don't have a college degree, you actually have to do some work. Kulamani Parida had to inspect tracks for two years before he could concentrate on his off breaks. He'd leave home at the crack of dawn, and travel 15 kms by bus to the stretch of track that was his little domain. He had to walk up and down 6 kms of line, checking and oiling the tracks, and climbing electric poles to make sure the wiring was okay. During home games, the Railways team stayed in a rather insalubrious dormitory at their ground in Delhi. When their captain, Sanjay Bangar, was playing for India in Delhi and Railways had a home game, he'd sometimes sneak off from his five-star hotel room to stay in the dormitory with his mates.

In the big cities, cricket is increasingly structured and organised. With their academies and coaches and parents wanting their little boy to be transformed into a Tendulkar, it brings to mind the US junior tennis system with its camps and gung-ho coaches and pushy parents. The old ways of self-help may be on the way out, which might explain why so many of the new stars are coming from places where success requires struggle and sacrifice.

Until the financial rewards began to mushroom, pushing one's son into cricket was looked upon as something of a risk. Ordinary Indian families have very little in the way of discretionary income, and Indian teenagers don't take a gap year to travel overseas. You study, you get a qualification, you get a job and you do it for life. There's no dole: families look after their own.

Making it changes everything. Harbhajan was clearly a great talent and had played for India at the age of 17, but he ran into trouble with his action, missed some tours and was suspended from the NCA. When he was 19, his father died. His career had hit the wall and he had no real qualifications, but as the only son he was expected to support his mother and five sisters. Before the Australian series in 2001, he was planning to go to the US and drive trucks. Ratra's father sold eggs wholesale. Ajay built his family a new house and tried unsuccessfully to persuade his father to give up work.

Be careful what you wish for, as they say. These players work and sacrifice to follow their dream of playing for India, but getting there can be an unnerving experience. They may be prepared for the on-field challenges, but they're not always ready for the circus. Srinath's early experiences sent him into what he calls 'seclusion'. He sat out a lot of early games for no good reason, didn't feel as if he had a mentor in the team, and couldn't understand why so much was made of him being a 'vegetarian fast bowler'. He believes that if he'd been given more support in his first few years, and had been told where to pitch the ball in what conditions, he would've taken another 100 test wickets. Instead, he had to find his way by trial and error. One of his more notable errors occurred in South Africa in 1992 when he rushed on to the field wearing Kapil Dev's trousers — with Kapil at the dressing room window demanding his trousers back at the top of his voice. Srinath practised what he preached: when he became a senior figure in the team, he took the younger bowlers under his wing. He could give them a rev-up and then go into bat for them in a team meeting. I'm sure there was a time when Srinath was shy and introverted, but it ended long before I got there.

I once heard a player say jokingly that it took newcomers at least three or four matches to feel at ease in the dressing room, because that was how long it took to stop observing Tendulkar's every move and start relating to him as a team-mate.

Ratra made his debut in a one-dayer at Eden Gardens, which can be an intimidating environment for experienced players, let alone a rookie. Every time the crowd did a Mexican wave, he felt the ground vibrate. He was so nervous that he appealed for a stumping every time he whipped off the bails and, sure enough, ended up before the match referee Dennis Lindsay, a former wicketkeeper, for excessive appealing. If it hadn't been his first game, he would've been banned for two matches.

They were young men, little more than kids in some cases, but from the moment they made the Indian team the expectations and demands on them were huge. They felt pressure to be successful because they didn't come from rich backgrounds, and pressure from the media, who they believed could make or break them. Yes, they always had the choice of opting out and regaining their peace and privacy, but they would pay a heavy price for that, not just in lost income but in loss of face and self-esteem. They were more than just sportsmen in their home towns and regions; they were achievers, success stories, role models, heroes, almost gods.

The Green, Green Grass of Home

The highlight of our 2002/03 New Zealand tour was a jet-boat trip up the Shotover River. I have a photograph taken that day which is an absolute collector's item because everyone's smiling. It was that kind of tour. An unkind person might say that all it proved is that when Indians come to New Zealand, they should stick to sightseeing.

Beforehand there seemed plenty to look forward to: Christmas at home with the kids, catching up with family and friends, roast lamb and mint sauce, cold beers around the barbecue and watching my team perform in front of my compatriots. I knew there'd be result wickets, as there always are in New Zealand, but we were on a roll. Friends had e-mailed to say how much they were looking forward to seeing 'all your hot bats'. I was looking forward to my hot bats turning it on for them.

I'm a fiercely patriotic Kiwi. I gave it everything I had when I played for my country, but now I was proud to be the Indian coach and I wanted my team to play well in front of my family, my mates and my fellow Kiwis. But there was no happy homecoming. By the end of the tour my team couldn't wait to get out of my country. My private joys were overshadowed by professional trials and tribulations that tested me as a person and a coach.

Perhaps the tour was a bridge too far. We'd been playing non-stop for two years and the World Cup, which we'd been talking about in planning meetings and informal discussions for months, was looming. I'd wanted to have the bulk of the probable World Cup squad for the whole tour so that we could start gelling; specifically, I wanted the two young guns, Yuvraj Singh and Mohammad Kaif, and felt that we could do without a third specialist opener, given that there were only two tests. My view didn't prevail, and while Kaif was picked for the whole tour, Yuvraj was picked only for the one-day series. When he joined the tour he wouldn't talk to me because one of the selectors had told him Kaif had got the nod ahead of him on my say-so.

But things had started unravelling much earlier. On our arrival at Auckland International Airport, Sourav Ganguly and Harbhajan Singh were fined by Customs for bringing dirty cricket boots into the country. Normally we get VIP treatment and are whisked through airports, but they went over us with a fine-tooth comb. Every step of our snail's pace progress through Customs was tracked by TV cameras. By then I was so used to operating in the media spotlight that I didn't think anything of it, but when I was back in New Zealand a few months later I happened to see a fly-on-the-wall documentary about the Customs, the centrepiece of which was them giving the Indian cricket team a working over. Even though the documentary dwelt at length on our captain's and champion off spinner's unwitting embarrassment, no one had bothered to tell us what was actually going on. I couldn't imagine it happening to the All Blacks, but I could imagine the outcry if it did.

In the programme, Harbhajan is obviously fuming, although given his forthright personality he was reasonably restrained, restricting himself to the comment that next time he was in this part of the world, he'd get off the plane in Australia. Watching them zero in on his dirty boots, I thought of his post-tour lament that 'in New Zealand they made us play in gardens'.

We kicked off with a game of Cricket Max in Christchurch on the best wicket we struck all tour, then got skittled in three days in the first test at the

Mid-day, India

The BCCI office in Mumbai, perhaps the greatest feat of camouflage since a wolf put on sheep's clothing.

Mid-day, India

A.C. Muttiah (left), the BCCI President at the time I was hired, with his point man Raj Singh Dungarpur.

Mid-day, India

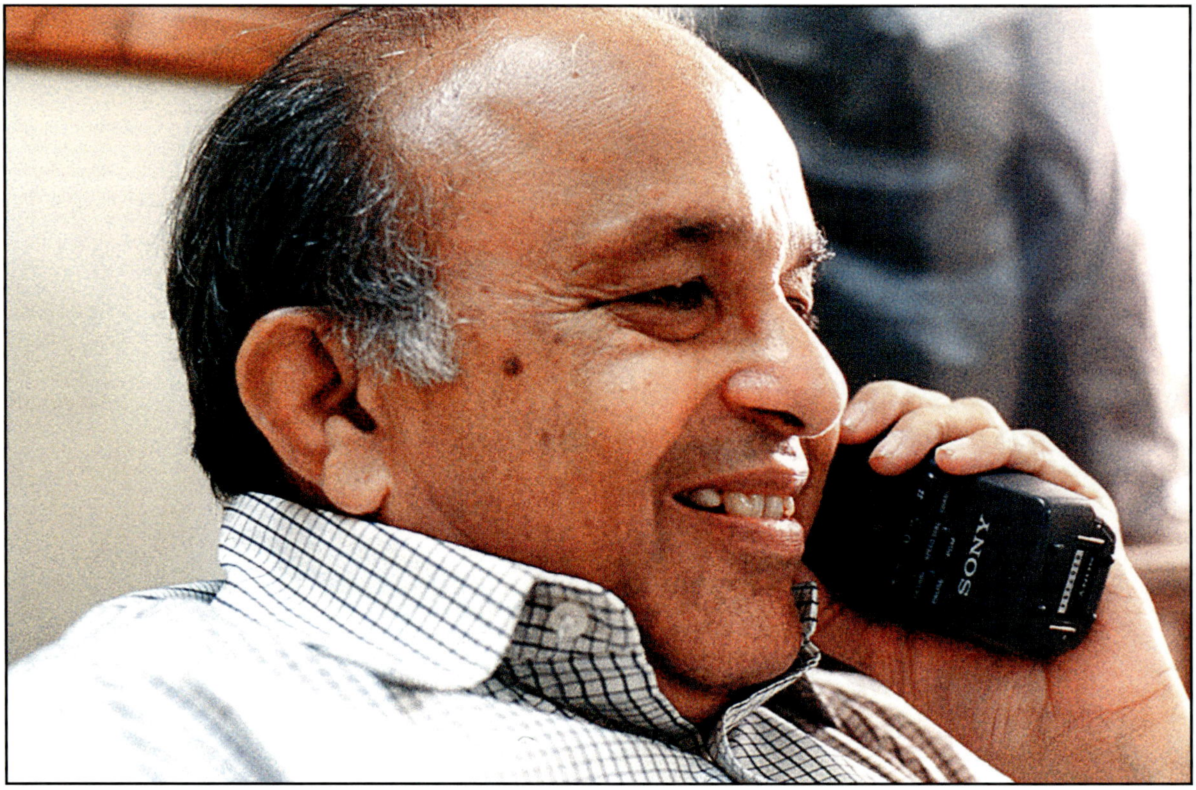

'John, you must take the hunter in the hand and the stick.' BCCI Secretary J.Y. Lele on the mobile he used exclusively for badgering the coach.

Mid-day, India

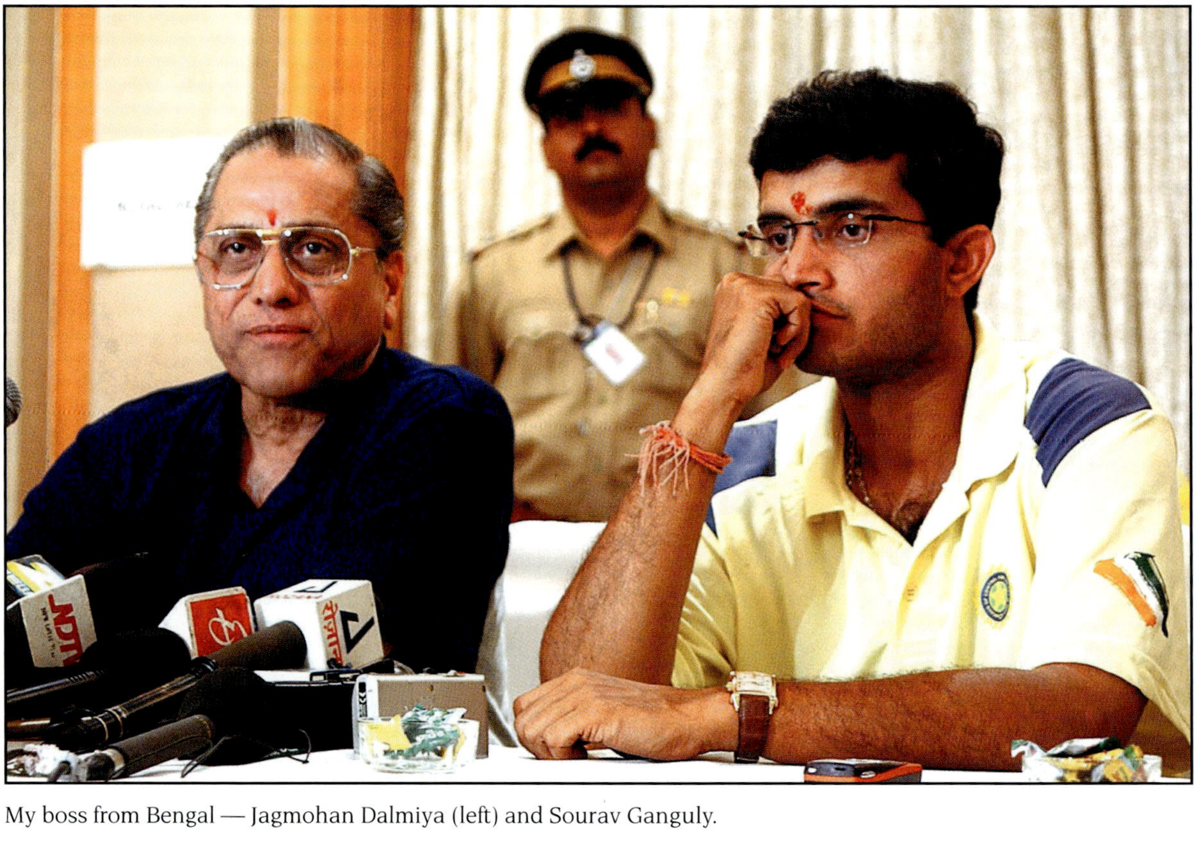

My boss from Bengal — Jagmohan Dalmiya (left) and Sourav Ganguly.

The sign that sent me hot-footing it back to Zimbabwe.

'Coach, I feel like bowling today. I got five-for last week.' With the police inspector I mistook for the groundsman (centre) and a member of the Georgetown Police Club.

Send lawyers, guns and money. Rahul Dravid finds himself stuck on the wrong side of the Zambia-Zimbabwe border.

'Free runs: you don't have to pay, just collect.' Dinesh Mongia (front left) with the net-bowlers-cum-commentators in Guyana.

I didn't coach Sachin Tendulkar; I gave him gentle advice when he asked for it.

This man did coach Sachin. Ramakant Achrekar ferried the 13-year-old Tendulkar around Mumbai on the back of his scooter so he could bat in two games on the same day.

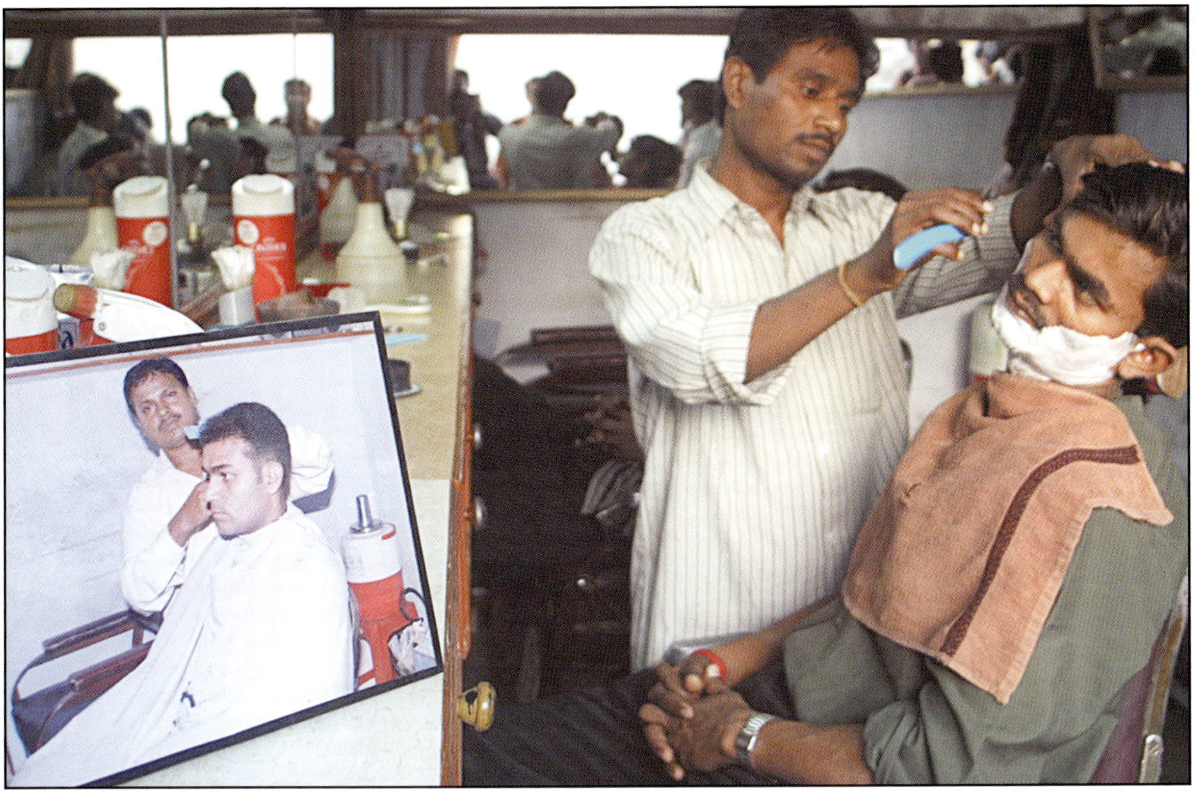

Times of India

He's Virender Sehwag's barber and he's got the picture to prove it.

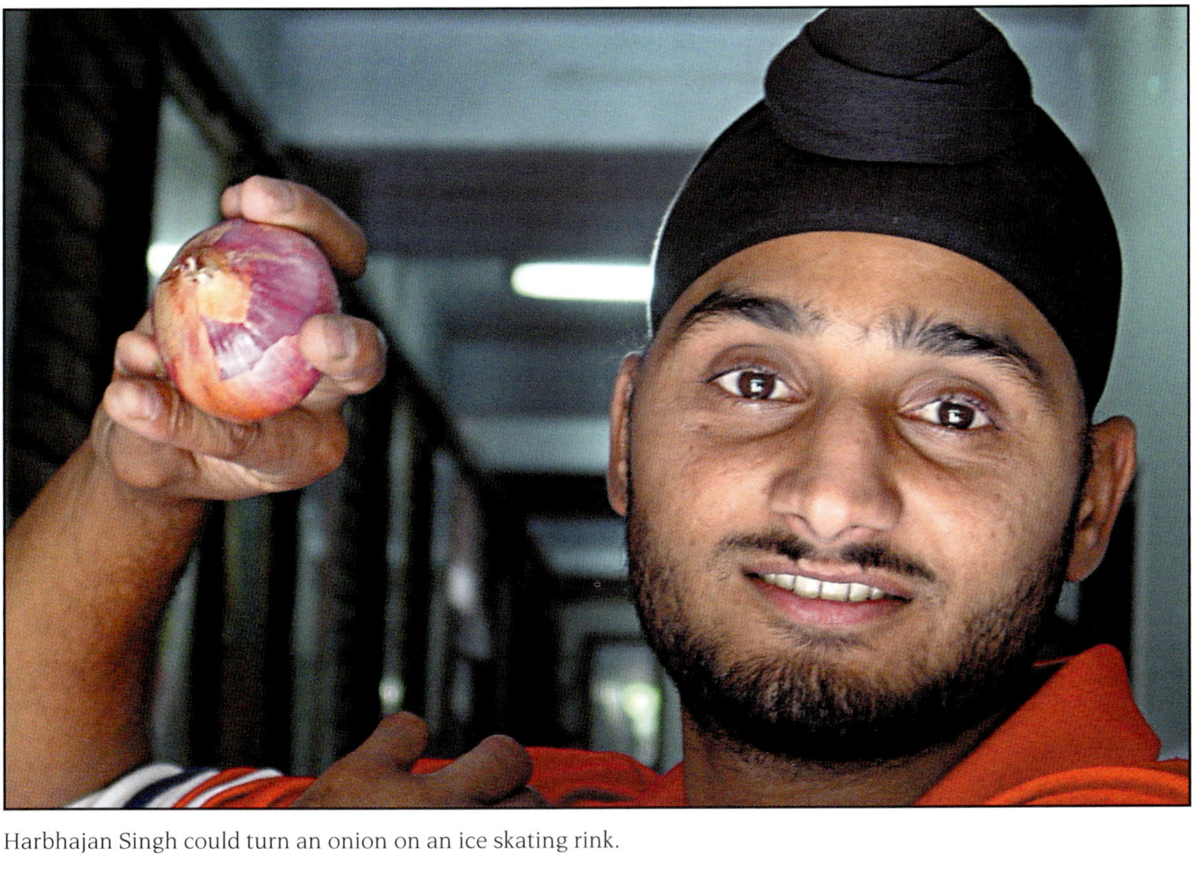

Times of India

Harbhajan Singh could turn an onion on an ice skating rink.

Rule Number One: when the coach points his camera at you, you smile. Clockwise from top left: Mohammad Kaif; Virender Sehwag; Rahul Dravid and Sachin Tendulkar.

John Wright Collection

It was a fine day at Lord's when we beat England in the NatWest Trophy final, so fine that Sourav Ganguly took his shirt off.

Adrian le Roux

Party time in the Lord's dressing room. The happy little bloke behind our fitness trainer Adrian le Roux (front left in the white top) is my son Harry.

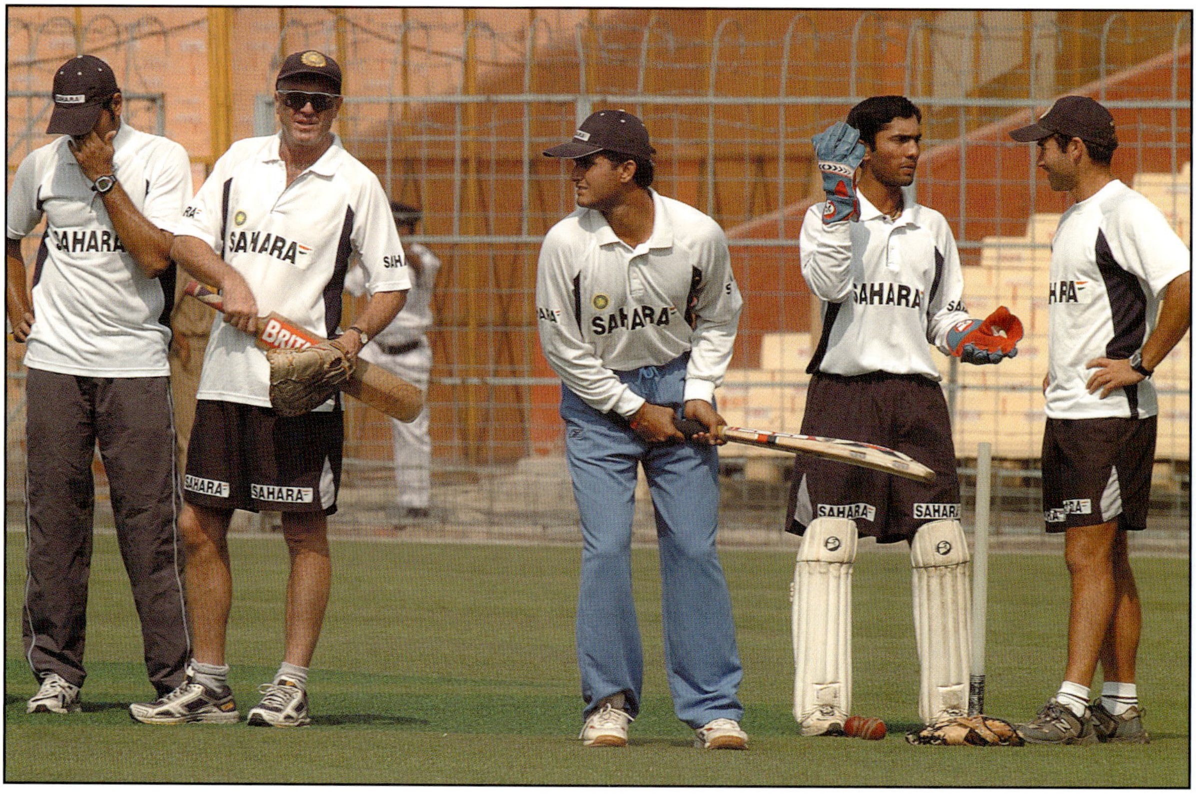

Look at me. I admire Sourav Ganguly's stance but, from left, V.V.S. Laxman, Dinesh Kartik and Greg King have their own preoccupations.

John Wright Collection

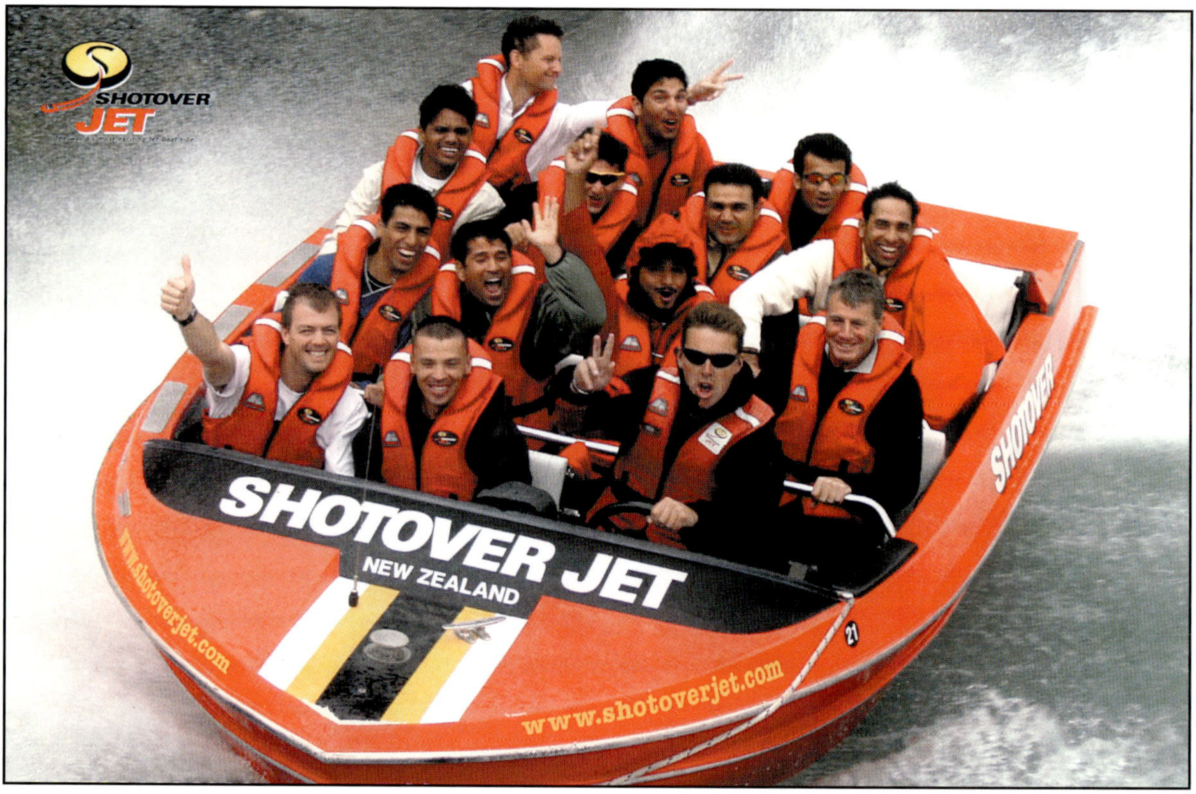

All downstream from here: the jet-boat trip on the Shotover River was the highpoint of our 2002/03 tour of New Zealand.

Basin Reserve. We had an open wicket practice on what would have been the fifth day and it was still seaming around. When the game finished early we got an informal request to play a one-dayer; but that was the last thing the players felt like doing, they would have taken a lot of persuading that you could have a fun game on that wicket. Little did we know. Chatting to people I knew in New Zealand Cricket, I expressed the hope that the wickets would improve. They didn't beat around the bush. 'This is the way it's going to be,' said one of them. 'You're going to be on green seamers.'

Two days before the Hamilton test was due to start, the wicket was wet. Unless global warming kicked in with a vengeance and Hamilton got Delhi's climate overnight, there was no way the test would begin on a dry wicket. The groundsman had a theory that sounded like it came from the back of a box of Betty Crocker cake mix: put X amount of water on the pitch two days before the game, and roll it so it sets. He reckoned it would be a fast wicket with good carry, even bounce and a little sideways movement, that would settle down after the first day. To this former opener, who'd suspiciously monitored many a wicket in the lead-up to a test, it looked like a seam bowler's wet dream. Unless something dramatic happened, we were in for another short test. What actually happened was that it rained for the next two days, an eventuality the Betty Crocker theory didn't allow for.

We lost the toss and were invited to make first use of a damp, very green pitch in overcast conditions. We got 99, New Zealand got 94; both innings lasted 38.2 overs. It was the first time in test cricket history that both sides had failed to make three figures in the first innings. There was a real opportunity to square the series if we could bat with guts and determination, put away the airy wafts and get behind the ball, and have someone dig in and get a score we could construct a decent total around. We got 154, with a top score of 39, and lost by four wickets. When Daryl Tuffey was knocking us over like ninepins, I pulled out the 'in my day' line, telling the boys it was just as well Richard Hadlee wasn't playing because we'd have been lucky to get 50.

It was a devastating disappointment. We'd played badly and I knew my compatriots would judge me accordingly. We were being flayed in the press, and by those of my former team-mates who'd won the game of musical chairs for those sought-after seats in the commentary box. There wasn't a lot I could say, but I made the point to anyone who'd listen that it was important for both teams that the wickets for the ODI series were a lot better. The World Cup was around the corner, and I assumed the New Zealand camp shared my view that it was critical for batsmen to go into that tournament with some confidence.

Things went from bad to worse. Before the first ODI, Sachin Tendulkar did his ankle bowling in the nets, putting himself out for four games. When he came back, he made scores of 0, 21 and 1. The first one-dayer in Auckland was on a drop-in wicket that had it all really: it was two-paced, with a lot of sideways movement and tennis-ball bounce. We just couldn't handle it and were all out for 108. The Black Caps lost seven wickets getting there.

People were starting to give me pitying looks and were asking what was wrong with the team. Well, most people: a woman in a shop in Napier told me she found it exciting 'when they're coming and going'. There was more coming and going at McLean Park the next day, although Sehwag got a century. (There were only two scored in the seven matches and he got them both.) We still lost. In Christchurch, the practice wickets were beautifully flat, but the match wicket was another minefield and we got rolled for 108 again. The batsmen were contributing to the situation by continuing to bat as if we had to get 250-plus, instead of adjusting their sights and aiming for 180-odd. You could see their confidence draining away.

Not surprisingly, after the test series fiasco and losing four ODIs on the trot, we were copping it from all quarters and being blamed for the public not getting their money's worth. Stephen Fleming waded in, questioning whether some of our batsmen deserved their high reputations, while others suggested we'd given up. Inevitably, my coaching ability was called into question, and I suppose those who'd decided I wasn't up to the job of coaching New Zealand were congratulating themselves on their sound judgement.

We scraped home at the Stadium in Wellington, and in the second game at Eden Park, before the tour straggled to its merciful conclusion in Hamilton, where the Betty Crocker theory still held sway. When the groundsman approached me, I told him he could do what he liked, as long as it produced a good one-day wicket. I might as well have asked for a world in which no child goes to bed hungry. We lost the toss, were invited to make first use of the pitch and were knocked over for 122. In baseball manager Yogi Berra's famous line, it was déjà vu all over again. New Zealand had the silverware, but some of their players didn't seem ecstatic about the way the series had gone. Craig McMillan and Chris Cairns both conceded that not many of the Kiwi batsmen were brimming with confidence. A former team-mate, now an administrator, admitted that he thought they'd got it all wrong. Certainly, looking ahead to the World Cup, it seemed a strange way to prepare for a tournament that would be played in batter-friendly conditions.

I've done a lot of batting on New Zealand wickets. There's nothing new in them seaming — in the 1980s we often went into test matches without a spinner, as John Bracewell will remember only too well — but I'd never seen wickets like these. The drop-in wickets had what I call 'stopping-bounce', meaning that the ball didn't come through at a consistent pace. There's no escaping the facts that we didn't adapt and we lost our fight, but I believe that international sport deserves international conditions. Here we had one of the most attractive batting sides in world cricket reduced to ineptitude, while the New Zealanders, who had the advantage of familiarity with the conditions, weren't much better. Batting was reduced to a matter of survival, and mere survival seldom makes compulsive viewing. The Indian fans were irate, but at the risk of sounding self-serving I believe the real losers were the New Zealand public. Cricket in New Zealand isn't so secure in the sports marketplace that it can afford to take the public and sponsors for granted; on the contrary, it needs to offer a vibrant and attractive product to maintain its position, particularly as rugby encroaches further and further into its season.

It was hard to salvage any positives, but we tried. With games finishing early, we had a lot of time on our hands, which Adrian le Roux used to really crank up the players' fitness. And with the wickets tumbling, our quick bowlers got into a good rhythm and went to the World Cup with a lot of confidence.

It was a very tough tour for me. When things are going badly, you try anything and everything: gentle encouragement, the call to arms, the blowtorch. I pulled out every trick, emptied the bag, but nothing seemed to work. We worked even harder in the gym and the nets, but the runs didn't come and the headlines became more caustic. With each failure, confidence and self-belief shrank a little further. The batsmen went out wearing haunted looks, thinking about what the ball was going to do, rather than what they were going to do. Coming off a year in which he'd scored 1200 test runs, with five centuries, Rahul Dravid said he had to get back to India to learn how to bat again.

It made me realise that there were advantages in being a foreign coach. Sure, I got criticised in India, particularly by the ex-players brigade, but my kids didn't see it, my family didn't know about it, and the wider cricketing community was largely unaware of it. When things got tough there, I'd tell myself that if it ended badly, I'd go home, get on a tractor and forget about it. But when it's your own country, and it's as small as New Zealand, and you're being slated in the media every day, there's nowhere to hide. Everyone who matters to you sees it, so it's much harder to deal with. It made me understand why the players took the criticism they got at home so personally and sometimes put up a wall between themselves and everyone else.

Mind you, there's something to be said for the old adage that if you're playing badly, don't read the papers. And there's a lot to be said for never losing sight of the fact that it's hard to quibble with performance and success. Every time you go out on the field as an individual or as a team, you have the opportunity to answer the critics and create a positive headline.

Through it all, I tried to stand up for the players. When things are grim, the coach has to go in to bat for his team. What you say in public isn't necessarily what you're telling the team in the privacy of the changing room (in fact, it's often the exact opposite), but you've got to be — and be seen to be — inside the circled wagons with the beleaguered pioneers, rather than outside with the Apaches.

And the players reciprocated. In Queenstown, Tendulkar invited me to his room for a chat. He opened a bottle of wine and asked me how I was bearing up. He said the team knew they'd been playing poorly and thanked me for not giving up on them. 'It must have been very tough,' he said, 'but you've stuck with us.'

In Christchurch, I was in a meeting with Ganguly when my parents arrived to see me. The captain and I sometimes didn't see eye to eye on cricketing matters, but he's a nice guy, with impeccable manners. My father was very ill and Sourav's warmth and concern was something I'll always remember.

The World Cup squad was named in the middle of the one-day series. The tour selectors — me, Ganguly, Dravid and Tendulkar — had communicated our thoughts to the selection panel back in India, and the captain and I waited by the phone for them to ring through with the final team. It wasn't a cosy chat; they made no effort to hide their disgust with us, our results, and probably our views on selection. Two players who were with us — V.V.S. Laxman and Rakesh Patel — didn't make the cut, but had to remain on tour even though we weren't going to play them, which was a bad mistake. They should have been allowed to go home immediately. It didn't help them, and it didn't help us.

Laxman was devastated. He'd never played in a World Cup and now maybe never would. He felt let down, and most of that sense of betrayal was directed at me. This is when a player's trust in his coach is shattered. I felt for Laxman; he was a wonderful bloke to work with and until then we'd had a good relationship. I tried to talk to him, but couldn't make much headway.

Getting dropped is horrible, but it's even worse when you're a big-name player and an established figure in the team, as Laxman was. You think it's a bullshit call, but there's nothing you can do about it. I was the New Zealand vice-captain for a long time, but got passed over for the captaincy on several occasions because the selectors didn't think I was officer material. Eventually

I got the job because Jeff Crowe was struggling for runs and they'd exhausted most other possibilities. I didn't want to have much to do with the people who'd made those decisions, so I knew exactly how Laxman felt. You carry that hurt with you till the end of your career.

This is the coach's burden: you drop a guy, and from then on your relationship is tainted by his resentment or perhaps even hate. It's easy to 'lose' that player, and I didn't want to lose someone as valuable as Laxman. Restoring the relationship took a year and a lot of hard work on both sides, and it was never quite the same. It didn't help that, about a year later, I made the most egregious faux pas imaginable. It happened in the dressing room in Ahmedabad: the TV was on and there was Sehwag in yet another advert — the players had been inundated with advertising opportunities after the World Cup. I ribbed him, saying that it wasn't as good as his last one, then turned to Laxman and asked, 'Why don't you do some of these ads, Lax?' Sehwag stared at me, as if to say *what planet are you from?* and reminded me that Laxman hadn't been at the World Cup. I forced a sickly smile, fled to the toilet and banged my head against the wall.

After the last one-dayer we had a two-hour meeting in our Hamilton hotel. I told the players that while we'd performed poorly, we'd played good one-day cricket for a year leading up to the tour. The boys were low on confidence, but I sensed that the core of self-belief remained intact. Anil Kumble, who often inspired us with his serenity and wisdom, did so again, and we left the room believing we could win the World Cup.

In my last press statement I said: 'We could have played better in the conditions provided, but the New Zealand batsmen haven't coped particularly well either. We're all very disappointed with the outcome. I'm particularly disappointed for the New Zealand public who didn't see the best of our batsmen. However, I'm sure if they switch on their televisions and watch us at the World Cup or on tour in Australia next summer, they'll see us at our best.'

It's not often that a coach gets to say 'I told you so'.

The Whole World in Our Hands

There was a definite touch of frost in the air when we got back to India after the New Zealand tour. Normally, there'd be a chauffeur-driven car waiting for me, but this time I had to queue for a cab like everyone else.

The batsmen didn't emerge from my tour report in a shining light. In all official correspondence I strove to be objective and discreet, which meant not naming names. There was no way of knowing where confidential BCCI correspondence would end up, and the front page of a newspaper was always a possibility. All coaches have to work with a few players they have reservations about, but if you commit those views to paper and circulate the document by letter, fax or e-mail, there's always a chance of it ending up in the public domain, whether by accident or design. The upshot of that is a poisoned relationship with those individuals, and a polluted team environment.

However, when we met I gave Jagmohan Dalmiya the unexpurgated, not-suitable-for-children version. He agreed to some of our requests, such as an extended pre-World Cup training camp in South Africa and extra white balls for practice, but not others, like additional training for players who hadn't achieved their fitness targets. He also had plenty to say on his own behalf.

I left the meeting with the distinct impression that if we didn't make the World Cup final, I wouldn't be seeing him again.

The patrons at Kolkata's Olypub, a no-frills drinking den that served a clear whisky that had to be approached with caution and handled with extreme care, were more encouraging. When one of them discovered my star sign was Cancer, he declared that the World Cup was ours; it was written in the stars. Sourav Ganguly was a Cancer, Sunil Gavaskar was a Cancer, John Wright was a Cancer; the planets were aligned and the World Cup was in the bag. An elderly bloke told me I was the spitting image of that John Wright, the cricket coach; I should check it out next time his photo was in the paper. Everyone knew how many days it was until our first game at the tournament and had a tip to pass on. In a restaurant, a 10-year-old boy sat down at my table, addressed me as 'Uncle' and put forward a persuasive argument for restoring Sachin Tendulkar to opener.

Drugs are a huge issue at any major international sporting event. While we were in New Zealand the BCCI had paid for the New Zealand drug-testing agency to test the entire team. Beforehand, Andrew Leipus instructed the players to load up with all their regular supplements and medicines. It was an expensive exercise but worth it; everyone came out clean. However, the Sports Authority of India's (SAI) anti-doping people weren't prepared to sit this one out; they turned up, unannounced, with their drug-testing gear on the day we were leaving for South Africa, which was already fairly hectic, as days like that tend to be. It was a slow process because there were only two doctors, and a couple of players missed the team photo because they were off somewhere peeing in a bottle.

We were based in Durban, which was ideal. It had great weather and the largest expatriate Indian community anywhere, which meant plenty of Indian restaurants. When we were there 18 months earlier, I'd beaten most of the players in a run along the beach. Now I came last, which I'd like to think was more a reflection of Adrian le Roux's impact than my physical decline. I talked at length to Phil Russell, who'd been my coach at Derbyshire and had gone on to coach Natal. His firm view was that in South African conditions the decisive period in one-day games was from over 32 on, and you had to go into those crucial last 18 overs with wickets in hand. All the South African provincial sides had a policy of bowling first in day games and batting first in day-night games.

At training we divided the squad into two groups and had two sessions a day, with one group fielding while the other batted and bowled. The focus was on getting the batsmen back into form; long net sessions required a constant supply of net bowlers. A friend of Raj Singh Dungarpur's, a wealthy tea importer based in England, was ready to pick up the tab for flying in a crew of quality net bowlers from India but it would have meant pulling them out of the Ranji Trophy, the main domestic competition. Instead, our friends in South Africa organised net bowlers for the entire tournament; wherever we went, they were waiting for us. All we had to do was tip them for doing overtime.

I had a vague sense that we'd overlooked something. I went over and over it in my mind, trying to put my finger on what we did differently when we were winning. Was it the way we trained, the order we did things, the personnel, the mood, the words? As a coach you're always searching for the key that will unlock the performance you know the team is capable of; it might be a little thing or something that at first glance seems utterly irrelevant to what happens on the field. Finally, the penny dropped: we weren't having our bowlers versus batters volleyball games. On the tour of England they'd become part of our routine, a ritual which the players had come to associate with winning. We'd stopped in India because it was just too hot and hadn't started in New Zealand, perhaps because it wasn't hot enough. As soon as we reinstated them, the mood became more relaxed.

Sandy Gordon had prepared a World Cup mission document that focused on mental toughness and getting into the right frame of mind for a long tournament that would get progressively more intense. We had batting, bowling and fielding captains who were in charge of planning and analysing our performances. We spent a lot of time talking about body language: Indian players tend to be mercurial, and we wanted to get into a mode where observers couldn't tell the state of the game from our body language in the field. The players were particularly taken with Gordon's point that during competition great teams and great players move into a 'f**k you' mode and stay there.

We had to give up our team room for the Hurricanes Super 12 team, who were staying in our hotel; a reminder that in South Africa, as in New Zealand, rugby rules. The two teams formed a mutual amazement society: the Hurricanes couldn't believe how small Tendulkar and some of the other Indian players were, and the Indians were equally astonished by the size of Jonah Lomu and his mates.

We had two practice matches against KwaZulu teams. In the first we got 265 before the rain came. The second was at Chatsworth, home to much of the local Indian community; 8000 people turned up, and we certainly turned it on for them. The opposition, essentially a KwaZulu third XI, scraped together 190, which prompted Ganguly to ask his opposite number if we could bat through the full 50 overs for practice purposes after we'd knocked off the required runs.

We got 158. I was apoplectic. Our media liaison spokesman, Amrit Mathur, reckoned my face was the colour of a new Duke cricket ball. This was what we had to show for eight days of solid training, with a strong focus on batting and all the positive discussion aimed at putting the New Zealand nightmare behind us: our vaunted batting line-up, boasting tens of thousands of test and ODI runs, skittled by the KwaZulu thirds. We'd supported the batsmen when they'd done little to deserve it, but it seemed to be a one-way process.

I consulted Javagal Srinath and Anil Kumble, two wise old heads, telling them I'd had enough; the batsmen had been batting like lottery winners for months, and it was time they were told a few home truths. They advised me to hold my fire, but if it happened again, then by all means let rip.

They had a question for me: where did Tendulkar want to bat? Their view was that if we were going to do well in the World Cup, our best player needed to be batting where he wanted to bat. The issue wouldn't have come up if we were playing well, but we weren't, and what we needed above all was some leadership with the bat. That evening I went to see Tendulkar and put the question to him. 'I'll bat wherever the team wants me to bat,' he said. 'Wherever they need me the most.' 'Fine,' I said, 'but forget the team for a moment; where do *you* want to bat.' After some toing and froing, he finally said, 'Well, if you really want to know, I'd like to open.' The next step was persuading Ganguly and Rahul Dravid that that was the way to go.

We travelled down to Cape Town for the less than memorable opening ceremony, having drifted back in the betting, which wasn't a bad thing. Our first game was against Holland in Paarl, where we were joined by Sandy Gordon who was in South Africa for a conference. He worked with us for two days, doing team sessions and one-on-ones for those who wanted them. With his help, the players came up with a theme for the tournament — 'Now or Never'. I had mixed feelings about it: it had a nice ring, but was uncomfortably similar to Dalmiya's parting message.

Gordon also suggested that at various times, such as the fall of a wicket, the team should get together to gee each other up, pass on information and prepare for the new batsman. His point was that because things happened so quickly and the crowds were so noisy, it could be difficult to communicate as a team and keep the team vibe going, unless you took the opportunity to bring everyone together. The players took it a step further, adopting the huddle which some of them had seen in county cricket. It certainly caught on in India, where it was interpreted very imaginatively and became the centrepiece of a cola commercial.

We dismissed Holland cheaply, which enabled us to get away with another undistinguished batting display. But there was no such let-off against Australia. Having won the toss, we lurched to 125, and lost by nine wickets, upon which all hell broke loose back in India.

In Kolkata, a mob burnt Ganguly in effigy, while a more sombre group staged a mock funeral procession, complete with all the paraphernalia used during actual Hindu cremations, for the Indian team who'd 'died' at the World Cup. It concluded with a makeshift camp cot adorned with pictures of the team being set on fire outside Eden Gardens. Black paint was thrown on Mohammad Kaif's house in Allahabad; his parents and sister moved out, fearing more violent attacks. In Bangalore, Dravid's car was vandalised. Ganguly even copped a serve from his brother, who contributed a scathing article to a Bengali paper, and there was a campaign to boycott products endorsed by the players.

That amounted to a lot of products. Before, and during, the World Cup, virtually every advertisement and promotion in India was cricket-related. Pepsi introduced 'Pepsi Blue', blue, of course, being our team colour. The corporate spend was estimated at NZ$540 million, with related advertising reaching NZ$280 million. A boycott would have caused a few sleepless nights for marketing directors who'd sunk big money into promotions linked to the World Cup.

Whether a boycott campaign was needed was a moot point. How many Indians would be rushing out to buy products endorsed by players who they'd just watched capitulate? Some of the players blamed the TV commentators, believing they'd stirred the public up with their vitriolic criticism. At the opening of Parliament, the Indian President wished the team luck, prompting derisive laughter from some MPs; a minority, presumably, since Parliament agreed to post policemen outside the players' homes and provide special security for their families.

Even though we were out of India, we weren't entirely spared. The 100-strong Indian media contingent was becoming increasingly hostile and the atmosphere at press conferences increasingly adversarial. Ganguly and I made statements, but the one that made people sit up and take notice came from Tendulkar. It was like a papal pronouncement. On behalf of the team, he addressed the well-wishers of India: 'We ourselves are disappointed with the kind of performance we all have put up. I also understand the disappointment you've gone through. I'm just here to assure all of you that we'll be fighting till the last ball is bowled.' Having said his piece, he left without taking questions.

The game against Zimbabwe in Harare was make or break: if we lost, we could be goners. A debate was raging about whether teams should be playing in Zimbabwe, but it wasn't an issue for the Indians. Frankly, at that stage, if there were World Cup points on offer, we would have turned up on the dark side of the moon and rolled and marked the pitch if necessary.

At the pre-game team meeting I began by saying that no matter what was being said and written in the media and regardless of the ructions in India, I still had faith in them, but it was time for that faith to be repaid. Then I turned the blowtorch on the batters, telling them that the rest of us had had enough: we'd tried this plan and that plan, and we were still getting rolled for 120. 'There are some chairs out by the pool,' I said. 'Go out there and sort it out and when you've done that, come back and tell us what you're going to do about it.' They returned half an hour later, having decided that Ganguly would drop down to three to allow Sehwag to open with Tendulkar, and vowing to start performing.

The next day Tendulkar led the charge, scoring 81. He and Sehwag put on 99 in 16 overs and we made 255, then bowled Zimbabwe out for 172. Against Namibia, Tendulkar got 152, Ganguly also got a century, and we won by 181 runs. We felt like we were back on track, but no one was taking much notice of us because we were dining out on minnows and there was so much else going on, what with Shane Warne's drugs bombshell, the ruckus over England playing in Zimbabwe, and New Zealand refusing to go to Kenya. We were quite happy to be ignored; we felt as if we were building momentum and sneaking up on the blind side.

We targeted the game against England in Durban, believing that a win would set us up for the tournament. This was Ashish Nehra's moment in the sun. He was a real character, who'd had to play through a lot of pain. At the end of a day's play he'd have his leg in ice from the knee down, and Andrew Leipus would wire him up to the interferential machine on a setting that would have most people climbing the walls. Nehra and Leipus spent so much time in each other's company that the players would ask them, 'so when are you two tying the knot?' On his day, though, his left-arm swing was a real handful. Against Namibia he was given the new ball and sent down two deliveries before twisting his ankle. Asked at the press conference why he'd opened with Nehra, Ganguly replied, 'We wanted to see what Ashish did with the new ball. We found out that he falls over.' It was still sore in Durban, but he passed a fitness test and assured us he'd go the distance. After Ganguly won a good toss, we told him to bowl Nehra straight through. He took 6 for 46, and won the game for us.

In these sorts of tournaments everyone says they're taking it one game at a time, but that's not always the case. We did. We stuck to our routines; we debriefed the same way after each game, and prepared the same way for our next one. Sticking to our routines and staying focused was comparatively easy when we were a sideshow, but now we were well and truly back on the radar. Our next opponents were Pakistan, and things were about to get a little crazy.

It was my first exposure to cricket's fiercest rivalry. There's nothing else quite like it; the Ashes has the tradition, but India versus Pakistan has a sharper edge. India and Pakistan were one country until independence from the British in 1947, when they were partitioned into two separate states. The event had lasting political repercussions, and no other cricketing rivals have been at war with each other three times in the last 50 years, the last time being as recently as 1999. Cricket was hostage to the political climate between the two countries at the time; India and Pakistan didn't play each other very often. While the players get on reasonably well, there's always tension beneath the surface. For the fans, however, these clashes are far more than games of cricket; national pride is at stake.

The talk about it being 'just another game' was developing a hollow ring; Tendulkar admitted later that he'd been thinking about it for a year. Leaving aside the historical and political overtones, we knew that if we won we were through to the Super Series stage of the tournament, and Pakistan would be struggling to go any further. And there was the small matter of India having never lost a World Cup match to Pakistan. I didn't want to be the coach who blotted that record.

The media and fans in both countries certainly weren't buying the 'it's just another game' line. The headline writers dusted off the war analogies, labelling it 'the Mother of All Matches'. If an India-Pakistan World Cup game is held on a working day, either you don't get too many people into work, or you don't get too much work done. The streets empty out as the game begins, and some Indian cities even declare a public holiday. Politicians, businessmen and movie stars flew over for the game, and we were told that 85 coach-loads of foreign spectators arrived at the Supersport Stadium in Centurion, where 1100 policemen were on duty, 200 more than normal. The extra security might have been a bit over the top, because Indian and Pakistani fans don't go to games to get drunk. In fact, whenever India or Pakistan played in Centurion bar takings were down 30 per cent.

Our team room was our place of refuge, a place where we could escape from the hype and bubbling anticipation. We covered the walls with Indian flags and posters made by the staff at the Taj Mahal hotel in Mumbai. The posters were decorated with slogans: 'We are India, we can'; 'The next game, our best game'; 'We are World Cup winners, get comfortable with it'; 'Expect success'; 'Love the moment'.

The team room in the Pretoria Holiday Inn had been used by the All Blacks before the crucial match at Loftus Versfeld Stadium in 1996 when the quest for New Zealand rugby's holy grail — a series win in South Africa — finally came to fruition. It meant nothing to the players, of course, but I hoped it was a good omen.

Sanjay Bangar, who didn't play a single match in the tournament, gave a very effective team talk, reminding the boys that Pakistan would try to intimidate them early on. We had to ride out the bluster, he said, and ensure that when things started to go our way, we didn't take our foot off the pedal. Listening to him reinforced my conviction that we had the right mix of people. The attitude and demeanour of players who aren't getting on the field is a pretty good indication of the tightness of a team. Like Bangar, Parthiv Patel sat out the whole tournament, and we rotated Harbhajan Singh and Kumble, but there was no moaning. Harbhajan was disappointed not to be picked for the Pakistan game, but you wouldn't have known it from the way he was fizzing around before the game. Our policy was to field first in day games, but Harbhajan got it into his head that Ganguly might opt to bat first and came running up to me before the toss. 'We have to win this, John,' he said. 'Make sure we field.'

The match referee Mike Procter gave us a little speech about keeping things calm and the players had to shake hands out on the field to set an example for the fans. Everyone kept saying it was 'just another game', but no one was treating it like one.

The Centurion wicket was slower and had less grass on it than the strips we'd encountered on the 2001 tour. Groundsmen had been given the word from the tournament organisers to provide decent batting wickets that would produce high-scoring games and entertain the vast international television audience.

Pakistan won the toss and made 273. India's highest successful World Cup chase was 222, and the Pakistanis oozed confidence at the lunch break. The simmering tension led to a verbal skirmish in which a Pakistani player made a provocative remark to one of our guys who wasn't inclined to turn the other cheek. Srinath had to step in to prevent a breach of the peace. As our openers walked down the long flight of stairs to begin the chase, Sehwag told Tendulkar, 'Don't say anything to me about my batting except "go and lagaao"' — basically, go for it. Tendulkar replied, 'I'm going to get these guys.'

Shoaib Akhtar went for 18 in his first over, and they put on 53 in 5.4 overs. Sehwag got out, but Tendulkar charged on. He loves a big stage and on this, the biggest, his batting was explosive. He and I chatted about batting now and again; he talked a lot about having a relaxed mind, heart and body. When he was at the crease, you could see him putting his fundamentals in place: he'd watch the ball from the bowler's hand on to and off the bat, and adjust his backlift for different bowlers. He stressed the need to be comfortable at the crease, and was quite prepared to change his stance or grip to that end.

He made 98 off 75 balls, cramping quite badly towards the end. The dressing room he limped into was silent out of respect, and perhaps also by anxiety brought on by his dismissal. But Kaif played another valuable hand, and Dravid and Yuvraj Singh got us home by six wickets in 45 overs. As we cruised to victory, the flag-waving got wilder and the cheering got louder. There were supposedly 22,000 at the ground, but it sounded like twice that many. People who'd worked at Centurion for years said that they'd never seen or heard anything like it.

The celebrations began amidst phone-calls from the high and mighty, including the Deputy Prime Minister and head of the army. The usual sequel to India-Pakistan games is that the victorious nation's troops stationed on the shared border let off a volley of gunfire to send a message to their counterparts on the other side. That day, Bill Clinton was speaking, via satellite hook-up from New York, to a high-powered conference in Delhi; they put him on hold until the match finished.

We weren't a drinking team by any stretch, but that day the boys cleaned up a couple of dozen cans of beer, practically a binge by their standards. Some of the empties were named after ex-players in the media who'd put the boot in after the loss to Australia, and the boys lined up to trample them flat. Back at the hotel, the foyer was jam-packed with delirious Indian supporters. A middle-aged man wrapped me in a bear-hug. 'That's it,' he said, 'that's our World Cup. We've beaten Pakistan — it doesn't matter what happens now.' I felt utter contentment and relief, as if I'd shed a huge burden. The players went off for a night out on the town — there were parties all over Johannesburg — and I had dinner by myself in a little Italian restaurant across the road. The oysters were great.

No one had more reason to be pleased than the players' families, who gave them the news of the ecstatic reaction back home. When the boys called home, their family members held their mobile phones outside their windows so they could hear the noise of the fireworks going off in their neighbourhood. In the space of a fortnight, they'd gone from being national disgraces to national heroes. As a South African administrator put it, 'When you do well for India, they name a street after you; when you do badly, they chase you down the same street.'

Before we played Kenya in the first of our three Super Six matches, I reminded the team that the critics, all those crushed beer cans, hadn't gone away; they were just lying low. 'They're waiting, boys,' I said, 'waiting to hammer you.' Srinath replied, 'John, we don't play for them.'

Kenya was a tough game. We had to chase 225 under lights at Newlands, which is often a recipe for disaster, as the wicket, having behaved itself during the afternoon, can play tricks in the evening. When we were 24 for 3, it was impossible not to think back to our loss to Kenya at Port Elizabeth in 2001. It was the stuff of nightmares: getting through to the Super Sixes, then failing to make the semis because we couldn't beat Kenya. The 2001 team might have lost this game, but we were more resilient now. Ganguly made an unbeaten century, Yuvraj played well again, and we won by six wickets.

Having scaled a few peaks, we were brought down to earth by an escalator at Johannesburg Airport. Someone's case got jammed on the top step, the guy coming up behind tripped over it and the dominoes started tumbling. You had the choice of hurdling the pile-up — no easy feat — or becoming part of it. Most of us took the latter option and the pride of India was reduced to a heaving, swearing human pyramid.

At the Wanderers, Sri Lanka won the toss and put us in. The top order fired, with Tendulkar stroking his way to another 90, and we posted 292. Srinath reduced them to 3 for 3, and we rolled them for 109, using only three bowlers. All in all, a resounding vindication of the 'bat first in day games' theory. We were through to the semi-finals, and New Zealand had to beat us in our final Super Series game to stay in the competition. People were talking about revenge and calling it a grudge match. We didn't really see it that way, but there was certainly no need for 'up and at 'em' speeches after Shane Bond's performance against Australia and Stephen Fleming's comments about 'reopening old wounds'. We were 21 for 3 chasing 146 before Kaif and

Dravid settled in. It mightn't have been a grudge match, but knocking New Zealand out of the World Cup certainly laid a few ghosts to rest.

We played Kenya again in the semi-final, winning by 91 runs. After a 20-year gap, India were World Cup finalists again.

While all this was going on, my father's health was deteriorating rapidly. It had really come home to me on my last visit. Seeing me off at Christchurch Airport, he'd asked me to close the car door for him because he didn't have the strength to pull it shut. He was a cricketing man and proud that I was coaching India, so at the back of my mind was the thought that our progress towards the final might help to keep him going. The day before the final the local paper ran a photo of him and Mum, proud parents looking forward to their son's big day. Sadly, our World Cup campaign ended with a whimper rather than a bang.

Beforehand, our plan was to bat first if we won the toss. When Sri Lanka put us in at the Wanderers, we'd got a decent score and skittled them. I also felt that we were better off batting first against Australia. When we'd played them in 2001, we'd beaten them twice batting first before losing a very tight series, 2–3. We'd got to the final playing four bowlers and batting down to seven, but I felt that in a one-off game against the Aussies a fifth bowler would be more valuable than a seventh batsman. I didn't win that argument.

It was a cloudy morning and there were damp spots on the wicket that the groundsman was drying with a hair-drier. After Ganguly, Dravid and Tendulkar had looked at the wicket, I asked them what they thought we should do. They wanted to bowl first, and it seemed worth a punt. You hope for some early life, and the dew spots suggested that there was moisture in the pitch. Our quick bowlers had done very well throughout the tournament, and if we could get a couple of early wickets, the pressure would be on them. Needless to say, if I had my time over again, I'd argue in favour of batting first till I was blue in the face.

They got into us from the word go, taking 15 off Zaheer Khan's first over. He was charged up and bowled a couple of no-balls and Adam Gilchrist was able to put us on the back foot. Again, in retrospect, I should've urged Ganguly to open with Srinath, the old campaigner.

We should have been smarter on the day, and I should have argued more forcefully for what my head and gut were telling me: bat first, and make sure you've got bowling depth, because if your top six batters don't get the runs, you won't win anyway. But there are some lessons you only learn through bitter experience. Afterwards, people were saying we put them in because we were gun-shy after what their bowlers did to us early in the tournament. But that didn't come into it at all.

Ricky Ponting was simply magnificent. To score 140 off 121 balls in a World Cup final is the epitome of performance under pressure and the hallmark of great leadership and great batsmanship. Chasing 340, Sehwag went out hard. There was a brief window when he was blazing away and the clouds were rolling in that the Duckworth-Lewis system, which like God moves in mysterious ways its wonders to perform, might have saved us, but the moment passed, just as the opportunity had.

Defeat was hard on everyone. I particularly felt for Srinath, who knew it was his last World Cup, and Kumble, who found the whole tournament hard going because warriors don't enjoy sitting on the sidelines. He never showed it though, and as a coach you feel privileged to work with a man like him, a great player blessed with grace and humility and dedication to the cause.

I flew home the next day. For some bizarre reason, they'd scheduled a tournament in Bangladesh almost straight after the World Cup, but I'd flagged my unavailability to the BCCI. I arrived in Christchurch on my father's birthday and had ten days with him. He wasn't impressed that I'd opted out of the Bangladesh tournament, telling me, 'You're going to bloody Bangladesh, because I'm not ready to die yet'.

He died the next morning.

There's No Business Like Cricket Business

Bodyguards, police escorts, sneaking out the back way to avoid being mobbed by star-struck fans . . . Just another day in the life of Sachin Tendulkar.

Early on, he invited me to accompany him to the adidas store in Chennai. We slipped in unobserved, as far as I could tell; Tendulkar collected his shoes (I also scored a free pair; the sponsors' largesse sometimes spilled over onto the coach) and we had a courtesy chat with the owner. When I suggested we needed to be on our way as we had a practice to get to, the owner said it wasn't quite that straightforward. He took me over to the window: there were hundreds of people milling around outside the store. Don't ask me how they knew Tendulkar was there. We had to stay out of sight in a back office until the cops turned up. They brought the car right up to the door, and we made a dash for it.

Tendulkar thought nothing of it; this was his everyday reality. He was a sporting hero and showbiz star rolled into one. As Andrew Leipus said, 'Every time Sachin gets injured, the whole of India gets an anatomy lesson.' Whenever he had a niggle, the media would run graphics of the affected body part, with a detailed diagnosis and prognosis, sometimes on the front page. When he was having trouble with his toe, the BCCI doctor appeared on the national news with a medical model of the foot's skeletal structure to explain the problem and soothe public anxiety.

One of the most fascinating, and sometimes challenging, aspects of my job was dealing with players who'd gone, almost in the blink of an eye, from the relative obscurity of the first-class scene to the fishbowl existence that went with playing for India. If the newcomer then produced a couple of good performances, they were like rocks rolling down a mountainside, the prelude to an avalanche. The media focus on a new star was so intense that within a matter of weeks he could be a household name. With the headlines came the hangers-on, and next thing, agents would be sniffing around. Then came the adverts, then came the billboards . . .

Nothing can possibly prepare you for this kind of instant fame. In the space of a season, Irfan Pathan went from being a promising junior to India's strike bowler. He was forever changing his mobile phone number, and his parents were hounded for interviews almost as much as Irfan. After making the Indian team, many players moved their families out of the old, crowded neighbourhoods, into new houses in posh areas, and bought them their first car. This was the uplifting part of overnight success: grateful sons repaying their parents for their support and sacrifice.

It all begins with the little screen in the corner of the room. Early in 2006 the BCCI global rights package was sold for NZ$991 million for four years, and Nike paid NZ$69 million to sponsor the team's kit. In 2004, India and Pakistan played their first full series for 15 years; the anticipation was phenomenal, as was the attendant commercial activity. Marketing experts reckoned the corporate advertising spend was around NZ$115 million, three times the usual figure for a series. Late ad spots during the ODI series cost more than they had at the business end of the previous year's World Cup. An eleventh-hour commercial slot during the World Cup cost NZ$6500 for ten seconds; a similar slot during the Pakistan series cost NZ$16,500. When India and Australia were playing off in the finals of the 2003/04 VB series,

ESPN-Star supposedly sold a last-minute 30-second spot for NZ$33,000. According to *Time* magazine, the India-Pakistan 2005 series attracted 'pay for view' subscriptions worth US$50 million, thanks to the 2 million people of South Asian origin living in the States.

Nobody hard-sells cricket like India's sports channels; anything that can be sponsored, branded or packaged, is. I've heard it said that in the course of the extended coverage of an ODI, a brand name can appear on the screen up to 340 times. Accommodating the demand and beaming out this barrage of brand names requires a lot of airtime, hence the lengthy pre-game build-ups and post-game analyses. There's a lot of time to fill, so the front men and pundits give a whole new meaning to the term talking heads. And because it's such a competitive industry, everyone's searching for an edge, and the men with the mikes have to go the extra mile.

Thus the pitch report might be presented by the Pitch Doctor, aka Michael Slater, complete with white coat, stethoscope and attractive 'nurse'. Pre-game analysis might take the form of Professor Deano's University of Cricket, courtesy of Dean Jones in an academic gown and mortar board scribbling on a blackboard set up inside the boundary rope. The Prof wasn't everyone's cup of tea: when he was doing his thing before one game, a spectator held up a sign which read, 'Deano, you say it best when you say nothing at all'.

Just as Channel 9 has Daddles the Duck, some Indian channels have animated characters, such as a dancing Sikh who pops up on screen every time there's a boundary, and a cross-legged guru who levitates when a run-out is referred to the third umpire. These are all accompanied by corporate logos. For the post-game wrap, the action is packaged in pre-sold capsules of catches, fours, sixes, wickets and man of the match performances. And when the sports channels finally sign off, you can switch over to one of a number of news channels for a replay, and more discussion and analysis from another line-up of pundits.

There are ten 24-hour national news channels, three in English and seven in Hindi. All of them have their in-house experts, ex-players who pop up in bulletins and during breaks to give their take on the game. After the day's play, they air cricket shows in prime time, mostly featuring a line-up of experts analysing the game from every perspective. Some of the criticism can be brutal; in line with international trends, the more aggressive and controversial the approach, the higher the ratings and the greater the advertising revenue. Interestingly, this constant and often highly critical analysis seemed to affect the wicketkeepers more than other players. India is perhaps the toughest place in the world to keep, because the wickets tend to keep low and take a lot of turn, and keepers spend a lot of time up at the stumps. As soon as a keeper dropped a few, the media would get on his back, replaying the damaging footage over and over again. Not surprisingly, the player would get very tense and uptight; 'don't make another mistake' became their key thought, instead of 'I'm going to catch the next one'. The media experts operated as judge, jury and executioner, with the result that in my time we had no fewer than seven test wicketkeepers.

Some of the cricket shows verge on the bizarre. One that ran in my last season was called 'Match Ka Mujrim'. Roughly translated it means 'Villain of the Match', although I'm told a 'mujrim' is actually someone who's been tried and found guilty in a court of law. Regardless of how well or badly we'd played, four members of the Indian team would be in the dock. Counsel for the defence was former chairman of selectors Syed Kirmani, while the redoubtable Bishen Bedi, who called a spade a shovel as a matter of course, was chief prosecutor. The show was filmed in front of live audiences, with viewers acting as the jury, voting via text messages, of which anything up to 10,000 would be sent in. Ganguly seemed to be a marked man, particularly if Bedi was on top of his game. The show changed to 'Match Ke Sitare' ('Stars of the Match') when one-day results improved the next season.

The Indian mass media, both print and electronic, is so huge that there are plenty of opportunities to make a living out of cricket once your playing days are done. If you haven't got a face for TV, there are always newspaper columns, although that's a very competitive sector because current players, both local and visiting, are in on the act. When I left, Sourav Ganguly, Rahul Dravid, Anil Kumble, Virender Sehwag and Harbhajan Singh all had syndicated columns, although Harbhajan's public musings weren't half as entertaining as the stuff he came out with in the changing room. The going rate for columns tended to be between NZ$1250 and NZ$1600. The insatiable demand for credentialed opinion enables some former players to earn more by sitting in judgement on their successors than they ever did playing the game.

Under the terms of my contract I wasn't permitted to write syndicated newspaper columns, which was fine by me. The likes of Ian Botham have found out the hard way that the flipside of a cosy, exclusive arrangement with one newspaper group is that all the others regard you as fair game. As the national coach, I had to be available — or unavailable, as the case may be — to all media outlets.

A new and highly lucrative media sideline is the ten-minute TV interview at the end of the day's play. All these rather superficial little chats could add up to NZ$330,000 a year for the Indian captain. Tourists were also sought after, albeit at slightly lower rates, say between NZ$500 and NZ$850 per interview. That's still pretty good money for answering a few tame questions, so it's little wonder some big-name cricketers have cottoned on to the fact that India can be a very friendly place in more ways than one. Steve Waugh does a lot of charitable and commercial work there, and Brett Lee's face appears on more than a few billboards. Brian Lara, Glenn McGrath, Ricky Ponting and even Heath Streak are others who've picked up advertising work while on tour in India. The going rate for visitors is closer to the amount paid to younger local players.

If the opinion industry exists primarily to cut the cricketing heroes down to size, the advertising industry is there to build them up and line their pockets. It's virtually impossible to watch television in India for any length of time without seeing a cricketer in an advertisement. I've seen Ganguly, in one ad, trying to look menacing in medieval armour, and in another trying to dance like John Travolta; it's hard to say which of these incarnations was more ridiculous. I've seen Dravid in a black *Matrix*-style outfit leaping metres into the air while brandishing a bat, an image designed to convince people to buy a certain brand of engine oil. Sehwag was Superman in one ad and a man about town on London's Oxford Street in another. Tendulkar's adverts were less contrived, and therefore more persuasive, focusing on his engaging smile and selling everything from bank cards to motor bikes. A Tendulkar campaign could increase sales by several percentage points, which in India amounts to a lot of product. I switched on TV one sleepless night and there was Parthiv, who was so new to the scene that he must have been signed up as he was having his Indian blazer fitted.

There was a strict pecking order for endorsements: Tendulkar was the king, followed by Ganguly, Dravid and Sehwag. These guys would pull between NZ$250,000 and NZ$550,000 per contract per year. The younger players got about half that. It only took a couple of reasonable ODI performances, particularly if they involved some flashy shot-making, for a player to attract an agent and score a contract at the beginner's rate of NZ$105,000. These aren't negligible sums anywhere in the world; in India, they're similar to the annual salaries of middle and upper management in the top 100 companies.

Not long before he left, Andrew Leipus was signed up to do promotional work for Gatorade that involved press advertisements and appearances at gyms around the country. He thought he'd hit the big time, until one of the players rang him, pretending to be the big cheese at Powerade, to say they would have paid three times as much.

I'll admit there was the odd moment when the team was winning and the players were being flooded with offers that I secretly hankered to be invited to join the Pepsi team or to team up with Ganguly in some imaginative television advertisement — as Batman and Robin perhaps, or Laurel and Hardy. I did get a call from an agent, but the product in question turned out to be an ointment which treated one or more of the various indignities associated with old age, and the fee was about a tenth of the going rate. It was just as well really; I wouldn't have enjoyed seeing myself on TV flogging shaving cream when we were going down the gurgler, and I'm sure the Indian fans would have enjoyed it even less. Anyway, I didn't go to India to sell things.

After the fame and the endorsements came the fashion statements. It started with a trendy pair of sunglasses, followed by designer gear and a new hairstyle. The boys loved their gadgets, so the cell phone would be upgraded and the discman traded in for an iPod. And sometimes, after the fashion statements, came the attitude. When a player first came into the team you'd tell him that his job was to look after the drinks or keep an eye on the batters in case they wanted something. Nothing would be too much trouble because they were so thrilled to be playing for India. The first sign that there was too much stardust in the air was when you had to ask them twice.

I didn't mind — in fact I encouraged — a little strut in the step, as long as they understood that their cricket and the team were the priorities. I also encouraged them to work hard and play hard. They weren't big drinkers, so there were no issues with alcohol. They had their own ways of relaxing, sitting around talking in their hotel rooms or corridors, places where no one could get to them. Some of them enjoyed a night on the town, and that was fine by me. There was a kind of synergy between Bollywood and the Indian cricket team, so they got invited to film industry parties and award functions. Movie stars gravitated towards them and vice versa.

The celebrity stuff was harmless, as long as it wasn't taken too seriously. From a team management point of view, we knew we had a problem when a player started going to ad shoots instead of doing his practice. In the lead-up to the World Cup, we wrote to Jagmohan Dalmiya asking him to ensure that players didn't take time out for commercial work, but it was an impossible demand and unenforceable. Under the terms of their contracts the players were committed to their sponsors for a fixed number of days a year. Clearly, the bulk of that commitment took place when we weren't playing, during the breaks when the players could have, should have, been preparing for the next series or the new season. When we reassembled after one ten-day break, I asked a player if he'd done enough practice. 'How could I?' he said. 'I had four shoots last week.'

My most challenging times were when the team had been successful and then had a few months off. This happened with the 2003 World Cup and a year later, after we'd won the series in Pakistan. The players returned home to find themselves in huge demand, both socially and commercially, and they were lavished with adulation and money on a scale some of them couldn't have imagined. Next time I saw them at the pre-season camp, some were distinctly more casual and self-confident.

They'd entered a comfort zone where selection was taken for granted and anything related to cricket was approached with less intensity. The tightness and unity within the group had loosened, and all the disciplines and good attitudes and habits that had helped us achieve success were being paid lip service rather than being put into practice. At the post-World Cup camp, I told a number of players that they weren't putting cricket first. Their responses ranged from agreement to 'I'm tired of listening to this bullshit'. It's no coincidence that after those heady successes and the subsequent breaks, we played some very ordinary cricket. The 2004 hangover didn't lift until we'd lost at home to Australia.

At those times, I really wished I was a selector, as opposed to an adviser to the selection panel. All it would have taken to get the players' attention was to drop a couple of them; the bigger, the better. After some indifferent displays at the 2004 Asia Cup, I told one player that if I'd been a selector, I would have dropped him; he admitted that he would have deserved it. But I wasn't a selector, and he wasn't dropped.

As the coach it's your job to improve attitudes and work habits and make a difference for the better, but you have to understand what's going on. These are young men whose lives have been turned upside down. Twelve months ago they were playing for peanuts in front of the proverbial two men and a dog; now they're being watched by 50,000-plus crowds and millions of TV viewers, they're recognised and fêted everywhere they go, and they're rich, with the prospect of getting a lot richer. That's bound to have an effect on the way they think and behave, and how they see themselves and other people — including the coach.

The players know that if they make it, they're set up for life. In terms of earnings, the Indian players are better off than their counterparts in most other cricket-playing countries because the bulk of their income is from endorsements rather than match fees and cricket contract payments. It means their earning power, particularly their ability to generate advertising income, is linked to performance; so, theoretically, the sky's the limit. The real professionals, like Tendulkar and Dravid, understand this equation: if you get your game in order and perform well, the rewards will flow from there. Some get it the wrong way around and neglect their cricket because they are overly focused on the rewards. It's understandable with the young guys, because at the outset the performance/reward relationship is completely skewed: a handful of promising performances triggers a tidal wave of adulation and some fat endorsement deals. This is where overnight success can be a trap for young players. Recognising the unreal nature of that initial windfall, and understanding that a career at the top level and its attendant rewards require sustained performance, rather than a few cameos, are part of every young star's growing-up process. Indian cricket's double-edged sword is that success can be your enemy.

Another troubling aspect is that some of the best players and greatest contributors don't get as big a piece of the pie as they deserve because of their less glamorous roles or the fact that they don't cultivate a rock star image. Javagal Srinath and Anil Kumble never became billboard heroes, even though they were strong individuals, who achieved great things over the long haul, and were among the rocks on whom the team was founded. Srinath always told young fast bowlers that they had to bowl well for India for 10 years; anything else was an underachievement.

Sometimes I felt trapped in a bubble of bullshit, where media and public perception, public relations, commercial imperatives and board politics seemed to matter more than actual performance. Because the volume of commercial activity swirling around Indian cricket is so huge, the bottom line isn't necessarily dependent on the team's performance, and that can breed complacency and scramble priorities. The problem comes when the quality of performance doesn't match the quantity of promotion. When a batsman has just got out playing a reckless shot in a tight situation, who wants to see his grinning face and listen to him plugging a soft drink five minutes later? And five minutes after that? And every five minutes for the next seven hours? People resented it, and who could blame them?

In a café in Mumbai, the old man at the table next to mine was sipping a beer as he watched a replay of the previous day's game, which we'd lost. Every time a wicket fell, he'd mumble to himself, 'They're only in it for the money.'

He was wrong, but it was an easy mistake to make.

Running Hot in a Sunburnt Country

In November 2003 we played an ODI tri-series at home against New Zealand and Australia. In the final, against the Aussies at Eden Gardens, we chased 236 against a bowling attack without Glenn McGrath, Jason Gillespie and Brett Lee. We lost by 37 runs, hardly an ideal note on which to embark on a tour of Australia a few days later. Afterwards, I was in the hotel bar with the Australian batsman Jimmy Maher. The previous week the Wallabies had knocked the All Blacks out of the Rugby World Cup; Maher, who has a booming voice, kept bellowing 'Spencer-burger', which he seemed to think said all there was to say about that fateful semi-final.

Having exhausted that subject, he turned to the forthcoming tour. 'Wrighty,' he thundered, 'why are you guys coming to Australia?' I can't remember what I mumbled in response, but it was a rhetorical question anyway, and Maher supplied his own answer, 'To win bloody cricket matches and nothing else'.

He was right. If you go on tour anywhere, let alone Australia, without that clear mindset, all the impressive averages and finely-tuned game plans won't help you. I remember an English player saying before an Ashes tour that they 'hoped to compete'. If they all thought that way, the Ashes were lost before they left Heathrow.

At least the players were coming down from their World Cup high. If it served no other purpose, the drawn two-test home series against New Zealand had brought them down to earth. Making the World Cup final had triggered an outpouring of adulation and corporate largesse, which went as far as a team sponsor giving everyone in the squad the keys to some flash condominiums in an exclusive gated compound near Pune. I couldn't get to the function, but told Andrew Leipus to make sure mine had a good view. As I'd suspected, there weren't quite enough condos to go around.

At the pre-tour camp, the fast bowlers were scoring seven in the bleep test; 12 is acceptable. Clearly, for some players the break had been all play and no work, and that attitude carried over into the camp. I had to take a hard line; as I wrote in my diary: 'As soon as they know the tail can wag the dog, the team is history, and I'm afraid so is the coach.' On the other side of the coin was V.V.S. Laxman who was fit, determined and hungry, but still sore about not making the World Cup squad.

To my intense disappointment we'd lost Adrian le Roux. I'd told Jagmohan Dalmiya that, regardless of what happened to me, it was imperative that India retain Leipus and le Roux because they were top-quality operators. But the BCCI didn't tie Adrian into a contract, and the South Africans poached him. We'd made a good team; le Roux was a complete professional, who made sure the players understood he was there to do a job, not to be their friend. They never knew if he was pleased with them or not. As it turned out, his compatriot, South African Greg King, proved to be a very worthy replacement.

By the time we left for Australia, cricket had been restored as everyone's top priority, but no one was giving us a chance. My old friend and sparring partner J.Y. Lele had been BCCI secretary when India last toured Australia in 1999; he'd gone on record then as predicting that India would be whitewashed in the three-test series. When that transpired, he was regarded as something of a seer; people would ring him at home to get a sneak preview of all sorts of events. This time Lele was bit more optimistic, giving us a show of drawing a test. 'Where are the bowlers who will bowl Australia out twice?' he asked. 'According to me, 100 per cent, India will lose.' One pundit saw the series as an opportunity for Australia to blood some up-and-comers after they'd softened us up in Brisbane. The players certainly weren't thinking that way; their theme for the tour was 'Change the Trend'. India hadn't won a test in Australia since 1981, so this was a chance to make some history.

On our arrival, we practically put our technical analyst, Ramki, under house arrest in his hotel room so that he could study footage of Australia's last three seasons. Just as freedom beckoned, Sourav Ganguly turned up with another 18 tapes. By the end of it, he must have been seeing Justin Langer's wagon wheel every time he closed his eyes. Sandy Gordon joined us for a few days before the first test to get us focused on the mindsets and habits we would need as individuals and as a team. He observed that the older players were developing a new, tougher culture, with more accountability, but made the point that, while we'd come a long way as a touring team, we had to be single-minded about becoming the best Indian team ever to tour Australia.

I drew on my own experiences as a player in Australia. In the early days, the New Zealand team had to guard against the tendency to look up at those great players with daunting reputations. 'That's not how you play Australia,' I said, clambering up on a chair and drawing myself up to my full height. 'You don't look up to them, you look down on them.' The players looked up at me with bemused expressions, probably wondering if I planned to jump or fly.

I'd requested a bowling coach on the tour; someone to work with the young fast bowlers. I suggested someone to Dalmiya, but he seemed to think Kapil Dev was the only Indian who was up to the job. As Dev was too busy, Dalmiya suggested I look elsewhere, and we agreed it made sense to have an Aussie who knew the conditions. We signed up the former Australian left-arm quickie Bruce Reid, whose career was curtailed by fitness problems, but who was one of the very best bowlers I faced. He proved to be a great asset and companion, relating well to the team, and helping the bowlers to get the ball to swing.

He and Ashish Nehra kept up an entertaining dialogue. At one lunch break Reid asked, 'Are you swinging it, Ash?' 'It's not that type of a wicket,' was the reply. Although bewildered by some of Nehra's theories, Reid communicated well with the bowlers, geeing up the laid-back characters, and ensuring energy and enthusiasm were productively channelled. He stressed the importance of field placements and bowling in partnerships, and gave some impressive PowerPoint presentations on how to bowl to various batsmen. After one such presentation, he sat there open-mouthed as Ganguly proceeded to do the exact opposite of what had been recommended. Having been through this many times, I predicted that a wicket would soon fall, which it did. In sport you can have a Plan A and a Plan B, but sometimes it's about going with gut instinct and having gambler's luck.

Reid sometimes doubled up as a net bowler and generated enough pace and bounce off a creaky six pace run-up to hit Rahul Dravid on the helmet. Dravid takes the nets very seriously, and I'm sure he didn't enjoy having his lid rattled by a 40-year-old coach with a dodgy knee. He was one of the few players I've worked with who approaches a net like an innings; he never wastes one, because he's always working on his technique and mental habits. The thoroughness of his preparation has helped him become one of the best batsmen in world cricket.

In the build-up to the first test in Brisbane we got the 'Welcome to Australia' treatment that is meted out to every touring team. Matthew Hayden's mouth seemed to have become as wide as his bat: he was quoted as saying that most of the Indian batsmen were loose outside off stump and afraid of short-pitched bowling; Dravid was slow and didn't have many shots; Laxman was windy; and Sehwag just threw the bat and hoped for the best. The captain always gets singled out, but Ganguly was even more of a marked man because he hadn't kowtowed to Steve Waugh during the 2001 series.

And as if we didn't have enough problems, we also had a 'popgun' bowling attack, who were intimidated by the Australian batters. It was almost a case of asking when would it be convenient for us to surrender.

It goes with the territory. In fact, it's so predictable it should be listed on the itinerary. Some well-known ex-player starts the talk, then one of the current team chips in with his view. Depending on your view, it's either psychological warfare (or to give it its new and portentous name, mental disintegration), cheap points-scoring, or the same old bullshit. Whichever way you look at it, if it has any effect, then you're far too sensitive to be taking on the Aussies on their own turf. And as usual, we copped a bit of friendly fire as well, with Bishen Bedi telling an Australian paper that Sachin Tendulkar didn't have as much endurance as Hayden, and ran out of puff when he'd got to 50 or 60.

To be fair, our performances in the warm-up games hardly made people sit up and take notice, but we knew that if we could get out of Brisbane unscathed, we'd be in business. So often touring teams go into the Brisbane test underdone, cop a hiding and never recover. The Aussies are very good at keeping their foot on the throat, and their media aren't too bad at it either.

There was rain about, so we put them in, which didn't look like a tactical masterstroke when they were 262 for 2 at stumps. But we rolled them for 323, in itself quite an achievement, given how often the Aussies run up 400-plus in the first innings of the series and grab the initiative. We were in trouble when we lost Dravid and Tendulkar in the same over to be 62 for 3, but Ganguly and Laxman put on 146, the tail wagged, and we ended up leading by 86 on the first innings. Ajit Agarkar, who'd made seven successive ducks against the Aussies, got a warm welcome from the crowd and when he got off the mark, he raised his bat to acknowledge their encouragement. Before the series, Ganguly had been to see Greg Chappell about his batting, and at the Gabba he produced one of his very best innings. It was his defiant 144, rather than an Australian performance, that set the tone for the series.

There were strong rumours that ESPN-Star Sports, the broadcaster screening the matches live in India, had booked commercials for the first three days only, on the assumption the game wouldn't go any further. For all their bluster, the Australian media and public like to see a contest, and most recent series had been hopelessly one-sided. The previous year's Ashes series, for instance, had been decided in 11 days. We got out of Brisbane with our self-belief intact, and having earned a little respect from a public eager for competitive cricket. We didn't get away scot-free though: Harbhajan Singh had a finger problem that made it difficult to grip the ball, and was out of the next test at least.

The rain had prevented the test from ever really coming to life, which only served to increase the intense focus on Steve Waugh's extended swan song. This was his last series, and there were moments when the actual cricket was reduced to a sideshow, not always in ways that flattered the great man. Some observers felt he was too quick out of the blocks when he came out to bat following Langer's dismissal for 121 — thereby depriving the century-maker of the ovation he deserved. When Damien Martyn, who was well set, was run out, some reckoned he'd sacrificed himself for Waugh. Two balls later Waugh was out for a duck; dismissed hit wicket for the first time in his career. It was an interesting phenomenon — one that became more marked as the series progressed — and probably worked to our benefit. It was certainly a nice change to have the Aussie media fixing their beady eyes on their own mob. We were happy to play a part in the farewell celebrations, as long as we could write our own script.

It seemed a rather sentimental, self-indulgent and, given the traditions and ethos of Australian cricket, unusual way to retire. Usually a bloke lets it be known that this is the end of the road, you clap him on and clap him off, he waves to the crowd as he departs for the last time and that's that. See you when we see you. As retirements go, this one seemed modelled on Frank Sinatra's, and the series became a very long goodbye. The standing ovations and fluttering red handkerchiefs became as routine as drinks breaks.

Australia is a wonderful environment for playing cricket. Everything is organised and runs to a timetable, and the practice facilities are excellent. As a coach you can't ask for more. We were also able to do things we wouldn't dream of doing in India before a test, like going for runs along the Torrens River and walking from our hotel to the Adelaide Oval.

Zaheer Khan, who'd taken five wickets in Australia's first innings at the Gabba, broke down, which meant the 19-year-old left-armer Irfan was pitched into test cricket having come straight from an Asian age-group tournament. At stumps on day one of the second test in Adelaide, Australia were 400 for 5, having put our attack to the sword. 'Indian Summer Over' was one headline. The match rattled along at an extraordinary pace, and just after tea on the second day we were 85 for 4, replying to 556. If we were going to change the trend, it was now or never. Lightning, in the form of a Dravid-Laxman triple century partnership, struck again, although this time it was Rahul who got the double hundred.

Even though both sides had posted over 500, Australia was batting again on the fourth morning, and rather sloppily at that. With Akash Chopra taking a great catch to get rid of Ricky Ponting, and Tendulkar chipping out a couple with his leg spin, we had them 112 for 5, at which point Adam Gilchrist launched one of his trademark blitzkrieg counterattacks. But Kumble knocked him over and Agarkar cleaned up the tail, with the last five wickets going down for 13 runs. Agarkar had hit Langer on the gloves with his first ball of the innings and decided then that he was going to have a good day. He took 6 for 41, making it his best day in test cricket to that point. Crucially, our intensity in the field never dropped. A few minutes before stumps on that long and unrewarding first day, Virender Sehwag ran like hell and dived to take a catch as if the game were only five minutes old. Throughout the series, the boys grabbed pretty much everything and actually out-caught the Aussies.

Leipus and Harbhajan had gone to see a specialist about Bhajju's finger. The wickets started tumbling during the taxi ride back to the Adelaide Oval, and they burst into the dressing room wreathed in smiles of utter delight, even though they'd just been told that Harbhajan needed an operation and was out of the series. Leipus hails from Adelaide, so his homecoming was proving happier than mine.

The swiftness with which the game had opened up was breathtaking. Suddenly it was stumps, and we were 37 without loss, needing another 193 to win on the final day. The next morning Sehwag was going along smoothly, waiting for the bad ball and putting it away, until Stuart MacGill came on. He immediately charged down the wicket, tried to bash it over the cathedral, and was stumped by five metres. The trouble with Sehwag is that he doesn't think spinners can bowl — or should be allowed to bowl. Often the opposition would introduce spin out of desperation because he'd made such a meal of their quicks. His first thought was, 'Oh, goody, dessert', which is why I always felt that this was when he was at his most vulnerable. I'd be thinking, 'Please, Viru, have a look; get through the first two overs'. But he usually — and often successfully — tried to smash them from the very first ball. God help them if he ever does decide to take his time. We'd had the momentum, but now the player generating it was out and a new batsman was in. This time I didn't wait for Sehwag; I vacated the dressing room and went for a walk around the ground.

Dravid made that test a personal mission. Each night, he said, he went to bed thinking about how much more there was to do. Most people, I think, would say this test proceeded at breakneck pace, but to Dravid it felt like it lasted a month. Little wonder: he was on the field for all but a couple of hours, which included 835 minutes at the crease for 305 runs once out. There was a little wobble at 170 for 4, but Laxman restored the momentum by hitting three boundaries in a MacGill over.

Agarkar couldn't explain what victory meant to the guys who'd been steamrollered in 1999, when they'd really only competed for one session in the entire series. 'The floodgates have opened' was our manager Shivlal Yadav's current catch-phrase, and they certainly did that night. The next afternoon, I got a copy of the music that had been pumped out over the PA system during the match. One of the songs was Dido's 'White Flag', which I'll always associate with Adelaide. The Australians who'd expected us to be waving a white flag by this stage of the tour were having to revise their opinion of this bunch of faint-hearts and pie-throwers from the subcontinent.

Shane Warne, who was still serving his World Cup ban, was quick to predict that the Aussies would bounce back to win 2–1. There was, however, nothing from Lele. Perhaps his reputation had taken a dive; a seer is only as good as his last prediction. A letter in which coach John Buchanan told the Australian team that their performance was 'soulless, un-baggy green-like and immature' found its way into the press. I understood the sentiments, but it was another reminder of the danger of putting forthright criticism in writing.

In the third test, there was early life in the Melbourne Cricket Ground wicket. Brett Lee hit Chopra on the head, but he didn't have to be talked into staying at the wicket; as he said later, 'I didn't want them saying an Indian batsman was scared.' He and Sehwag made just 24 in the first hour, but were still there at lunch. Their opening partnerships in the 2003/04 series averaged 57, compared to 9 in the 1999 series. They were mates, two Delhi boys who had good chemistry, and they ran well between wickets even though their calling (in Hindi) was apparently conducted in elaborately courteous conversational exchanges: 'All right, Viru, let's take a single now' and 'Why don't you go back, Viru?' when a simple 'yes' or 'no' would have sufficed.

Chopra was dropped the following year, but it would be an utter waste if he's been consigned to the scrapheap, because he delivered the goods in the toughest environment and is the best bat-pad catcher I've ever seen. I heard later that the night before the first test, he'd been buttonholed by one of the doyens of Indian cricket writing, who'd proceeded to tell him his grip and stance were all wrong and he was basically doomed to fail. With friendly advice like that who needs criticism?

Sehwag played an extraordinary innings — 195 off 233 balls, with 25 fours and five sixes — but the last six wickets went down for 16 runs and 366 was well short of what we needed. The runs we didn't get then were the runs Australia didn't have to get in the fourth innings, when the wicket was deteriorating.

To my mind, the key dismissal was Tendulkar's, in that if he'd got in, we probably would have got close to 600. A lot of critics, though, pointed the finger at Sehwag; they reckoned he'd thrown it away because he got caught in the deep trying to hit part-time spinner Simon Katich for six. I guess that's one way of looking at it; another is that he didn't get to 195 before tea by pushing slow full tosses for a single. I sometimes wished he'd pick the part of the ground where he didn't have to clear a fielder, but then again Sehwag doesn't clutter his mind by worrying about where the fielders are.

Whenever the opposition announced that they had a plan for Sehwag, we'd look at each other and smile. Most teams have had a plan for him, but good players can adapt, and special players, like Viv Richards and Sehwag, can make a mockery of the most astute and logical tactics by knocking bowlers off their line and length, and reducing all those carefully placed fielders to statues.

Australia powered home by 9 wickets on the back of big scores by Hayden and Ponting (his second double century of the series) in the first innings. Summing up on television, Mark Taylor said everyone had forgotten Sehwag's innings. 'An opener shouldn't get 190 before tea on the first day,' he said to fellow ex-opener Bill Lawry. 'That's just rude.'

Tendulkar was having a quiet series, with just one 50. Before the Sydney test, we talked about his batting, which didn't happen very often as he knew his own game inside out. People would often ask me how I coached Tendulkar, and I'd say, you don't, you give gentle advice when it's asked for. In Sydney, he decided he was going to keep it very tight; he wouldn't play through cover or square off the front foot because that was where he'd been getting out. Having formulated a plan, he went out and executed it, making 241 not out, his highest test score, of which only 53 came on the off side. The word gets done to death, but this was an awesome display of technique and discipline. A month later his wife Anjali, who'd listened in on our conversation, got in touch to say thanks for the chat in Sydney. Coaches are never really sure whether what they're saying is getting through, so it's gratifying when someone tells you that you did make a difference.

The Australians went into the test thinking that normal service had been resumed. It had, in the sense that Laxman was involved in another triple century partnership. And after Laxman's epic stand with Tendulkar, little Parthiv Patel trotted out and smashed 62 off 50 balls. We batted into the third morning, making 705 for 7, India's highest-ever total.

Rocky 'Balboa' Harris, the man in charge of the visitors' dressing room at the Sydney Cricket Ground, has his own honours board. It dates back to a Sheffield Shield game in the late 1990s, when a disgruntled player booted the door off Rocky's cupboard; he got the guy to sign the dent and put the date on it. A bit later Jason Gillespie told Rocky he was going to get eight wickets that day; after he'd duly done so, he offered to record it on the cupboard door. It became an SCG tradition, even though there's now a formal honours board in the visitors' dressing room. Rocky's cupboard door records visiting teams' centuries, big partnerships, and five-wicket hauls. By the time we were done, India was well represented.

Rocky was in his 70s, an ex-army man who'd served during the Malay insurgency in the 1950s and found himself in charge of the visitors' dressing room when his predecessor died suddenly. He'd enjoyed the Indian team in 1999, and the players had enjoyed him, making a habit of speaking English when he was around so that he could follow the conversation. He'd write a thought for the day on a whiteboard in the physio's room — 'If you think education is expensive, try ignorance'; 'The vacuum which forms in a batsman's head is balanced by the lead which fills his feet'. When Tendulkar and Laxman were sailing along, Rocky whispered to me, 'I love a good slaughter and so do you.'

We couldn't finish it off, though. The Aussies hung on for a draw, thanks to Katich and Waugh, who came in at 196 for 4 and made 80 in the last innings of his career. After he was out, the crowd watched the last half-hour in nervous silence. With Harbhajan sitting in hospital after his surgery, Anil Kumble took 12 of our 16 wickets in the match.

We were never intimidated, which is the key to competing in Australia. If you give a hint of being overawed, you're gone. Our batsmen might have seemed serenely detached, but the opposition understood what was happening. Langer said the Australians could learn from the patience of the Indian batsmen, who batted 'like they were in a meditative state'. They were beautiful to watch, but they were also relentless: when they got going, they kept going.

Laxman got three more hundreds in the ODI series. He can play one-day cricket as long as he bats in the top three, because he's a boundary hitter and needs the field up to get momentum. I always felt more comfortable with him in the side, especially when we were chasing. By the end of the tour, some Aussies didn't want him to leave.

The series also marked the return of Kumble, the patient predator who stalks batsmen and senses when it's time to move in for the kill. He was our leading wicket taker, and used the series as a springboard for what was to be the best year of his 14-year career: in 2004 he took more test wickets than anyone else. In my observation, it's no coincidence that fit players, or players who have made the effort to get themselves really fit, perform more consistently. Getting fit requires time, effort and self-discipline, and if you can get there, you feel happier, sharper and in control of yourself, all of which increases your chances of playing well. Kumble has often said that he wished he'd understood the importance of fitness when he was a young player.

He hadn't played much of a part at the World Cup, and may have even contemplated retirement. He could have walked away or felt sorry for himself, but instead he worked bloody hard to prove us all wrong. He shouldered an enormous workload in Australia, but when he had his hunter's look on, you had to be a brave man to try to take the ball off him. Our running joke was the old US presidential election slogan: 'Four more years, Anil,' I'd tell him, 'four more years.' It was appropriate because he was a statesman in the team.

Changing the trend became a fixation. The players were utterly determined to break the pattern of Indian tours of Australia. I didn't have to chivvy them along: if it rained they went to the indoor nets; if it wasn't nets, it was the gym. Ramki reckoned the batsmen were so focused, he had to get them to snap out of it just to get a reply to a simple question. It was his first tour, so perhaps he hadn't quite realised that some of them could be absent-minded and a bit otherworldly. Before he went out to bat, Laxman used to lie under a table and listen to music on his headphones.

The series, particularly the contest between our batsmen and their bowlers, was another riveting chapter in the burgeoning India-Australia rivalry. A lot of teams came to India with the mindset that a draw was a win, but not the Aussies. Of the teams who toured India in my time, they were the ones who came with an attitude of wanting to enjoy it. They didn't gripe and groan like some teams, and their open-mindedness and spirit of discovery were genuine. No doubt the commercial opportunities contributed to that positive frame of mind.

In 2004, they came back to India and beat us on our patch. Our batsmen were searching for form and weren't the well-oiled machine they'd been the previous season, whereas the Aussies were more patient. They said they'd learnt that from us.

Written on History's Page

I'd heard the stories and got the message: when India and Pakistan go head-to-head, the stakes are very, very high.

In 1989, the Indian captain Kris Srikkanth was attacked on the field in Karachi, and the Indian team bus was the target of angry demonstrators. During a one-day tournament in 1997, stones were thrown at the players in the same city. Before Pakistan toured India in 1999, the BCCI's office in Mumbai was vandalised. After he'd been appointed Indian captain for a series against Pakistan in 1960/61, Nari Contractor received a letter that said, 'Let's hope you win the series. If you can't win, let's hope you draw. But if you lose, I'll kill you.'

Now we were on our way to Pakistan for an ODI series and three tests, and the hype and drama were just as intense. Just before the tour, I'd gone to my favourite fish restaurant in Mumbai with Deepak Gautam, a great friend and helper, without whom I wouldn't have survived in India. A waiter said to us, 'If you don't win, you can't come back here.' It was a joke in the sense that many a true word is spoken in jest. When we went back after the tour, Deepak suggested that, under the circumstances, the least they could do was give us a free meal, but they didn't see it that way.

We'd been due to go to Pakistan in December 2000, but feelings were still a little raw after a border flare-up the previous year. The Government vetoed that tour and a few months later put the kibosh on a proposal to stage an India-Pakistan match in Sharjah to raise money for the victims of an earthquake in western India.

Given the political and military tensions between the two countries, it was by no means assured that our scheduled 2004 tour would take place. When we were in Australia, news came through of an assassination attempt on the Pakistani President General Pervez Musharraf, and that caused a renewed flurry of doubt. The players had understandable concerns; they wanted assurances that if the tour went ahead, there'd be appropriate security measures and they'd be going as cricketers, not as pawns in a diplomatic game. I was more philosophical, if not fatalistic. When I joined the New Zealand team in Sri Lanka in 1992 after a bomb blast had persuaded some guys to head home, I realised that it would be hard, if not impossible, to guarantee absolute security against suicide bombers — for instance, if a motorcyclist with a bomb strapped to his body tried to crash into our bus.

The Indian elections were coming up and it seemed as if the tour was being looked at as an opportunity to measure the apparent improvement in India-Pakistan relations. It was something of a gamble for Prime Minister A.B. Vajpayee and the Government: if it went off well, they could expect to accrue a few brownie points, but if it somehow went wrong, they wouldn't be popular. There was a lot riding on it, on both sides of the border. In the jittery international climate some cricketing nations were reluctant to tour Pakistan, but if a tour by India passed off without incident, it would send a strong signal to the rest of the cricket world. For the two uneasy neighbours, with their fraught and volatile history, a cricket tour was to be a test of their ability to put their squabbles aside and behave in a neighbourly fashion.

In the space of three weeks the tour was almost cancelled, then postponed for several months, then put back to its original schedule give or take a week.

They swapped the order in which the tests and ODIs were to be played, then they changed the dates, then they changed the venues. There were rumours the Government didn't want the one-dayers to be at the end of the tour because they'd be too close to the elections; if they went badly, the voters wouldn't have time to forget whose idea it was to have the tour. The players used to say that we wouldn't know for sure that the tour was going ahead until the plane took off.

Tit-for-tat publicity campaigns got under way. It came out that Imran Khan had attended the Pakistani training camp and passed on 'useful tips' — which tend to be the best sort. The next day the BCCI announced that Kapil Dev would attend our three-day camp in Kolkata in the capacity of bowling coach. See your legend and raise you one. On the second morning of the camp I bumped into the former Indian off spinner Erapalli Prasanna and asked what brought him to Kolkata. 'I'm here for the camp,' he said. No one had informed me. 'Great to see you, Pras,' I said. 'The spinners are over there.' Being the furthest Indian city from Pakistan, Kolkata seemed an odd venue for the camp, but then again it was the home town of both the captain and the BCCI President.

If anyone needed a reminder that this wasn't your run-of-the-mill cricket tour, the morning of our departure provided it. First there was a Ministry of External Affairs briefing, then a security briefing, then we went to see the Prime Minister.

The ministry spokesman said things had changed and there was a real desire among people in both countries to increase contact. 'Your tour is an important part of this Indo- Pakistan revival,' he told us. The head of the VIP security division in the Ministry of Home Affairs, Yashovardhan Azad, who'd made an inspection visit to Pakistan, briefed us on security arrangements. We were given a 16-point list of do's and don'ts which included not discussing plans, programmes and engagements in public, not having a routine of going to the same place at the same time every day (bad news for those with regular toilet habits), and taking precautions before opening unidentified mail.

For our computer analyst, Ramki, the visit to the Prime Minister's residence was another reminder of his uncertain status: he didn't have a security clearance, so he had to sit on the bus while we went into the reception. This was a continuation of the demeaning and perplexing treatment that had begun with the computer analyst being booked into different and inferior hotels to the team. When we finally got that resolved, there was a furore over clothing because some BCCI officials didn't want him wearing official team gear.

I ended up chatting to Prime Minister Vajpayee, and I found him a man of few words. When I asked him if he was planning to come to Pakistan, he chuckled and said he had his own test to think about, referring to the elections. Within a few months he was out of office. Like coaches, politicians don't have much in the way of job security.

Eighteen years after my first visit, I was back in Pakistan. While Ian Botham famously described it as a good place to send your mother-in-law, I enjoyed touring with New Zealand in 1985 and was looking forward to doing it again. While it's definitely the case that results on tour have a big bearing on the enjoyment factor — when you're winning even the sky seems a little bluer — this would prove to be, without doubt, the most well organised tour I've ever been on.

We were told that the President's secretariat was responsible for our security, and there were no half measures. Our convoy from Lahore Airport included an ambulance and 'jammer' cars to block radio frequencies in case of remote-controlled bombs along the route. There was also a decoy bus that took a different route to our hotel. The security arrangements meant that there was no dead time. When we went to practice, they simply blocked off the route so that what was normally a 30-minute stop-start chug through traffic became a ten-minute dash. It was the same on the return trip, and it didn't matter whether we finished practice 20 minutes earlier or later than we'd indicated: when we were ready to go, they closed the roads and we went. We were surrounded by tough-looking hombres from the Punjab Police's Elite Squad; they carried machine guns and wore black T-shirts with the No Fear logo on them. I believed them.

Twenty-four hours into the tour, news came through of the commuter train bombings in Madrid. Our security chief talked about terrorist sleeper cells and warned us not to go anywhere on our own and to keep our security details informed of our movements. I couldn't help noticing that the players hung on every word of these security briefings, which wasn't always the case with my team talks. Our hotel even had a couple of food-tasters, health department officials whose job it was to make sure we weren't poisoned. It was nice to know, but it did slow up room service.

The security guys were most worried about Karachi and Peshawar, so we didn't spend any longer than we had to in those places. The convoy back to Lahore Airport, en route to the first ODI, included a fire engine rather than an ambulance, which wasn't altogether reassuring. Karachi seemed a little tenser, and the security was ratcheted up even further.

When our manager, Professor Shetty, Sourav Ganguly and I went for a routine meeting with the match referee Ranjan Madugalle, there was more hardware in evidence than at the gunfight at the OK Corral. Ahead of our little van were two motorcyclists and two pickup trucks; two motorcyclists were alongside us, and three more trucks and three motorcyclists brought up the rear. Each truck had two guys in front and six in the back, all carrying guns, and another man on the roof with a mounted machine gun. The Indian security guys called this the 'box formation'; the Pakistanis called it 'the capsule'. Whatever you called it, it was a lot of trouble to go to just so that we could have a cup of tea with the match referee.

Every time we hit the road in Pakistan, it was like we were late for a plane. The speed was determined by the pilot car after consulting the local police and depending on the importance of the 'targets'; a head of state's capsule apparently travelled at 110 to120 kph, on the theory that the faster you went, the harder you were to hit.

Our liaison officer, Masood, had done the same job for New Zealand in 1985, so it was like linking up with an old friend. He reckoned an Indian team was 200 per cent more work than an Australian or New Zealand team, because the Indians had people to meet, places to go and things to do. Whatever they wanted, Masood knew where to find it. When the tempo of the tour slowed after the ODIs, the players were able to relax and explore their surroundings, and Masood was the man with the key to many doors.

The tour theme was obvious: to be the first Indian team to win big in Pakistan. India had won just three ODIs in Pakistan in 19 years, and hadn't won a single test on five tours going back to 1954. It was going to take a lot of courage and commitment, as the pressure on and off the field would be relentless. The fact that the security situation would keep us pretty much confined to our hotels wasn't necessarily a bad thing because it would keep us tight and together. We were a quiet team on the bus going to games. There was no need for big speeches about representing your country and the importance of the occasion; everyone understood.

In a practice game against Pakistan A we got 335, but they got to 100 in 7.1 overs and won with four overs to spare. The message was loud and clear: 'Good morning, India; this is your wake-up call.' The South Africans and the Kiwis had played Pakistan recently, and I'd touched base with both camps. New Zealand coach John Bracewell reckoned we should keep it simple: pack the point, gully and cover region to stop them going through that area and bowl back of a length. Some of the players didn't think the New Zealand game plan was relevant to our situation, but no one was under any illusions about the magnitude of the challenge.

It was only the third ODI in Karachi in more than a year and a half, and was India's first appearance there for six years. A helicopter hovered over the ground during the warm-ups. There were about 3000 security men on duty in the city: sharpshooters on rooftops along our route to the ground, cops in uniform, cops in plain clothes, and even Pakistani Rangers, members of a special forces outfit, who wore beige uniforms with their first names stitched on, like the staff at your friendly neighbourhood hardware centre. Spectators had to travel the last kilometre to the ground on foot and were screened five times before they were allowed in. During the morning, our security guys were taken to the control room to see video footage of a group of demonstrators being rounded up and removed with no beg-your-pardons.

We made 349, but won by just five runs. The bowling was fine in the first 15 overs and progressively less fine after that. The boys were desperate though, and in the end that probably got us home. What came out of the game was the fact that when India played Pakistan, everyone lifted: you saw extra effort and extraordinary performances from both sides. One of the players remarked that 30 runs against Pakistan were worth 50 against anyone else. It should have been easier, but at least our batting had looked in good nick.

We didn't hang around in Karachi. Pakistan International Airlines held the scheduled flight to Islamabad for two hours for us, and the cabin crew lined up and clapped us onto the plane, a gesture as gracious as it was unexpected. Two days later a car bomb consisting of 900 litres of liquid explosive was defused outside the US Embassy. The newspapers said that if it had gone off, it would have caused damage over a 2.5 km area. The original itinerary had us staying in Karachi for 11 days and Peshawar for eight, but the Indian security people had vetoed that because you can only lock down a city like Karachi for a day or two at the most.

In the second ODI, a day-night game in Rawalpindi that was watched by the Pakistani President, we chased 329 and came up just short, despite Sachin Tendulkar getting 141. This time, our bowling in the first 15 overs let us down. The next day we were invited to the presidential palace. Decked out in military uniform, General Musharraf spoke of the two teams setting an example of co-existence. Once he'd got the serious stuff out of the way, he had both teams in fits of laughter, referring to the sweets we were being served as 'weapons of mass destruction'. He said he knew the Karachi match was getting tight when he saw Inzamam-ul-Haq dive for the crease for the first time in 14 years.

One of the players said afterwards that the Indian and Pakistani leaders were exact opposites: one said too little and the other said too much.

Musharraf's press secretary reckoned he and I were in the same boat: 'When things go well, no one says anything,' he said. 'When things go bad, everyone looks at me.'

We lost the next ODI in Peshawar, and he was dead right: everyone was looking at me. Chasing 244, Pakistan were 59 for 4 when an edge went between the keeper and second slip — in other words, exactly where first slip would have been had there been one. It's one of my pet hates: if it's worth having a second slip, then it must be worth having a first, whether it's a test match or a one-day game. My diary note reads: 'Could have been 63–5. Shit. Uphill from here.' The media were saying it was all over because the last two games were in Lahore and Pakistan had never lost a double-header there.

Like Karachi, Peshawar was a high-anxiety venue in terms of security. After we'd made a quick exit, three rockets were fired into the town. I'd been there in 1985 and loved the place; it felt like a frontier town, something out of the Wild West. Not much had changed: from the air, it still looked the colour of sand, and it was still famous for Afghan rugs. Before our first practice, Andrew Leipus, Greg King and I visited the best-known carpet shop in town. (Because security tended to focus on the players, we support staff could come and go without attracting too much attention. In similar circumstances in Bangladesh the following year, we were able to stroll out of our fortress-like hotel by telling the security guys we were TV cameramen.)

We were working our way through the shop's 75,000 carpets when the owner emerged from his back office. Abid Ali cut a dapper figure in his Savile Row suit; I told him I wouldn't be buying a carpet off him because I could see too much margin in his suit. He informed us that Peshawar was also famous for its food and before we got down to the serious business of buying and selling carpets, we had to eat. One of his workers was dispatched to fetch barbecued lamb and chicken, and we sat on piles of rugs having lunch and listening to Abid's life story. We promised to come back and buy something later on in the tour.

Game four: chasing 294 to win, we were 94 for 4. The run-rate was fantastic, but we'd lost too many batters. Professor Shetty was looking queasy, but the players were serenely confident. One of them told him we couldn't lose because Mohammad Kaif was still to come. When Yuvraj Singh went in the 24th over we were 162 for 5, over halfway there but only one wicket away from having a bowler at the crease. I was almost as calm as the rest of them. For some reason there was an air of inevitability about the Dravid-Kaif partnership; perhaps it was simply that they were the coolest heads in the house. They both got unbeaten 70s and we won with five overs to spare.

The air was thick with moths. The floodlights at the Gaddafi Stadium seemed to have attracted every moth between the Gulf of Oman and the North-West Frontier. It was an eerie scene. From where we were sitting at ground level, it looked like a light fog had descended and we could hardly see the pitch. Having to bat in that haze, which Dravid and Kaif did with absolute certainty and precision, made their achievement even more meritorious. It's the match-winning innings, rather than averages or the number of centuries, that define players and their careers in the eyes of their team-mates and coaches.

Rather than getting credit for fighting back to square the series, that performance triggered a rash of stories about match fixing. The big rumour was that it had been settled in advance: it would be 2–2 going into the last game. It's something teams from the subcontinent have to live with, but it's not easy. I made no comment because I didn't have any that were printable.

Match fixing had raised its ugly head when we suffered a spectacular defeat at the hands of Kenya during a triangular tournament in South Africa in 2001. After beating the hosts, only their fourth defeat in 23 home games, and slaughtering Kenya, we had one of those days against the Kenyans in Port Elizabeth, losing by 70 runs. Next thing, people were nodding knowingly and talking about a NZ$65 million dollar bet that had supposedly been placed in Sharjah. Gambling is banned in India and Pakistan, but everyone knows there's an illegal betting industry. According to an official ICC report,

NZ$830 million was bet on every game in the 2005 India-Pakistan ODI series. The former Pakistan wicketkeeper Rashid Latif gave the witches' brew a few vigorous stirs, as he often does. It was deeply unfair on the players, who couldn't win whatever they did.

By this stage, the atmosphere was incredible. Thousands of Indian supporters, including the usual movie stars and socialites, had travelled to Lahore. Also in the crowd was Dina Wadia, the daughter of Mohammed Ali Jinnah, the founder of the state of Pakistan. It was her first trip across the border. There were a lot of flags, both Indian and Pakistani, being waved in the stands. The players said that even five years earlier it would have been impossible to imagine this scene.

It felt like we had the momentum going into the decider. Batting at three, V.V.S. Laxman got a hundred, and we scored 293. The Pakistan coach, Javed Miandad, was sitting a few seats away from me; in three hours one of us would be getting patted on the back and the other would be watching his back. When the chase began, I wrote in my diary: 'I'm not nervous but sort of uptight . . . They've just lost their first wicket, which is a start, but it looks flat . . . The stakes are just too high for all of us. I'm hoping they have an average or off day — we've all had them.' Sometimes this is what coaching boils down to: after all the practice, the planning, the fielding charts, the computer analysis and the team talks, you're reduced to hoping like hell the other mob has an off day.

I tried to stay as detached as possible, knowing there was nothing I could do. Writing in my diary was one way to take my mind off the game and relieve the tension; working out exactly where in my house outside Christchurch I'd put all the carpets I was going to buy, was another. But I was quickly sucked back into the drama: Ganguly hurt his back diving to stop an Inzamam off drive. He was stretchered off by what looked like the entire cast of 'ER'. The dressing room resembled an emergency ward as Leipus tried to attend to our injured captain and cope with the influx of medical experts, who looked ready to operate on the spot.

Inzamam was out to a running catch on the boundary by Tendulkar, an amazing piece of anticipation, presence of mind and determination. That made them 87 for 5, and another wicket fell soon afterwards. Their lower order fought hard, but it always looked beyond them and we won by 40 runs. It was an immense relief; whatever happened now, we wouldn't be going home empty-handed. The next day a local paper ran the headline, 'India end "chokers" tag by winning first one-day series against Pakistan'. When our bus left the ground shortly before midnight, the crowd of about 100 people standing outside the stadium gates began to clap and wave.

Multan, the venue for the first test, isn't a place you'd forget in a hurry. The old ground, the Ibn-e-Qasim Bagh stadium was in the middle of the city, which is centuries old and, being full of Sufi shrines, attracts many pilgrims. According to a Persian rhyme, Multan was famous for four things: dust, heat, fakirs and burial grounds. Now there's a fifth: Inzamam-ul-Haq.

When New Zealand played a one-dayer there in 1985, there was a ticketing botch-up which resulted in genuine ticket-holders being locked out because the ground was full. As Bruce Edgar and I were knocking up on the outfield we heard these dull thuds: the people outside the ground were throwing rocks onto the field. They forced open a gate and surged in, and a riot ensued. The police laid into them with batons and when that had no noticeable effect, they tear-gassed them. My other memory from that game is of people sitting in front of the sightscreen when we batted, but somehow finding other places to sit when Pakistan batted.

The air conditioning in my room at the Multan Holiday Inn sounded like a very old, overladen helicopter taking off. At least it drowned out the traffic noise. When checking in, umpire David Shepherd, who'd spent his career standing on one leg when the batting team or a batsman is on 111 because it's English cricket's unlucky number, was handed the key to room 111. He handed it straight back. Every morning the two teams would be ferried to the new stadium in a 20-vehicle convoy, racing through streets cleared of traffic and lined with waving crowds.

Captaining the team in Ganguly's absence, Dravid won the toss and we batted on a flat wicket. Just after lunch on day two Virender Sehwag belted his sixth six (there were also 39 fours) to become the first Indian to score a triple century in test cricket. Unbelievably, within a few hours this feat had been overshadowed. Midway through the final session Dravid declared, as you do when you're 675 for 5. What Indian captains don't tend to do, however, is declare when Sachin Tendulkar is 194 not out. The matter became a fully-fledged sensation when Tendulkar told a press conference he was disappointed not to get to his double century. He said he'd been taken by surprise by the timing of the declaration because he thought he had a few more overs to get to 200.

If I'd been captain, I would have declared a lot earlier. I'd advised Dravid to time it so that Pakistan had to face about 25 overs; at that point Tendulkar was about 170. Dravid wanted less time in the field, but got caught a bit betwixt and between. At tea he told the batsmen he wanted 15 or 16 overs at the Pakistanis, and after tea a couple of messages went out. As I sat there watching the innings grind on, it crossed my mind that Tendulkar needed to get a move on. A final message went out saying they had one more over. Then Yuvraj was run out going for a quick single and Dravid called them in.

There was fault all round. I should have convinced Dravid to declare earlier and he should have grasped that it's one thing to declare when a batsman's 170 or 180, quite another when he's 194. And Tendulkar should have pushed to get there quicker. The fact that we didn't get a wicket that night added to the jangled nerves. As soon as I heard that Tendulkar had publicly expressed disappointment, I knew we had a hot potato on our hands. I talked to Dravid, who agreed that he had to have a chat with Tendulkar before things got out of hand. That combination of steeliness and serenity, so evident in Dravid's batting, is the mark of the man: nothing fazes him. He's a mature and intelligent individual; all the hype and fuss goes over his head because he can stand back and put the issue in perspective.

Tendulkar felt let down. He'd been playing for India since he was 16;

he'd stood up for his country in bad times and tough conditions, and often been the only man to do so. Having given so much for the team, over such a long period, he probably thought this was one time the team could give something back to him. Even the greatest have their goals and dreams and milestones, and a double century against Pakistan in Pakistan would have been a memory to treasure.

In the middle was our non-playing captain who was about to return to Kolkata to get his back checked. He was worried that the issue would snowball and end up dividing the team. There was no doubt it was going to be a big story; it had apparent conflict between two of India's superstars in the already dramatic context of a series against Pakistan. And of course it was a rich source of conspiracy theories.

They came thick and fast: the timing of the declaration was Ganguly's idea because he was anti-Tendulkar; if Dravid couldn't get a double hundred, he didn't want Tendulkar to get one; Tendulkar had batted slowly on purpose to make life difficult for Dravid. Every hour, it seemed, there was another piece of sensational nonsense coming at us, because people prefer to believe these things are the result of careful — and usually malicious — calculation rather than accidents caused by a combination of miscommunication, misjudgement and Murphy's Law.

After a sleepless night, I spoke to Tendulkar who confirmed that he'd wanted the team to cut him some slack. Then he and Dravid talked it through and resolved the matter, and we focused on winning the test match. There were lessons in it for all of us, but in a way it was what Ian Chappell called it: 'A declaration of independence.' It was an important step in the team's development, in that the principle that no one is bigger than the team had been very publicly adhered to.

There was an ongoing issue surrounding Tendulkar: the view was that he'd become a percentage player rather than the dasher he'd been as a younger man. I was often told that, in effect, he wasn't the player he used to be. The facts are, that in my time with India he scored 12 centuries in

46 tests and averaged 60.89 and was every inch a team player. Pat Riley, the celebrated US basketball coach, observed that style can stimulate the player and thrill the crowd, but it's efficiency that wins games. I sometimes felt that style mattered more than results to the Indian media and fans. I hope the era that I was part of has gone a long way to changing that mindset.

We won the test, but had to spill a lot of sweat; the bowlers churned out 200 overs on the trot. Tendulkar dismissed Moin Khan with the final ball on day three, and I don't think I've seen him look happier on a cricket field. I usually saw every ball bowled, but before I was in my seat the next morning Irfan Pathan got Abdul Razzaq, the last of the recognised batsmen. It was a nice start to what turned out to be a very good day.

We made them follow on. There were two decisive moments in the field: Yuvraj running out Inzamam for a duck with a direct hit, and Akash Chopra taking an astounding catch at short leg to get rid of Razzaq. They were 207 for 9 at stumps, so we had to come back and finish it off the next morning: Irfan bowled a bouncer, Yousuf Youhana, who'd played a lone hand, top-edged it, and India had won its first test match on Pakistani soil. Winning these big games was what I worked and sacrificed for; it was difficult not to get emotional, but I really didn't give a toss if people took that to mean I cared too much.

After the photos and interviews, I sat on the balcony outside our dressing room, listening to the players' happy clamour and watching the nets going up. Javed was about to put his team through a punishment practice. The Pakistani players looked glum, and Javed was purple with rage. I thought, there but for the grace of God go I. Javed and I went back a long way; he'd been an extraordinary player and a great warrior for Pakistan, the cheekiest opponent I ever came across. I can still hear him giggling at first slip when I nicked Abdul Qadir to the wicketkeeper at Eden Park in 1989. We'd greeted each other with a hug in Karachi, but we both knew that when it was all over, one of us would be out of a job and we were both thinking, 'I hope it's you, old son, and not me'.

The staff at the hotel lined the foyer and cheered and clapped us in. Throughout the tour we were amazed at the genuine warmth and generosity of the reception we got. It was completely at odds with the stories we'd heard. The Pakistanis seemed really pleased to see the team and the 8000-odd Indians who'd crossed the border on 'cricket visas'.

Contact between the two peoples had been problematical at the best of times: mail sometimes went missing or arrived opened, telephone connections were unreliable and visa rules very tight. In 2004, all you needed was a match ticket purchased off the internet and the patience to queue with your papers. There'd been very few cross-border movements on this scale since partition.

Some people used their cricket visas to go back to the homes they'd left behind. Roshan Lal had fled Multan as a 16-year-old after his parents, grandparents and two sisters had been killed in anti-Hindu riots. He'd applied for a visa three times, but had had no joy. In 2004 his son bought tickets to the first test and Roshan went back to Multan after 57 years. He broke down when he saw his old neighbourhood, where one of the oldest residents, a woman in her 90s, recognised him. He spent five days in Multan, but I don't think he saw a minute of the test. There were hundreds of similar stories.

Many of the Indian journalists travelling with us had Pakistani links and took the opportunity to visit neighbourhoods that their aged relatives had told them about. Others broke visa rules that forbade them from deviating from the itinerary and went off into the countryside to visit villages where their grandparents had lived and owned fields. They'd arrive unannounced, ask for the oldest resident and explain their family connection, and before long they'd be surrounded by villagers who'd known their grandparents. A number of Indians told me that Pakistanis wouldn't allow them to pay for taxi rides or food. Pakistani families who'd made the shift in the other direction met the children of friends they'd left behind and saw photographs of people they hadn't been in contact with for decades.

To an outsider, Indians and Pakistanis seem to have a lot in common, including their sense of humour. The cricket was ultra-competitive, but the players got on better with each other than they did with other opponents. The younger guys on both sides called the veterans *bhai* meaning brother, so Inzamam was Inzy Bhai and Tendulkar was Sachin Bhai. A lot of the sledging got lost in translation, but this exchange between Shoaib Akhtar and Sehwag would work in any language: Shoaib was needling Sehwag, challenging him to take him on with the pull shot. This went on and on, until Sehwag asked, 'What are you doing, mate: bowling or begging?' (There seems to be something about Shoaib that brings out the good lines. During the ICC World XI test against Australia in 2005, he was strutting around the dressing room with his shirt off, displaying his admittedly impressive physique. The fact that he hadn't made an enormous contribution to that ill-fated campaign might have prompted Freddie Flintoff's comment, 'It's no good looking like Tarzan if you bowl like Jane.')

There'd been criticism that the Multan wicket had been too flat, so they juiced up Lahore a little. It looked like it would play well after the first day, so I thought we should field if we won the toss, figuring that would give us the opportunity to have them at 90 for 4 at lunch, but if they got 400, we could match that. Dravid preferred to bat and at lunch we were 107 for 4, after their debutant seamer Umar Gul had cleaned up our top order. We slumped to 147 for 7, before Yuvraj (112 off 129 balls, his first test hundred) and Irfan counterattacked. But 287 wasn't nearly enough. The next day, Pakistan put on 294 for the loss of two wickets, but I was proud of the players because they left everything on the field.

They headed us by 202 on the first innings, and we didn't bat any better the second time around, although some of the umpiring didn't help. I decided it was time to share my thoughts on the subject with the match referee and set off under a head of steam, realising too late that his room was right next to the press box. A dozen Indian journalists saw an obviously angry Indian coach, aka the Human Headline, enter the match referee's room and sure enough it made the news all over India and Pakistan. After that, I always used a mobile phone if the referee's room was anywhere near the press box. As Pakistan knocked off the handful of runs they needed in their second innings, I overheard the top-ranking police officer in the Pakistani security team tell a colleague, 'There might well be a happy ending to this tour after all.'

We went to Rawalpindi for the decider, knowing that if we won the toss, we'd bowl. Ganguly returned, having had his back fixed up; we knew we'd see him again because he'd left his gear behind. That created the dilemma of who to leave out: Yuvraj was coming off a hundred, but if Chopra got the chop it meant playing a makeshift opener. We agreed that unless we'd been in the field for two days, Parthiv Patel would do the job. However, in his final pre-match press conference Ganguly took everyone, including his coach, by surprise by announcing that he'd open the batting. The previous day, playing my cards close to my chest, I'd said that the opener would be either a left-hander or a right-hander. We got hammered for dumping Chopra, who'd been a real soldier and given us some solidity at the top of the order, but he'd failed twice in Lahore. Going with Ganguly, who hadn't played for a while, was something of a gamble, but experience would count in such a huge game.

The opposition had their problems: their fitness trainer had just resigned; Umar Gul, a star in Lahore, couldn't play because of a back injury; and there was talk that Shoaib and Inzamam weren't seeing eye-to-eye. As a coach, you use that sort of information to build your team's confidence and make every effort to ensure that any ructions inside your camp don't reach the opposition's ears.

We won the toss, bowled first and opened up their top order. They were all out for 224, with Lakshimipathy Balaji picking up four wickets. He was a joy to work with, a brave bowler and a kid at heart. Once when I was writing my diary he asked, 'John, if you write a book, will you mention my name?' He'd become something of a cult hero in Pakistan, perhaps because of some lusty hitting in an ODI. In Peshawar the crowd chanted his name and in Lahore he had girls singing Hindi songs to him. Part of his appeal was his seemingly permanent beaming smile. He was so unselfconscious that he told a reporter it was a result of jaw surgery he'd had as a child.

We lost Sehwag very first ball, but the new opener, Parthiv, scored 69. (The captain came in at number six.) Most of the other batters got a score, but they were just support acts for The Wall: Dravid batted for 12 hours 20 minutes to make 270, his highest score in test cricket, and swing the game and the series emphatically in our favour. It was cloudy and the ball did a bit when Pakistan batted again, late on the third day, and we got both openers before stumps.

Abid Ali came to see me with the carpets he'd picked out for me and we had some long conversations over drinks. He had an endless supply of proverbs: 'Wright Brother, my grandfather used to say there are three things in life that are difficult to find — a good wife, a good horse and a good carpet.' Another one went: 'Once you have a gun, you'll always know how to fire it.' We had Pakistan cornered — they needed another 327 to make us bat again; we'd finally got our hands on the gun. All the boys had to do was take aim and pull the trigger.

On the fourth morning, Balaji and Ashish Nehra got the ball to swing in the overcast conditions, but nerves and overeagerness got to the players. They had the gun, but they couldn't hit the target. The catching, which had been outstanding all tour, suddenly went to pieces: five catches went down in half an hour. It seemed like every time I looked up, I saw someone fielding out of position and dropping a catch. Yuvraj, our best point fielder, was at bat-pad, where he put one down; our best bat-pad Chopra, who was on as a substitute fielder, was at point. As I wrote in my diary, it was, 'stupid, stupid, stupid'.

Things got back on track and we started picking them off. When Inzaman went they were 94 for 5, and Anil Kumble grabbed a couple of wickets just before lunch. At the break I talked about finishing the job. They went back out, needing three wickets to write their names in history. I wrote in my diary, 'I'm feeling like I did when I was a kid going to bed on Christmas Eve, waiting for the presents to arrive in the morning.' Nine overs later it was done and dusted: victory by an innings and 131 runs. After all the hard work and the frustrations and the seemingly interminable wait, the fact that the overseas series win was achieved in Pakistan made it all the sweeter. In those euphoric moments in the Rawalpindi dressing room, the glittering prize seemed well worth the wait.

I wasn't in the habit of insinuating myself into team photos or presentation ceremonies, but Sehwag left me little choice. 'John, you are my friend,' he said putting me in a headlock, 'this time you're coming.' Then he marched me down the stairs and out onto the field. That night we went to a restaurant and then on to a party; I remember smoking cigars with Abid, and drinking Heinekens, and talking more rubbish than usual with Leipus and King. For a bunch of virtual teetotallers, there were an impressive number of sore heads the next morning. Three months later, a pair of my brown shoes and sunglasses which had been missing-presumed-lost turned up in the team gear, one of those inexplicable occurrences that often accompany vigorous celebrations.

I'd told the boys that on my test debut in 1978, I was part of the first-ever New Zealand team to beat England, and that being the first was something special, that it could never be overtaken or diminished. If they were the first Indian team to win in Pakistan, they'd have reunions in 20 years' time and remember when they made history together.

Just before we left for the airport, Shahryar Khan, the chairman of the Pakistan Cricket Board and a former foreign secretary, addressed the team, telling them they'd been wonderful ambassadors who'd brought great credit to India. The tour, he said, was more important than cricket: 'You have been part of history.'

Fitness trainer Adrian le Roux and I umpire a batters v bowlers volleyball game prior to the 2003 World Cup.

Last train to Pietermaritzburg — a symbolic journey on the train that Mahatma Gandhi was thrown off.

It mightn't be the oldest water fountain in Zimbabwe but it's still pretty impressive. At the Taj Mahal with fitness trainer Greg King (left) and Andrew Leipus.

'When you do well for India, they name a street after you: when you do badly, they chase you down the same street.' The fans celebrate our charge to the World Cup final.

Not just a cricket tour — an exercise in diplomacy. Jagmohan Dalmiya introduces me to Indian Prime Minister Vajpayee before the tour of Pakistan.

Tea with the General: meeting Pakistani President Musharraf. Rameez Raja, ex-Pakistan player and CEO of the Pakistan Cricket Board (dark jacket), and our liaison man Masood await his next one-liner.

Pradeep Mandhani

John Wright Collection

Snapshots of Pakistan. Clockwise from top left: a street vendor of memorabilia lies down on the job; the tough guys from the Punjab Police Elite squad; crowds line the streets of Multan as we drive to the ground in a 20-vehicle convoy; welcome to the Holiday Inn, Multan.

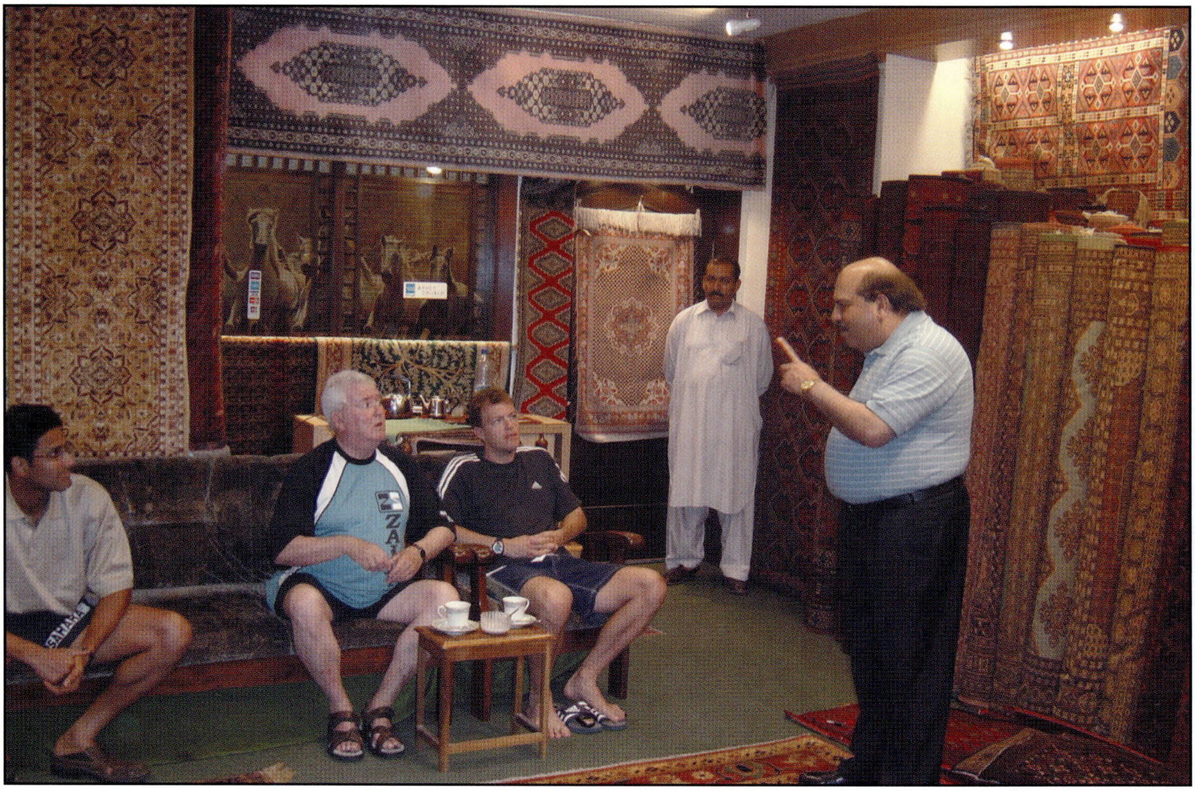

John Wright Collection

‘Three things in life are difficult to find: a good wife, a good horse and a good carpet.’ Abid Ali (right) holds forth in his carpet emporium in Peshawar to an attentive audience of, from left, Anil Kumble, umpire David Shepherd and Andrew Leipus.

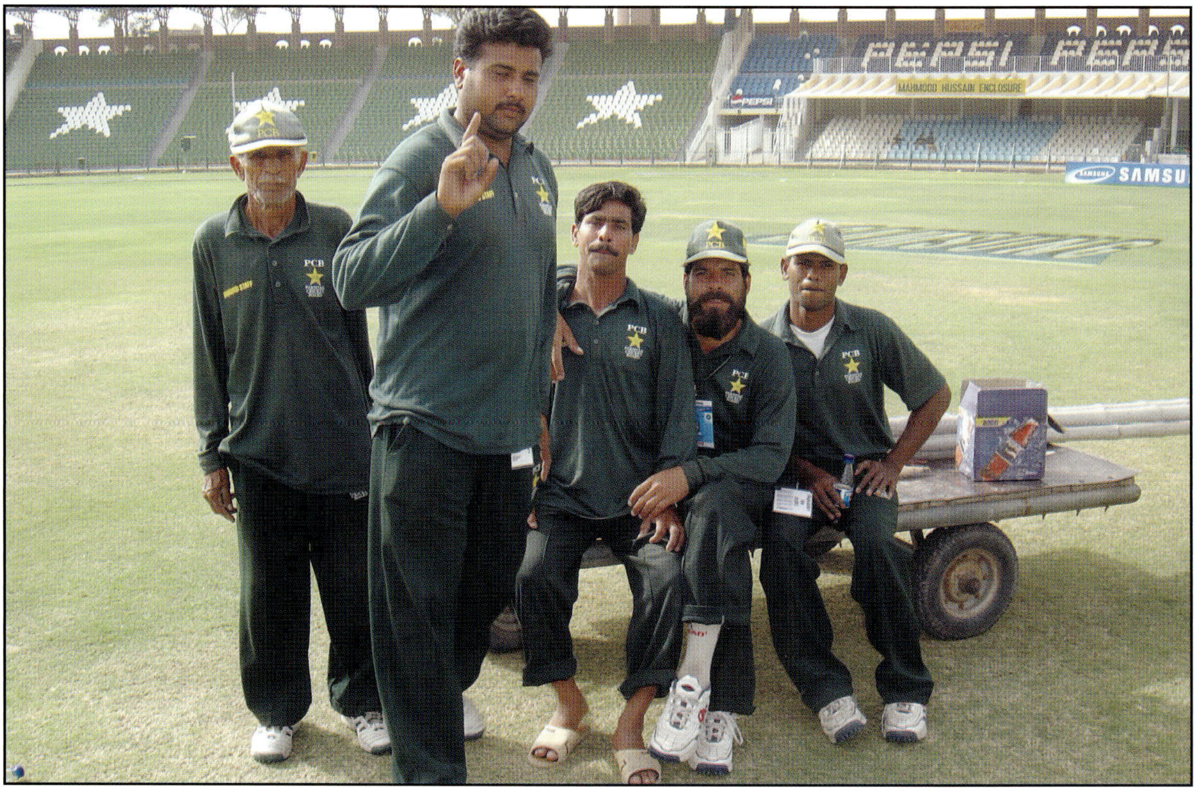

Pradeep Mandhani

‘Mr Coach, grass is always green!’ The groundstaff at the Gaddafi Stadium in Lahore.

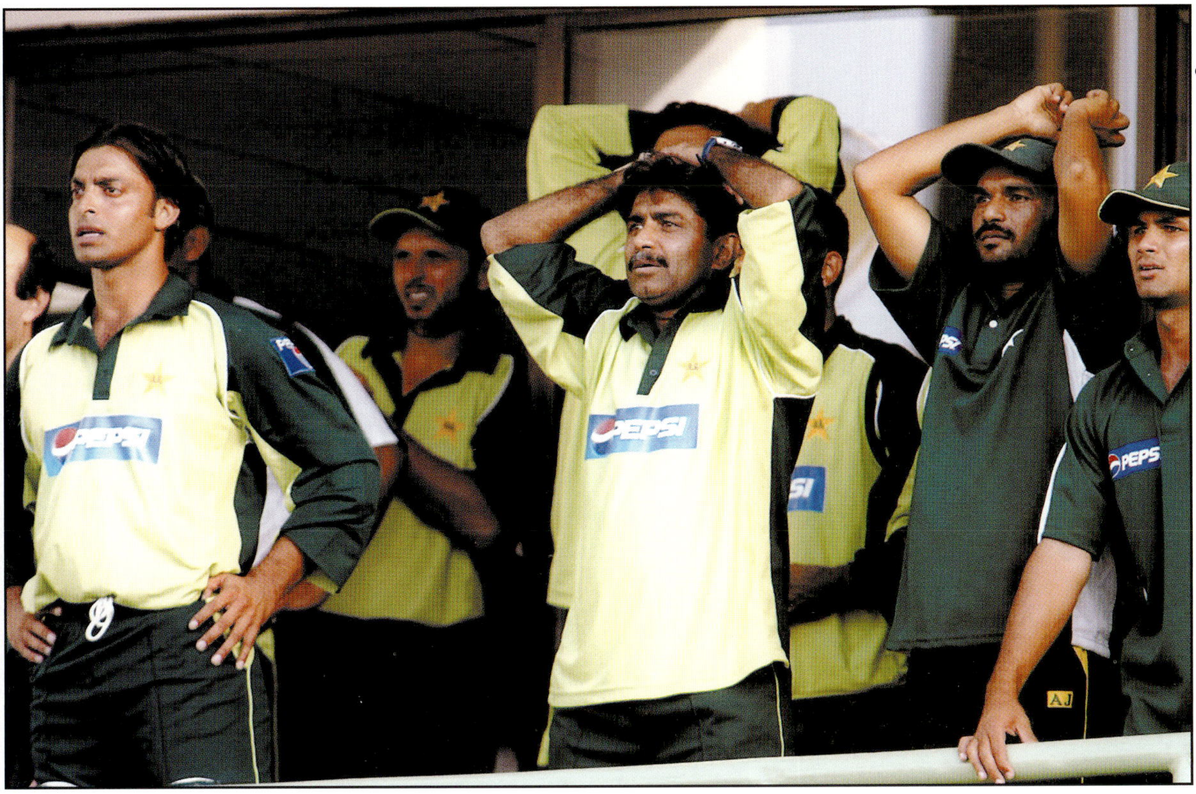

John Wright Collection

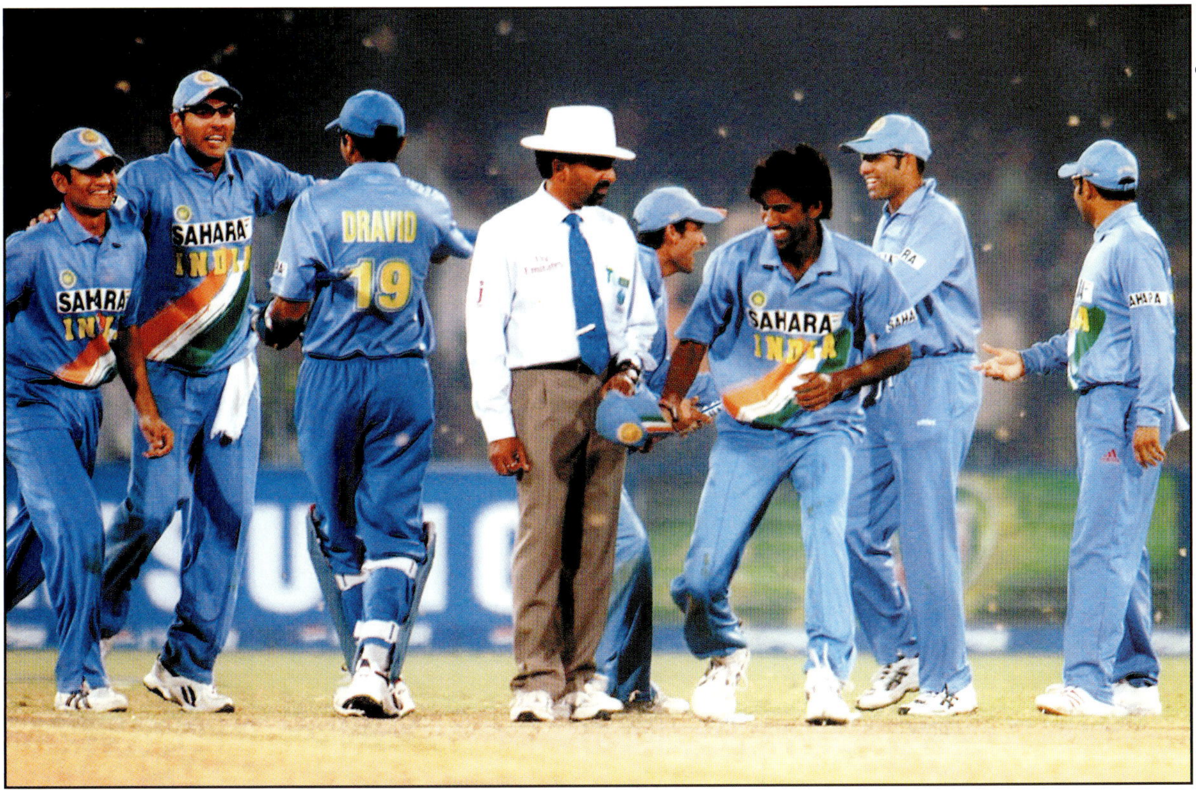

John Wright Collection

It's a fine line between pleasure and pain. India win a one-dayer and Pakistan coach Javed Miandad (centre with hands on head) suffers. At left is Shoaib Akhtar and behind him Shahid Afridi. Meanwhile, out in the middle the celebrations begin for, from left to right: Irfan Pathan, Yuvraj Singh, Rahul Dravid, Mohammad Kaif, Laxmipathy Balaji, V.V.S. Laxman and Virender Sehwag.

Where are the cherries? The Indian players had their cake and ate it too after winning the test and ODI series in Pakistan.

Homeward-bound heroes. From left, Sourav Ganguly, Anil Kumble, Virender Sehwag, Rahul Dravid and Sachin Tendulkar on the flight home after making history in Pakistan.

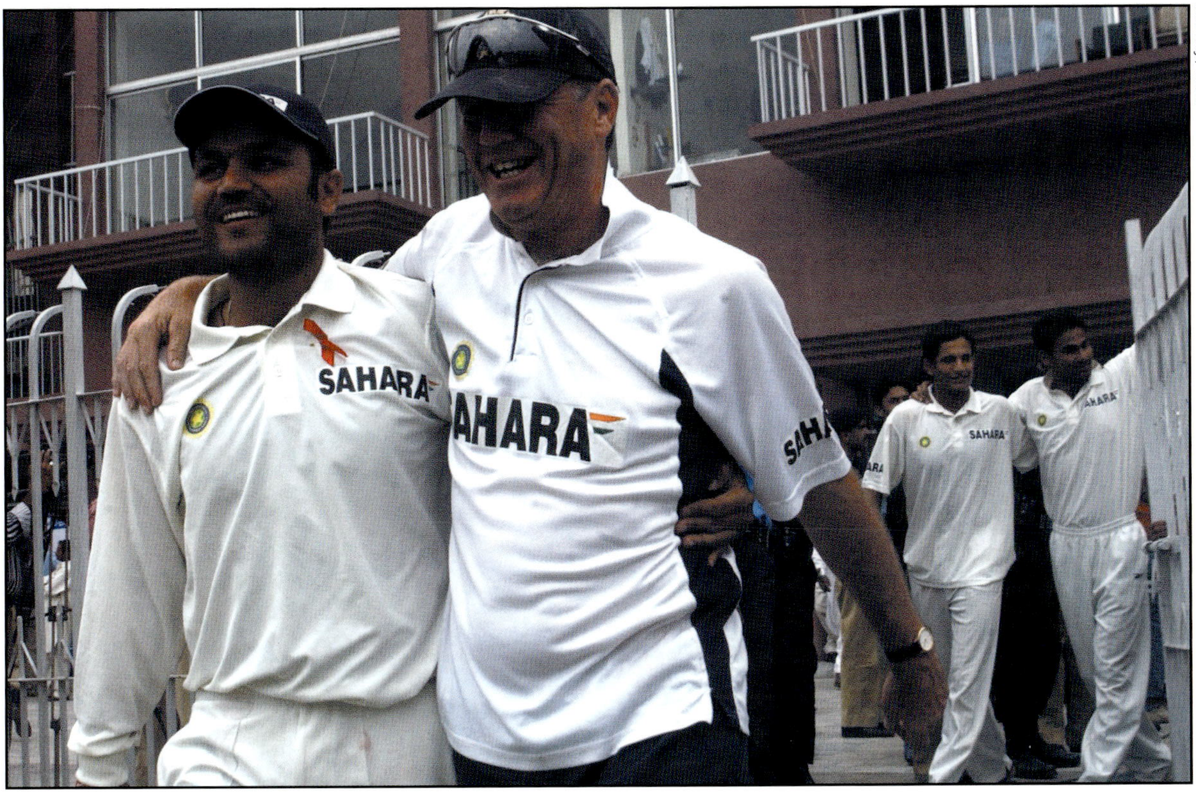

Mid-day, India

'John, you are my friend; this time you're coming.' Virender Sehwag escorts me out to the presentation ceremony after our series win in Pakistan.

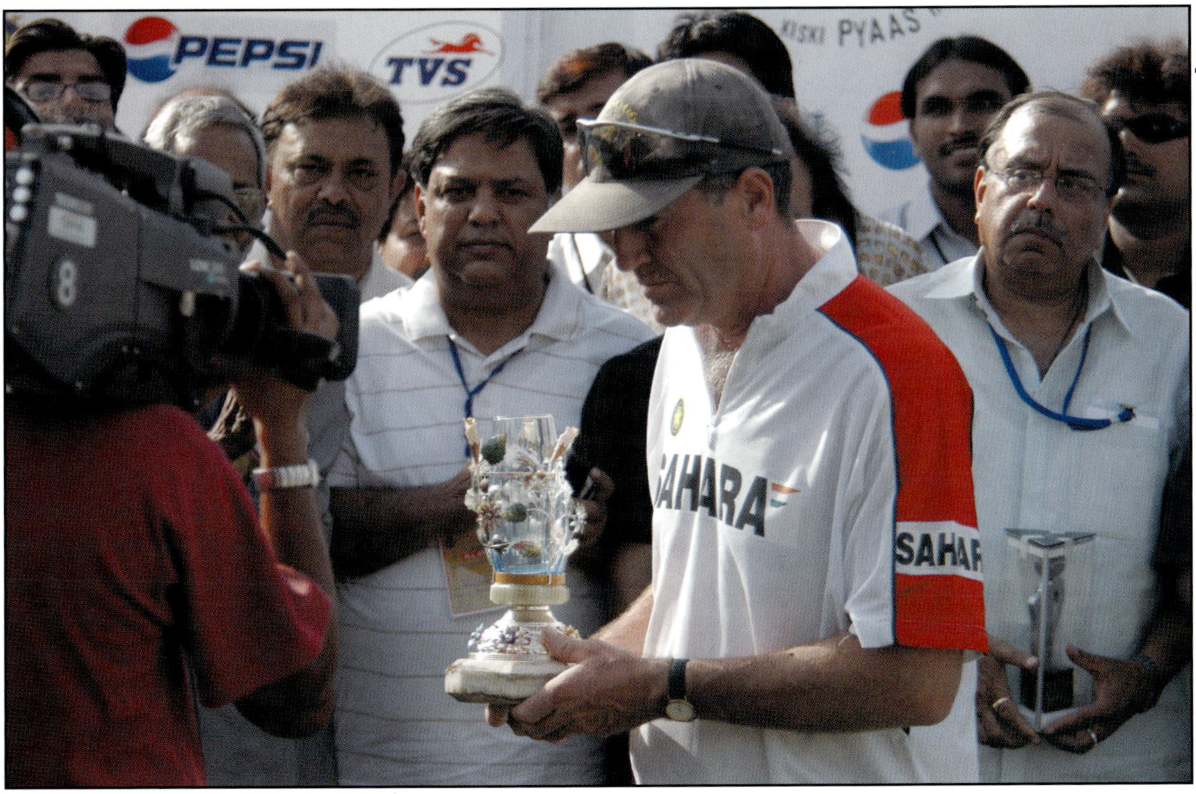

John Wright Collection

There are no happy endings: it's all over and I've got an ornament from the BCCI to prove it.

Don't dream it's over. I saw my job as helping to give the most passionate fans in the world the team they deserve.

A Process of Unnatural Selection

During my first TV interview in India, Ian Chappell mentioned that things could get pretty political in Indian cricket. It didn't really register with me. It was like one of those things you hear all the time that go in one ear and out the other — 'Please do not unfasten your seat belts until the aircraft has come to a complete halt.'

But at that stage I hadn't attended a selection meeting. After the intensity I witnessed at my first meeting, I approached the second one with some trepidation, given that we'd just lost a one-dayer to Zimbabwe. Nerves were raw, and it was another torrid affair, with people shouting and getting emotional. I didn't see the need for it because I didn't understand that the selectors not only had to fight for their players, but had to be seen and heard to fight for them.

The problem wasn't with the individuals, but with the structure they operated under. There are 27 first-class teams in India, divided into five zones — north, south, west, east, and central — and every year each of those zones elected a selector to the national selection panel. So a selector's tenure depended on keeping the powers-that-be, in and around the five or six states in his zone, happy. Each state was hugely passionate about the number of their boys selected for the team. It was a source of great pride to them. So each selector was pressured to get representation of the boys from their zones.

When Sourav Ganguly was dropped from the Indian one-day team, the East Zone selector, Pranab Roy, was hammered in his and Ganguly's home state of Bengal for 'doing nothing'. Because he'd failed to prevent Ganguly from being dropped, there were questions asked as to why Pranab didn't resign from the panel — the clear implication being that he'd failed to do his job. I often wondered what it was like for selectors to go back to their home states where they'd be labelled a failure or a success on the basis of how many local players were in the Indian team, rather than on whether they'd help pick the best possible team.

I doubt that many of them handled the pressure with Joel Garner's sang-froid. When we were in the West Indies, I had a night out in Barbados with Garner, who at the time was a West Indian selector. We ran into some of his mates and neighbours, who really ripped into him about selections. Garner gave the appearance of listening, although he didn't let it put him off his rum, fish and the kilo or so of macadamia nuts he worked his way through. When I ran into him the next morning, I asked, 'How're you doing, Big Bird?' He gave me a dazzling smile: 'Johnny, I'm fresh as a rose and ready to go.' I wished I could've said the same.

The selectors knew that, even if a candidate from their zone was unlikely to end up getting picked, they had to argue his case strenuously. Mysteriously, what was said behind closed doors in selection meetings generally found its way into circulation. The press often seemed to know which selectors had pushed for which players, and even when the details didn't appear in a newspaper, it seemed to be common knowledge among the cricketing fraternity, particularly the players.

The meetings had a certain ritual. We'd arrive and take our places, and the photographers would get their shots of the wise men — the panel,

Ganguly, myself and the honorary secretary, whose job it was to write down the names and announce the team afterwards — about to begin their august deliberations. Then the chairman would call the meeting to order: 'Gentlemen, we're all here to pick the best team for India.' The first six or seven selections were straightforward; names like Tendulkar and Dravid were never mentioned, they were just written down. So far, so good; the meeting would be proceeding in a calm and orderly manner. But when it got down to the marginal selections, those last three or four spots that determine the balance of the team and your ability to develop new players, the zonal factor kicked in and things would get interesting.

It was easy to tell when selectors had come to a meeting with an agenda, i.e. to do their damnedest to get one or two players from their zones into the team. If their boys weren't picked, they tended to cross their arms, clam up and take no further part in the meeting. After one meeting, the selectors had to make a long car trip together. They were so hacked off with each other that not one word was exchanged the whole way.

There was a meeting in Delhi at which we continually had to check the door for eavesdroppers, either photographers or snooping local officials. The debate reached a crescendo with one selector bellowing at another, 'You know Indian cricket like I know Indian cricket. If this player comes back, then you spit in my face.' After four or five of these verbal free-for-alls, I told them I couldn't come to any more meetings because there was too much yelling. They told me they had to yell because some of them had hearing difficulties.

There was a lot of rhetoric and posturing, and a conspicuous lack of rigour and hard information on paper. As a result, it was difficult to look seriously at big-picture elements, like succession planning, or to use the selection process to send out messages about attitude.

I was pretty passionate about selection because at Kent I'd learnt the importance of getting it right and the cost of getting it wrong. I strongly believed that winning was about getting the right people in the room. What made the situation more interesting, and at times immensely frustrating, was that neither Ganguly nor I had a vote. We could go to meetings and say our piece, but we had no way of backing up our point of view when it came to the crunch. Despite that, players tended to blame us if they were dropped. We got some pretty angry calls and text messages; relationships came under strain and one guy even threatened to retire. It was a classic no-win situation. Either the captain and coach should have a vote so that they can get the team they want and be more directly and justifiably accountable, or they shouldn't attend meetings at all and just work with what they're given. However, with the vagaries of the zonal system, the latter course would involve a fair degree of risk.

As it was, we just had to hope like hell that we got a couple of good selectors who'd take our concerns and perspectives on board. And hope like hell that they stuck around. Absurdly enough, five months out from the World Cup, four of the five selectors we'd worked with for the previous two years were replaced.

During our last home ODI series before the World Cup, one of the new selectors walked up to Ganguly and me ten minutes before the toss to tell us that we had to bat a particular player at number three. I didn't appreciate this last-minute, off-the-cuff strategic input that was contrary to what had been communicated to the players well in advance of the game, and I conveyed my displeasure in a vehement fashion. At the next selection meeting, he wanted it recorded in the minutes that the coach had used unparliamentary language, a quaint way of describing my barrage of fine old Anglo-Saxonisms — words that anyone who'd ever worked with me would've regarded as par for the course.

It could be a wearying business. Shiv Yadav didn't like flying, so when he became a selector he'd travel to the meetings by train. India's a large country and if the meetings were only a week apart — as they could be during a one-day series — he'd spend most of it on a train, travelling back and forth from his home in Hyderabad. When Jagmohan Dalmiya became President, most of the meetings took place in Kolkata. For me, that meant getting up in Mumbai at 6 a.m., an hour's taxi ride to the airport, a two-and-a-half-hour flight, and another hour in a car from the airport to the Taj Bengal Hotel. Afterwards I'd retrace my steps, getting back to Mumbai around midnight. There was a meeting at which only two positions — wicketkeeper and a fast bowler — were discussed, but it still went on for so long that I nearly missed the last flight to Mumbai. It was an awful lot of travel when you didn't have a vote.

When there were injury issues, Andrew Leipus would have to attend, although the players sometimes sent a doctor's certificate as proof of their fitness. These weren't always regarded as definitive; in my first year, for instance, we received one issued by a maternity hospital.

Sometimes it was a matter of reading between the lines, which I got better at. Before the team to tour Australia in 2003/04 was picked, a selector mentioned that he'd read an interesting article arguing that swing was the way to beat Australia. He went on to say that Laxman wasn't batting very well, so Sehwag would have to drop down the order. Given that Laxman was averaging 62 at the time, this was transparent nonsense; it took me about five seconds to work out where he was coming from. With Laxman gone and Sehwag down the order, there'd be a vacancy for an opener; this selector's zone happened to have both an opening batsman candidate and a swing bowler who, it must be said, was unlikely to terrorise the Aussie batsmen. If he could get both in the team, he'd be the toast of his zone. Two years earlier I would've jumped down his throat, but by then I understood what was going on, so I just smiled and kept moving.

I saw the system really exposed when the panel had to choose the Indian team and an A team at the same meeting. It took three hours to pick the top side; everyone had a plane to catch and it was an hour's drive to the airport, so India A was selected in about thirty minutes. They just went around the zones: two from here, three from there, and so on. It was just a divvy-up; you couldn't even call it horse trading.

There's a story, vigorously denied by everyone involved but which refuses to die, that selectorial confusion led to the wrong player representing India in an ODI series in Canada in 1998. They supposedly intended to pick J.P. Yadav, an all-rounder from Madhya Pradesh, but the player who got the call-up was J.P. Yadav, a left-hand batsman from Uttar Pradesh. Despite the coach at the time, Anshuman Gaekwad, insisting that nothing was amiss, the other players noticed that J.P. wore a nonplussed expression throughout the trip. It could be one of those stories that is somewhat spoilt by the facts. Or maybe not.

At state, junior, A team and even zone level, the same practices applied, only more so because there wasn't so much attention. Theoretically, the zonal teams should be the feeders to the national side, because they're made up of the best players from the 27 first-class squads. That should mean that India always has a pool of around 80 to 90 very good cricketers to choose from, but it doesn't necessarily work that way. According to one selector's reckoning, up to a third of the players were token selections from weaker teams that otherwise wouldn't have a representative in the zone team. Another third were probably journeymen who didn't have what it takes to cut it at the highest level. That left around 30 players with realistic international aspirations. The nature of the system meant that survival was the number one priority, so it was little wonder it produced cricketers who tended to play for themselves.

I heard stories of zonal selectors ganging up to isolate a colleague who was pushing for merit-based selections. A selector I worked with arrived ten minutes late for a zonal meeting to find that 14 players had already been picked. He was told there'd be no more discussion, but that he could choose the fifteenth player. In some zones, the selector from a weak state wouldn't bother to turn up, settling instead for giving 'his names' to another selector whose job was to try and 'get them in'.

I was told another story regarding the selection of an under-19 team to tour England. A quality batsman was out of favour with four of the five selectors because he hadn't got runs in the national tournament, and when the team had been finalised without him, the selector from his zone said he believed the batsman should tour because he was better than his statistics indicated. To demonstrate the depth of his conviction, he was willing to drop a player from his own zone to make room for the batsman. Even though they hadn't wanted this batsman, the other selectors were happy to go along with it because it was no skin off their nose. There didn't seem to be any recognition of what they were agreeing to: dropping a player they'd all chosen, to make room for one they hadn't wanted, and it was all acceptable simply because it didn't disturb the zonal calculations.

The selector making the supposed sacrifice had actually worked a double-bluff: realising his favoured candidate didn't have any support, he'd successfully pushed for another player from his zone just to nail down a spot in the team. The boy who got initially selected was just a pawn, to be sacrificed once the other selectors had fallen for the gambit.

When it comes to selection shenanigans, all roads lead to Delhi. The selection procedures there are more archaic than the 15th-century ruins next to Delhi's home ground, Ferozshah Kotla. Some years ago a dispute among the selectors culminated in two Delhi under-16 teams being picked to play the Punjab under-16s. Some boys were in both teams and had to decide who they should warm up with. Three captains went out for the toss, upon which the umpires declared, 'Three teams can't play one match', and walked off the field. The *Times of India* report on the incident the next day was headlined 'Pandemonium at the D.D.C.A.' The cricketer who related this story to me was only twelve at the time and says that's how he found out what the word 'pandemonium' meant.

It seems to be getting worse, particularly among the junior teams. One of the Delhi players in the Indian team was adamant that he wouldn't make it now, because his father didn't have the right connections. 'You know what Delhi's like,' he said. 'Even a rickshaw driver will tell you that he knows someone in the Prime Minister's Office.'

The term they use in Delhi, I understand, is an 'approach', and the question that is asked is: Do you 'have an approach', i.e. any kind of connection, to officials or selectors? Ambitious families and coaches use the approach to try to get their boys into teams, often because they knew that they weren't quite good enough to get there on merit. Familiarity could work, or a favour in return for selection would be just as handy. The family might know of someone in local government, or the education department, or a political party, who might be happy to ask a cricket official a favour. He, in turn, might find it very difficult to refuse. Of course, once an official gets a reputation for being 'approachable', approaches are likely to come thick and fast. It's reached the stage where, so the Delhi boys told me, people just assume that any Delhi junior team will include one or two 'approach' players. A recent variation on the approach is to ask the coach not to play your boy against quality opposition so that his shortcomings don't get exposed.

When I returned to India in early 2006 to do some TV work, there was a ruckus in Delhi that sounded like an episode of 'The Sopranos'. After an approach wasn't followed through, a couple of heavies turned up at the Delhi senior team's training, took the two coaches aside and made them an offer they couldn't refuse, supposedly involving threats to their families. At first the players thought their coaches had been abducted, but they emerged from the meeting somewhat shaken and the following day's training took place under police guard. A couple of journalists who reported the story got phone-calls suggesting they would be better off writing about dog shows instead.

A few days later the captain announced that he didn't want to lead the side in their next match and the coach, a friend of mine, and an ex-national selector, Madan Lal, washed his hands of selection of the playing XI because of the pressure being exerted to pick a certain official's son. The assistant coach had to pick the team, and Akash Chopra, being the senior player, was forced to captain the side and sign the team sheet. When the story broke, the Delhi and District Cricket Association bosses ordered the captain to lead the side, sacked the entire selection committee and announced a team that still included the official's son. Perhaps the saddest indictment of the situation was having a player from Delhi tell me that he wouldn't want his son to play cricket.

While the BCCI's tournament structure operates throughout the country, the local structure varies from state to state: Mumbai has a club system, Punjab has districts and Chennai has corporate teams. In places like Delhi or Uttar Pradesh (UP) where everything revolves around politics, political influence and interference come into the picture. And where political corruption exists, then pretty much anything is possible. In Kanpur, junior selectors usually switch off their mobile phones during trials to avoid being approached or threatened, and they are routinely given police protection. One official told me he'd avoided being kidnapped because he knew someone in the state's extortion and kidnapping task force, which picked up the three thugs sent to arm-twist him into picking a certain player.

You can take the view that the system works in spite of itself because quality players keep emerging, but you have to wonder how many slip through the net. The UP Ranji Trophy trials involve around 280 players; the UP junior trials (under-15, under-17 and under-19) involve from 500 to 800 boys over the three days. A kid might have ten minutes batting or bowling to convince the selectors he should go through to the next round.

As a 17-year-old, Javagal Srinath was picked from his hometown, Mysore, for an under-19 state trial. He travelled three and a half hours to Bangalore on a bus, bowled for ten minutes in a net, was 'all over the shop', and that was the end of his trial. He travelled back home again and missed selection. It didn't end badly for Srinath, but he said cricket for him was all about playing, and not representation or selection. Now, as he has witnessed in his role in his state's coaching programme, he says that when some good kid gets dropped from one level to another for no apparent reason, they frequently just decide to leave the game.

In Kanpur, I saw a 12-year-old leg spinner and a 15-year-old off spinner who weren't good, they were outstanding. I wondered what would become of them if they were competing for a spot with an approach player with political clout behind him; and if they weren't picked, who would even notice? I subsequently heard that the offie got picked, but the leggie failed to make the cut.

Selection in India is not professional and it's open to abuse in all sorts of ways. When we set off to tour Australia, the big talking point wasn't our prospects (perhaps because hardly anyone was giving us a chance) but a scandal surrounding a first-class player who'd been reported for trying to bribe two national selectors to get him into the team. On occasions, players have complained that 'their' selector, i.e. the selector from their zone, was leaning on them to do personal favours, such as making an appearance at the opening of a shop or giving an interview to a reporter who just happened to be related to the selector.

Cricketers in other countries can be pragmatic about selection, but in India it's a minefield. The players are acutely sensitive about it, and are very wary of upsetting anyone because they've seen and heard so many horror stories. The prevailing view is that if you get dropped from the Indian team, your chances of getting back in are somewhere between remote and nonexistent. 'Dropped' is code for 'gone for good'. Despair for an Indian cricketer must be seeing his name in the papers alongside the words 'test discard' or 'India discard'.

There are plenty of them. Pravin Amre made a century on debut in Durban, and his last six test innings were 78, 57, 52 not out, 21, 15 not out, and 21. He averaged 42 over his 11-test career. Vinod Kambli was in the Tendulkar league as a teenager: when they were 17 and 16 respectively, they put on an unbeaten partnership of 664 in a school match. He made his test debut at 21, but by the time he was 24 it was all over, despite an average of 54. He averaged 59.6 over a much longer first-class career. Injury interrupted Sadagopan Ramesh's test career, and it quickly reached the point where he seemed to be completely off the radar in selection terms, even though he averaged nearly 38 over 19 tests as an opener. The attrition rate and burnout caused by playing virtually year-round may provide a route back for some of these discards.

As is the case anywhere, some players are easier to drop than others. V.V.S. Laxman and Kaif are examples of outstanding performers who always seemed to be only one or two failures away from having their places questioned, and for some reason certain bowlers attract far more scrutiny than the batsmen. The exceptions are the superstars; there's still a reluctance to give an underperforming or unfocused big name a blunt message by having him sit out a tour or a few one-dayers.

I struggled with the fact that attitude and off-field behaviour didn't seem to enter the equation. I told a star who'd become casual, 'If you keep playing and practising that way, you'll get dropped.' He gave me a cheeky smile and said, 'John, tell it to the selectors.' You can try all sorts of things as a coach, but if a player still isn't scoring runs or smartening up his attitude, dropping him is often the best way of getting his attention. In my time, every player who got that treatment came back tougher, stronger, keener and more willing. When you make that call as a coach, you don't want to be told that form is temporary but class is permanent, you want a panel that trusts your judgement and will back you by making the tough decision.

Sanjay Jagdale, a selector I had a lot of time for, used to say, 'The job of a selector is to pick the right people at the right time.' And sometimes drop them. Selection must be dispassionate and objective. It's not that different from making a significant purchase: you have to be absolutely clear about what you want, and look for those qualities and attributes without getting distracted by alternatives that, however attractive, don't meet your criteria.

I felt sorry for those selectors who tried to do their best but were always under pressure, knowing they'd cop it if they were seen to have 'failed' their zone. As one of them said, 'We're like birds in a cage.' I felt for those players who dropped off the radar for reasons I never understood. I felt for the passionate fans whose existences are brightened when their team performs, but who aren't being served by a system that's outdated and at times downright unfair. Outside of the BCCI, I can't think of anyone who endorses the system, and I said so in my first major interview as Indian coach.

And I said the same thing when I finished. Friends who worked in administration and the media would tell me, 'It can't change; it's been this way for years; it's about the vote.' Well, that doesn't alter the fact that it needs to change, not just at the top level, but down below, as far as it can go. At the moment, the system is a handicap on Indian cricket, akin to starting behind the other runners in a 100-metre race.

The best comment I heard on selection was when I asked a group of players about how one particular batsman was going in a one-day tournament.

'Is he getting any runs?' I asked.

One boy replied, 'Does he need any?'

YOUR COACH IS READY TO DEPART

I should have realised that it was time to go when I went to Tony Greig's place for a barbecue.

When I walked into Tony's house in Sydney in early 2004, it hit me that I hadn't been in a normal home for seven months. I found myself taking in the surroundings — the furniture, the paintings on the walls, the homeliest kitchen items — with envy because it was all a reminder of what real life was like and what was missing from my unreal existence. I coached one of the most fervently and loyally supported teams in world sport, but it was the loneliest job I'd ever done. I understood the players wanting to go home between games and encouraged them to do so as often as possible, but popping home for the weekend wasn't an option for me unless I was prepared to spend 30 hours on a plane.

Touring gets tougher as you get older and it was starting to wear me down. I rarely hung out with the players in the evening; having spent the day with me, I figured they deserved a break at night. So I'd have a couple of beers and a meal, occasionally with company, mostly by myself, then hit the sack. That was my routine, and I'd grown tired of it. My 2003 Christmas dinner was fish and chips and a coke at a Melbourne sidewalk café. In 2004 it was the hotel buffet in Dhaka. I'd missed the kids' birthdays four years running. One year when I was home for Christmas, Harry said, 'Dad, my mates think it's great you're coach of India and I think it's cool too, but I wish you were home a bit more.'

People thought I had an apartment in India, but whether we were touring or playing at home, my existence boiled down to two suitcases, a guitar, and a room, either in a hotel or at the Cricket Club of India in Mumbai. On our breaks, the foreign support staff — myself, Andrew Leipus, and Adrian le Roux or Greg King — would head back to base and stay at the Taj, the grand old lady of Mumbai. I was always given room 477 and the hotel staff did everything they could to make us feel at home. But a hotel, no matter how familiar, can't be a home, and the staff, no matter how obliging and attentive, can't replace family and friends. And the novelty had worn off.

One of the curiosities of sport is that everyone wants to go out on a high, but so few manage it. I seriously thought about quitting after we won the series in Pakistan, but I really wanted to have another crack at the Aussies. They were coming to India again and to finish up with two wins and a draw in three series against the best team in the world would be quite an achievement. And the Pakistanis were making a return tour, so there was also the enticing prospect of back-to-back wins over the great rival. If we could beat both of them again, it wouldn't be forgotten in a hurry.

I came back for one more year because I thought we could take that next step. As it turned out, it wasn't a disaster, but we couldn't take the next step and I didn't go out in a blaze of glory. We lost to Australia, the only test series loss at home during my tenure. We drew the series against Pakistan 1–1 and lost the one-dayers. The loss to Pakistan in Bangalore was the only home test we lost to a side other than Australia in five seasons. We didn't play as well as we had the year before, which was another pretty good indication that it was time for me to move on and for someone else to have a go. I played 82 tests and 149 ODIs in 15 years; while I was coach, India played 51 tests and 130

ODIs. These days, four and a half years on the treadmill is a long time.

I was asked to continue, but that would have meant going through to the World Cup and I knew I couldn't do that. Besides, keeping going was a recipe for frustration because I would've wanted changes and more say in all sorts of things, including more influence over team selection, and that just wasn't going to happen. In some of the instant history, spoken and written, that's appeared since I left there seems to be a perception that I was a passive figure who accepted whatever happened and never rocked the boat. That simply wasn't the case: I'd tried everything, including banging my fist and being hard-nosed, and whenever the president or selectors sought my opinion, they got it without any equivocation or sugar-coating. Well, almost everything: one thing I chose not to do was argue my case in public. As much as I respect Sourav Ganguly and acknowledge his record as captain and contribution to Indian cricket, I believed there were sound arguments for a change of leadership towards the end of my stint. There might well have been times when he favoured a change of coach. What really mattered was that the two of us saw the bigger picture, worked as a partnership to provide leadership on and off the field, and got results. In that last season, though, the results dried up.

I've always believed in use-by dates and I'd reached mine. The team needed a new voice. And there were the personal reasons. When I signed on, I understood that loneliness went with the territory, but you can only live that way for so long.

When we regrouped in 2004 it was like the post-World Cup hangover, only worse. After winning in Pakistan, it was being said this was the best Indian team ever, and the air the players breathed had become even more rarefied. In the land that traditionally hero-worshipped great batsmen, even our quick bowlers Irfan Pathan and Lakshmipathy Balaji had become cult heroes. Our first assignment, the Asia Cup, was regarded as a *fait accompli* and there was a bit of swaggering in the media, such as Virender Sehwag suggesting that he could score 200 in an ODI if he batted 50 overs. It reminded me of what my old Derbyshire captain, the South African all-rounder Eddie Barlow, said to me after I'd followed a big hundred with three soft failures: 'If you take the piss out of cricket, cricket will take the piss out of you.' In his first 13 ODIs that season Sehwag got one fifty.

He wasn't the only one who took time to get going. We didn't need a training camp, we needed to play some competitive matches and select only those who performed; having made history in Pakistan shouldn't have given anyone a boarding pass for Sri Lanka. This was when I needed clout at the selection table, so that I could say, with the panel's backing, 'sort yourself out or have a rest'.

We made the final of the Asia Cup, but without a selectorial prod to jolt them out of their complacency there was no spark and no hunger. Ganguly was struggling with his own form and tinkered with the batting order, promoting himself back to number three. In the last ODI in Pakistan, V.V.S. Laxman had made a century batting at three that basically won us the series, but now he found himself down the order. It was Ganguly's prerogative, but I thought it was a bad move.

The biggest ODI event of 2004 was the ICC Champions Trophy. We played a couple of warm-up games in Holland, where the practice wickets were dire and it rained. Over in England things weren't much better; we couldn't get any momentum into our batting. I did some stern talking, reminding the team that success can be your biggest enemy. Some of the boys had returned with bigger wallets, but with lazy attitudes. They listened now because they knew we were in trouble, but there was no overnight revival. Sachin Tendulkar, one of the few who'd come back with determination and renewed ambition, injured his elbow; we thought it was minor, but it turned out he'd ruptured the tendon. All in all, it had been an unimpressive start to a season that was about to get a whole lot tougher.

Two days before the first test against Australia, I was notified that the legendary Sunil Gavaskar would be joining us as a batting consultant. Our one-day form was certainly patchy, but in the most recent test series, in

Australia and Pakistan, the batting had fired on all cylinders. From a coaching point of view it was perplexing, to put it mildly. I'd asked for some help for our young bowlers; I got help for our experienced batsmen.

I'd played against Gavaskar and respected him enormously, but I was also aware that he was one of the most powerful men in Indian cricket. Early on, I'd virtually given him an open invitation to have an input; he dropped in during a few camps and I had a couple of meals with him on tour, but generally the players and I found out what he thought about us by reading his newspaper column. I was used to having uninvited experts turn up at our camps, but this was a formal and ongoing arrangement and I couldn't work out how it had happened. Gavaskar solved the mystery by revealing in a team meeting that he was there because he'd had a text message from Ganguly, asking him to come.

I was far from happy. As the head coach, I should have had the final say on support staff issues and not had personnel thrust on me; the more people in the room, the more shoulders to cry on, the more chance of mixed messages, and the more potential for players to go off in different directions. But if the captain decides to bring someone into the camp two days out from a test against the best team in the world, there's not a hell of a lot you can do about it.

I used up a lot of emotional energy over this matter. I could have thrown my hands up and said enough is enough, but I coached for the players and I'd always told them that if we stuck together, we could face any opposition and prevail in any situation. So now that I'd been put in a difficult and unsatisfactory position myself, what was I going to do — walk away? In that situation you have to swallow your pride and make the best of it because any other course of action will have a knock-on effect and disrupt the whole organisation.

Gavaskar was there as the captain's confidant and was involved in selection and team issues, so the management group had expanded. It was a matter of managing the situation and using him as a resource, because when

Gavaskar says you have to bat five sessions, people listen. I did notice, though, that after we'd lost the third test in Nagpur, and therefore the series, largely as a result of our dysfunctional batting, Gavaskar's TV channel, ESPN-Star Sports, changed his title from batting consultant to plain old consultant.

It wasn't personal. I'd known Gavaskar for years and didn't care that he and the players traded jokes in Hindi. But it created an awkward dynamic: if a player talked to me, he'd feel obliged to go and talk to him, and vice versa. You don't want a dressing room with invisible barriers, where everyone's walking on eggshells. After Nagpur, I tried to clear the air and told Gavaskar that I'd be finishing after the Pakistan series, or perhaps sooner if things didn't improve. He said that he didn't want to coach the side. It was an unusual situation; one that I think will be seen for what it was and that will be judged accordingly.

The tour took place before Christmas, when it was cooler. The Aussies had done a lot of work since 2001 and their major batsmen had learned to play spin better. Ricky Ponting missed the first three tests, but was replaced by Simon Katich, who's a good player of spin, as was Darren Lehmann. Damien Martyn didn't get a game in 2001, but this time he played a big hand, scoring 444 runs and winning the 'Man of the Series' award. We were underdone, which is no state to be in against Australia. In 2001 we had lots of domestic cricket and a very hard camp, but this time we'd been playing one-dayers overseas.

In the first test in Bangalore our top six contributed 136 and 86, and it was our tail that took the game into the fifth day. This match was umpire Billy Bowden's first experience of India, where the crowd noise is so loud and constant that it's hard to hear the snicks; add in the fielders clustered around the bat on turning wickets and it's a demanding experience for someone unused to the environment. Bowden made some mistakes, most glaringly when he gave Sehwag out lbw off a thick inside edge. Those are the breaks and you accept them, but the Indian media and fans were unforgiving. Prasanna, a computer nut who'd spent two days travelling to Chennai to show me yet another upgrade of his cricket software program, told me that my friend from New Zealand, that Billy, was no good: 'They should change his name to Billy Burden.'

We knew we had the ability to fight back and even win the series, and in Chennai the boys got stuck in. Sehwag, who'd been struggling, scored 155 as only he can; he brought out the full repertoire, including the uppercut for six. He sets himself up very quickly and uses the pace of the ball and a wristy flick with lots of bottom hand. We had a 145-run lead on the first innings, but poor Parthiv Patel, who was having a tough time, dropped Matthew Hayden off the first ball of Australia's second innings. We had them at 145 for 4, but Martyn and the nightwatchman Jason Gillespie bought Australia time. It wasn't the first time Gillespie had held us up; the only consolation was that I could point him out to our tailenders as an excellent example of a bowler who'd made himself into a very useful lower-order batsman through hard work. We finished day four needing 210 to win with all wickets standing, but rain washed out the final day.

We would've liked to have gone straight into the third test, but the Aussies had negotiated a five-day break, which suited them more than us. The venue was Nagpur, in central India, where the pitch was usually slow and low, a draw wicket as opposed to a result wicket. For this test it underwent a dramatic change that had nothing to do with global warming. There'd been a BCCI election narrowly won by the Jagmohan Dalmiya faction. The president of the host association in Nagpur belonged to the anti-Dalmiya faction. In the lead-up to the match he was quoted as saying that the wicket was tailor-made for fast bowlers, and Glenn McGrath couldn't have asked for a better pitch for his 100th test.

We wanted to go to Mumbai with the series still alive, because that was a real Indian wicket; if it starts to turn, it goes quickly. One down in the series, without Irfan, who'd got injured in Chennai, and up against three quality seamers, we could have done with the standard Nagpur wicket. Instead, the Australian bowlers got the closest thing to a home wicket they're ever likely to come across on the subcontinent. I didn't really believe that the BCCI elections could have any bearing on a test wicket until we got to Nagpur three days before the game and found that the local officials were permanently unavailable and even the groundsman wasn't talking to us.

At the very last minute Ganguly developed a groin problem and had to pull out. Australia played the better cricket, and we lost the test and the series. Martyn led the batting; the pace battery of McGrath, Gillespie and Michael Kasprowicz performed at a higher level than in 2001, and Shane Warne, who had his best tour of India, was their foil. In Ponting's absence, Adam Gilchrist led the side with more innovation than Steve Waugh had shown in the previous two series. Having said that, I still wonder why we had to play this critical test in conditions that were tailor-made for our opponents. After the game, I asked umpire David Shepherd for his take on the wicket: 'John,' he said, 'it was as if they prepared it for themselves.' A foreign journalist called it 'a 22 yard suicide note'.

As we were going down the gurgler, the players received their official letters from the BCCI informing them of their selection for the first and second tests. Given the surreal nature of events in Nagpur, it was tempting to think that the powers-that-be had decided to wipe the slate clean and start the series all over again. The less fanciful explanation was that the BCCI had sent a slow courier to the wrong hotel.

By this stage my stocks were in decline and it was interesting to observe some of the movement on the periphery. Dean Jones, who has always been very keen on making the jump from commentary to coaching, spent about 40 minutes on the first morning in Nagpur talking to the injured captain while the rest of the team warmed up. It looked more like a job interview than a conversation. The Aussies' security man, Reg Dickason, had a company in Iraq that employed 200 people to teach the Iraqis how to protect their politicians. The staff did three-month stints, for which they were paid NZ$800 a day, and were provided with a flak jacket, an AK-47 and a belt of grenades. The way things were going, downtown Baghdad didn't look such a bad option.

When things are on the slide, everyone tends to go into emergency mode.

This is when the coach needs to display equilibrium, consistency of mood and behaviour, and a sense of perspective. There are times when you can hammer the team for losing, but after a defeat I preferred to keep quiet and take myself off to my hotel room. The boys would be hurting too and were well aware that there'd be an uproar and a hunt for scapegoats. Rather than have the coach climbing into them as well, they needed me to provide some quiet reassurance and honest assessment to help them pick themselves up and get back into the fray. In keeping with that logic, it's actually often better to give people a rev after a victory.

Mumbai was damp and cloudy, but Rahul Dravid took one look at the wicket and declared that we needed to play three spinners. We won the toss and were bowled out for 104 in 41.3 overs. By stumps on day two we were batting again, having conceded a first innings lead of 99; life had become even grimmer for the Indian team, its coach and, indeed, its batting consultant. We mapped our way back into the game, starting from a victory and working backwards, and reached the conclusion that we had to make the Australians chase at least 150 in the fourth innings.

Before the test I'd suggested to Dravid that we bat Laxman at three. He didn't think to do it in the first innings, but did so in the second. It was tough on Laxman getting shunted up and down the order, and tough on Dravid, given that he'd been voted international player of the year in the 2003/04 season for his batting at first drop. Under the circumstances, though, it was the right call from the team point of view, and that must always be the determining factor.

Laxman got 69 at a brisk clip and Tendulkar, who'd missed out in the first two tests, got 55. (Only this pair and Martyn passed 50 in the game.) It wasn't your normal test match and it became increasingly bizarre from the moment Michael Clarke came on to bowl his strictly part-time left-arm spinners. He picked up our last six wickets for nine runs in 6.2 overs. We'd left the Australians 107 to win, 50 too few, even given the way the pitch was behaving.

Early wickets are everything when defending small totals. If you can reduce the opposition to 20 for 3, then the pressure's on them and there's a chance that they'll choke. On the other hand, it only takes one partnership to settle the nerves and take the wind out of the bowling team's sails. Our three spinners did their job very efficiently and Dravid managed his bowling changes brilliantly. He opened with Harbhajan Singh and Zaheer Khan, who went for 14 off his two overs but got the early wicket. Then, instead of bringing on Anil Kumble, he turned to Murali Kartik, who got the big wicket of Martyn. When Gilchrist hit one down deep square leg's throat, they were 58 for 7 with only bowlers left, and it was possible to start believing in miracles. They were all out for 93, 13 runs short; 16 wickets had fallen in four hours.

The next day I got an e-mail from John Inverarity, the former Australian batsman and a renowned coach, who'd succeeded me at Kent. Among other things, he wrote that the level of interest in the series had been extremely high, and he congratulated me on my contribution towards 'making India such an interesting and mercurial team'. The thing about mercury, of course, is that it rises and falls with the weather. It was a relief to come out of the series with something, and the mood changed instantly. I'd come to understand what the players always knew: that no matter how bad things were, we were always only one win away from glory. That was the nature of the beast.

South Africa, who were up next, were a hard side to break down because they toured with the mindset that a draw was a win. The pressure that had tapered off after the win in Mumbai was back on and my kilometre count went up accordingly. I often jogged laps of the ground at the end of play, after the players had left for the hotel, trudging around the perimeter as the light faded and the reporters in the press box tapped out their copy. The joke was that you could tell how India was doing by how many laps the coach ran after the day's play. There was an element of truth in that, but I also found it peaceful; jogging around empty grounds at dusk was one of the very few ways of obtaining solitude and time to think. It was just me, the women sweeping out the stands, and the policemen who guarded the ground and sometimes gave me a round of applause and asked for my autograph when I finally ground to a halt.

When Greg King and I were leaving Eden Gardens one night, a police inspector came up to tell me that he played rugby: 'I'm a small prop.' He reckoned I looked pretty fit and wanted to know how old I was. Expecting to be flattered, I asked him how old he thought I was. He looked me up and down: 'Coach, I'd say you're 56.' King burst out laughing; two months before I'd turned 51.

South Africa are always tough, but they're too defensive and you really can't do well in India without a quality spinner. Winning that series was sweet, particularly because losing two home series in a row would have been the end of me. Their new and outspoken coach, Ray Jennings, said after the draw in Kanpur that the Indian fielders looked like they were carrying pillows. When we finished them off in Kolkata, the players autographed a pillow for him and sent it through to the South African changing room.

Christmas Day in Dhaka: just me and my guitar. I wrote a song which, while it's not exactly Bob Dylan, provides a pretty good snapshot of my existence and of a coach on his last lap.

Hotel rooms and smoky bars
Cigarettes and lost key cards
The elevator's jammed at floor fifteen
My bed is soft, my pillow's hard
And traffic noise is sounding loud
I long for those country silent sounds.

The friendly staff and the wake-up calls
My laundry's lost, it's my cotton shorts
The mini-bar has run away on me
The paintings hang like sleeping cats
They're staring down and I smile back
And the loneliness creeps on you in the nights.

Watch the world from a TV screen
Satellites all fully beamed
They tell me where I was late last night
They bombed Fallujah yesterday
There's forecast rain for Tampa Bay
And the movie's crap on channel fifty-three.

Moving on in two days' time
Bags to pack, it's a four-hour flight
Stadiums and games to win
Will this season be my last
Before this life becomes my past
Of living on the road with the team?

I've got those Christmas away blues
Long time from home blues
Wondering what the kids are doing now
Are they shopping are they sleeping?
Are they growing up and keeping
All the memories of the times we used to share?

The next day we lost an ODI to Bangladesh, demonstrating yet again our uncanny ability to play up or down to the level of our opponents. Back at the hotel I turned on the TV to watch unbelievable images of the tsunami and the initial — and, as it turned out, understated — reports of the cataclysmic destruction it had unleashed on Asia. It was the most emphatic reminder I've ever had that cricket is only a game.

Bob Woolmer had replaced Javed Miandad as Pakistan coach. Twenty-nine years earlier he and I were whizzing down the A2 to Canterbury for Kent's pre-season training. At that time Bob was trying to crack the England team and I was trying to get myself a gig in county cricket. Now here we were in Mohali, a long way from the green fields of Kent, rival coaches of teams from the Indian subcontinent. Woolmer took first blood, winning the battle of the cones: when we went out for our warm-up, we discovered that the Pakistani warm-up area occupied almost the entire ground.

I reminded the Pakistan captain, Inzamam-ul-Haq, that as a significantly leaner 22-year-old he'd given me and the rest of New Zealand a lot of grief in the 1992 World Cup semi-final. He was gracious enough to describe it as one of the best innings of his life. There's an air of inevitability and an economy of effort about Inzamam that brings to mind a galleon under full sail moving slowly across the horizon. When Inzy walks, nothing moves except his feet. These days Woolmer is also built for comfort rather than speed, so the Pakistan team is led by two substantial figures in both senses of the word.

It was the same story: India versus Pakistan meant that everyone found a little extra. We were well prepared, but this contest is always balanced on a knife-edge and we didn't take our chances. In Mohali we had them on the rack on the last day, but couldn't finish them off. We didn't drop a catch all day, but didn't have enough fielders in catching positions. I couldn't understand what was going on. A coach can send messages out, but he can't captain by remote control; apart from anything else, no captain worth his salt would stand for it. Rather than issuing instructions, it's more a matter of providing information that the skipper and the team can act on or ignore. They need the freedom to make their own decisions. The captain is the man on the spot; the coach is the bloke sitting in the grandstand getting more and more frustrated because the information he keeps sending out is being ignored and the game's starting to slip away. That's his lot.

I'd have my say at the team talk and check whether Ganguly wanted me to send out suggestions. Generally he did, and I'd let him know what I thought. Some coaches don't do it; it depends on the personalities involved, their relationship and individual styles. I don't imagine John Buchanan sends messages to Ponting. At Kent, Matthew Fleming didn't appreciate it and once sent the messenger back to tell the coach to get stuffed.

But then, whichever way you looked at it, Ganguly and I were an odd couple. Our strategic approaches to one-day cricket differed quite markedly. I placed huge emphasis on saving runs and applying pressure by cutting off the singles. If I were captaining a team with 300 on the board and the opposition were 100 for 2, I'd go for the jugular by bringing five or six fielders into the ring to force the batsman to take risks. Ganguly would rather strangle the batting side slowly. Similarly, when a tailender was in with an established batsman, I thought it was pointless giving the better player singles; by attacking at one end only, you reduce your chances of getting a wicket by 50 per cent. Sometimes my way and my hunches were right, sometimes they weren't. During this test and ODI series I was right more often than not, but that was no consolation. I'd rather have been proved wrong.

The way sport works at the highest level is that if you don't seize your opportunities, sooner or later the momentum will shift and the boot will be on the other foot. We went into the final test in Bangalore having dominated the series but only one-up because we hadn't finished the job in Mohali. That came back to haunt us: we had two bad sessions, which were the difference between winning and drawing the series. We were 90 for 1 at lunch on the fifth day, and previously we'd been able to bat out the last day when we had to. This time we fell in a heap. I kept wondering if I'd given them the wrong message. Things were going so well that nothing was said at lunch, but afterwards we made the mistake of just occupying the crease instead of playing normal cricket. I should've picked up on that at lunch and reinforced the need to be positive, and I should've also pushed harder for Laxman to bat at three. He would've played his normal attacking game and the Pakistanis wouldn't have been able to take the initiative and apply pressure. The wicket had started to turn, but we got negative and allowed the Pakistanis to bowl at us. Laxman's as good as any batsman in world cricket at keeping the game moving; if he gets a bad ball, it goes for four. Besides, Laxman at three had worked for us before, most recently against Australia in Mumbai. As they say, why are the old moves old? Because they work. In my scheme of things, having a series win snatched away in the last two sessions was as great a disappointment as losing the World Cup final.

We blew Pakistan away in the first two ODIs. The second at Vizakhapatnam was notable for Mahendra Singh Dhoni's 148 off 123 balls. Rather than knock politely on the door of international cricket, he booted it off its hinges. He made Sehwag look slow, which had never happened before. Results were going with the toss, a trend that was maintained for Pakistan's benefit in the third game, and something odd happened in the fourth game in Ahmedabad. When we left practice, Ganguly was having a chat with the groundsman. The next morning the start was delayed despite it being a beautifully sunny day, because, strangely, the wicket had been watered. When he saw it, Woolmer's face changed colour as dramatically as the wicket had. We got 316 but leaked singles in the field and Pakistan cruised home in 48 overs.

Ganguly had copped another over-rate ban, so Dravid was in charge for my last two games. It was fitting, since his stint at Kent was really when the Indian seed was planted. Now I was on my way out and he, I felt sure, was going on to even greater things. Before the fifth ODI in Kanpur I wrote: 'If there was any justice in this sporting world, Rahul would get runs and India would win.' Well, Rahul got 86, but Pakistan's Shahid Afridi went berserk, as he's made a habit of doing lately, smashing 102 off 46 balls. Victory and justice sailed out of the ground like one of Afridi's sixes.

My official farewell took place at a team dinner the night before the Delhi game. Dalmiya was there, along with some senior BCCI officials, but Ganguly couldn't make it because he was banned, and neither was Andrew Leipus, who had quit after the tour of Bangladesh. The players gave me three boxes of hand-cut crystal they'd had custom-made in Jaipur, and the presentation left me feeling as fragile as the crystal.

I'd already said some goodbyes — to the players who hadn't been required for the ODIs and those who'd been dropped in the middle of the one-day series. We'd spent so much time together that we were like a family. And, just like a family, they were a source of joy and fulfilment, but sometimes they drove me crazy.

We had to win at Ferozshah Kotla to square the series, but when Dravid and I looked at the pitch, it was obvious that the side winning the toss would have a big advantage. You never like to think that way, but in reality that's often the way it works. We lost the toss and the game, and that was that. They got 303, we got 144 in 37 overs. Afterwards, Woolmer described the wicket as a beach.

At the end of my press conference the media gave me a round of applause, which was nice of them considering that I hadn't exactly been a headline-a-day man. And at the presentation ceremony after the game, the BCCI gave me an unusual-looking ornament. It's hard to look happy when you've just lost a one-day series and I didn't really come close in the official photograph, but that was partly because I was trying to work out exactly what I'd been given.

After Pakistan had pulled one back in Jamshedpur, and we were 2–1 up with three to play, I had a few beers with Woolmer. 'There are no happy endings, John,' he said. 'There wasn't for me with South Africa and there won't be for you here.'

THE CONE MAN

Before the NatWest final at Lord's in 2002 I ran into Sir Tim Rice, the celebrated lyricist, who was then President of the MCC. He introduced me to his secretary as the coach of the Indian cricket team. When she asked him what I actually did, he told her, 'He's the man who puts the cones out, then brings them in again just before play starts.'

I've heard even less flattering definitions of the cricket coach's role. It would seem that the cricket community — players, commentators, fans and administrators — can't agree on what a coach does, let alone what makes a good one. If you put the secretary's question to Bob Simpson, John Buchanan and Duncan Fletcher, you'd probably get three different answers. Simpson has said that a coach's role is to teach the batsmen to get more runs, the bowlers to take more wickets, and the fielders to take more catches and save more runs. In a speech in Bangalore, Buchanan said a coach takes a team and an individual somewhere they haven't been before. Fletcher described himself as a consultant to the team. On any given day, my to-do list might have included finding a whiteboard for a team meeting and analysing Anil Kumble's run-up on a computer.

Coaching had always interested me and I knew I'd regret it if I didn't have a crack. I suppose I thought that having played test cricket for 15 years, and seen and experienced pretty much everything the game can throw at you, it would come naturally. I enjoyed leadership and teaching and had read widely on the subject, much of it from America, where coaching has a long history and the coach is king. I'd had time away from the game in which to reflect and get another perspective. With the benefit of hindsight and detachment I'd gained a deeper understanding of myself as a player: what I'd done well and what I could've done better. Last, but by no means least, I envied people who were able earn a living by coaching.

Nine years of coaching in England and India has left me greyer and, I hope, wiser. Coaching is a bit like captaincy in that the more you do, the more you learn and, providing the fire still burns, the better you become. In India, I started a process that my successor is continuing. I look at it as a massive sculpture that will take years to complete and is beyond the capacity of a single person; I chipped away for four and a half years, and now Greg Chappell is continuing the work. His approach may be different, but the ultimate goal is the same. If I proved anything at all, it was that a foreign coach could survive and achieve results.

At Kent, I was told by various people at various times that I was too tough on the players — particularly the young batsmen — put too much emphasis on fitness, didn't have much time for fast bowlers and lazy trainers, and overdid practice both in terms of frequency and duration. In India, I was accused of being too soft on the players and too close to them, of not knowing enough about the game and of not being able to speak Hindi. I'll plead guilty to that last charge.

An ex-convenor of selectors said publicly that I'd 'achieved nothing that we Indians couldn't have done ourselves'. After I'd left, Ashok Malhotra, who was on the first selection panel I worked with, said, 'Everybody says John Wright did a good job, but what exactly did he do? In five years he couldn't rectify Sourav Ganguly's problem with the short-pitched delivery.' Kapil Dev went on TV to say it was a pity 'that despite India having coaches of the calibre of Sandeep Patil, we have to import the likes of John Wright'. I grew on Dilip Vengsarkar, who was initially unenthusiastic, but after we made the World Cup final wrote, 'I feel John Wright has done a tremendous job. He has been a thorough professional and earned the respect of the team.'

Becoming a good coach takes time, but while you're learning on the job, your employers, the fans and the sponsors are demanding results. The pressure can turn you inside out, but you've got to stay true to yourself and your values. I was tested in India, particularly early on, when no one thought I'd survive and some people didn't want me to. I was tested when I sought to do things differently but didn't have the clout to get my way. And, of course, every loss is a test. There were times when I felt like packing up and going home because it seemed as if I were trying to shift an immovable object or there was a danger that my values would be compromised.

In simple terms, I saw my job as working alongside the players to help them improve their performances, both individually and collectively. A coach has to form a relationship with the team as a whole, and with the individuals within it, and that can be an interesting balancing act. Sometimes you get the balance wrong and overdo the team talks at the expense of one-on-one communication.

You get along better with some players than others, and of course it's easier to communicate with and coach those in the first category. While I found talking to the team to be the easiest part of the communication cycle, I believe one-on-one dealings are more valuable. There's nothing more satisfying than spending extra time with a player, whether that involves throw-downs in the nets or a quiet chat, and then seeing it reflected in his performance. If you can get on the wavelength of every individual in your squad — a big if — you're doing a good job.

In Durban, during our build-up to the World Cup, I went into a sandwich bar not far from our hotel. It wasn't flash, but the sign outside promised fresh sandwiches, which was what I felt like. I asked the old coloured lady for a tomato sandwich. She said they didn't do tomato sandwiches. The filling options were listed on the menu board behind her: tomato and cheese, tomato and ham, tomato and beef. I said, 'But you do tomato and cheese?' 'Yes,' she said, 'but we don't do tomato.' 'Tell you what,' I said, 'could you make me a tomato and cheese sandwich without the cheese?' 'Certainly,' she said. 'White or brown bread?'

As my father used to say, you can lead a horse to water but you can't make it drink. Coaching is about helping the player find his own solutions: he needs to buy into the change. People will resist change if they don't think it will deliver a benefit, so the key is to steer them to a point where they can see it will be good for them. And if you can persuade them that it was really their idea in the first place, they'll embrace it all the more readily.

At an India A camp, I noticed that Lakshmipathy Balaji had a problem with his front foot in the delivery stride. Instead of pointing straight down the wicket when it landed, it splayed towards cover, so that he opened up and fell away as he released the ball. I asked him how far he wanted to go in the game; he said he wanted to play for India 'with all my heart'. I explained that it would be very difficult for him to reach that goal if he didn't sort out his foot placement. Next time I saw him, it was fine. It's not easy for a bowler to change his foot placement, so it must have taken him hours and hours of practice, but he'd embraced the idea. Six months later, his bowling was a key factor in our success in Pakistan.

Three days before the start of the series in Pakistan, the umpires, David Shepherd and Simon Taufel, warned me that Irfan Pathan had a problem with running on the wicket. He'd got by in the ODIs, but if he did it in the tests, he'd get himself, and us, into trouble. At practice the next day I spelt it out for him, explaining that if he couldn't kick the habit pronto, he wouldn't be playing, and in fact he might as well go back to India. Forty minutes later the problem was fixed. When the umpires came to our nets the next morning they looked at me as if I were a genius. I told them Irfan had fixed it himself; my contribution had been to tell him he'd be going home if he didn't. Because many Indians learn the game by watching and copying, rather than through formal instruction, it tends to make them more flexible and adaptable.

Everything I read about coaching and mentoring stressed the importance of asking questions and listening with empathy, and I often found that the critical decision was whether to give an instruction or ask a question. Do you yell, 'Watch the bloody ball' or ask, 'Do you think you're watching the ball?' In my view, the question is much the better option. It makes players think their way through the problem, even if they don't always arrive at the correct solution. You also need to anticipate the reply. Asking the team early on whether they thought a 10 km run was a good idea wouldn't have increased their respect for my coaching ability or intelligence.

Young batsmen who'd just come into the squad would ask me, 'What do you think?', as if they expected me to give them a grade or a mark out of ten. I'd often turn it around, asking them what they thought, because their judgement of their own performance was more important than mine. If I noticed a technical problem — for instance, if I thought a batsman's head was falling over and he was struggling to play through the leg side — I'd ask him if he was happy with his balance. On the other hand, if the problem was sloppiness or lack of effort, I was more likely to bark than inquire gently. The trick was, firstly, in knowing which approach was appropriate to the situation and, secondly, asking the right question or giving a clear and consistent instruction.

The area I never really mastered was what Sandy Gordon termed 'emotional control'. I tended to live every ball. It mightn't have appeared that way on TV because I was able to maintain a deadpan exterior — I was once called 'a slab of granite', although that might have referred to my personality and/or intellect — but you can't fool those close to you. As Harbhajan Singh said, 'John, you always whistle when you're nervous.'

Watching what's going on out in the middle but being unable to influence it can push you into a strange mental space and make you nervous, angry and frustrated. The only way of avoiding that is to let go and let the players get on with it. As the coach, your role is often to challenge the team and individuals, but adding to the pressure on them with your demeanour or behaviour in response to what's happening on the field can do more harm than good. You're nearly always better off exuding relaxed confidence, almost nonchalance, as if whatever the minor setbacks you might be currently experiencing, the big-picture strategy is intact and on course.

It's not easy to do when every fibre of your being is straining with desire to win the bloody game, especially when things aren't going well. One of the greatest challenges I faced was to instil hunger and desire and intensity in players while not displaying those things myself. I felt much more in control of my destiny when I had a bat in my hands and was striving to make a difference and a contribution with my performance. And when the batsman can no longer influence proceedings, i.e. when he's out, and he's over the disappointment, he can switch off and read a paper. The coach can't.

It's tough, but as the saying goes, 'Out-of-control emotions can make smart people stupid'. It's also the case that old-school coaching methods and philosophies which incorporated a strong emotional focus and appeals to emotion are being challenged by new approaches that stress emotional control, if not detachment, and the need for clear minds. One isn't necessarily superior to the other, but the current generation of players don't seem to expect their coaches to live every ball and don't seem to respond to an environment with a high emotional content.

Looking back on my cricketing journey, I'm increasingly of the view that some of the most valuable knowledge you acquire as a player comes from your peers. When I first played for New Zealand, we didn't have a coach; we learned from each other and the opposition. Playing for Derbyshire against Leicestershire, who had a formidable spin attack, I scratched around for what seemed an eternity for an undistinguished 44. I hate to think what the paying spectators made of it. Over a pint that evening, I was telling the Leicestershire and former England captain Ray Illingworth that I'd made a bloody fool of myself, as if he didn't know. 'Aye, lad,' he said, 'you've got a way to go, but out in the middle is the best place to learn.' In Australia in 1980/81 I spent a lot of time in the Aussie dressing room drinking beer with Dennis Lillee and his mates, and listening to the great fast bowler describe in detail how he analysed opening batsmen and what weaknesses he looked for.

There's not as much interaction between teams as there used to be, which is a pity in a number of ways. In my day, spending a few hours in the Australian changing room was a guarantee of a hangover, but some of the knowledge I picked up in those convivial sessions was priceless.

I encouraged the players to coach each other and to seek advice from people with the proverbial runs on the board. For any young player wanting to learn more about batting, asking Sachin Tendulkar or Rahul Dravid wasn't a bad place to start. Ian Chappell and Mark Taylor have demonstrated that they know a thing or two about captaincy. Ian Healy was happy to help Parthiv Patel. Whatever you might think about the guys on the commentary circuit as commentators, the fact is that most of them have played and watched a lot of cricket at the top level. I've got no time for coaches who seek to reinforce their authority by restricting their players' access to information, and I encouraged my players to consult anyone whom they thought could be of assistance. No one knows everything. The only proviso is that you shouldn't accept advice indiscriminately because it won't all be equally valuable and some will be counterproductive if not downright loopy — like the suggestion once made to me that I should bat two metres out of my crease when facing Jeff Thomson.

One of the big changes since my playing days is the use of computer technology. Now that all international cricket is televised, coaches and support staff are able to do a huge amount of analysis. In fact, there's so much information out there that the challenge is to separate the wheat from the chaff, because there's no value in overloading your players with mindless information. There were a couple of dictums I liked to keep in mind when confronted by a mountain of analysis: 'Instinct is swifter and more accurate' and 'Simplicity is wisdom'.

Cricket starts with the guy who's got the ball in his hand. How and where he bowls the ball goes a long way to determining what happens next. Our research will have told us where an opposition batsman scores most of his runs and what types of deliveries he might be uncomfortable with, but it's no good having that information if you don't act on it by bowling the ball in the right place. Planning and analysis gives you a starting point but not necessarily much more than that, because good players adjust, great players dictate, and the captain and team have to read the situation and make tactical changes as and when they're needed.

A good reader of the game will spot weaknesses and strengths from the grandstand within a few overs. It didn't take an extraordinary level of technical expertise, or days of video analysis, to figure out that early in his innings Justin Langer wasn't entirely comfortable against Ajit Agarkar's inswing. We got him that way a couple of times, but he still made plenty of runs against us because any successful international batsman is acutely aware of his weaknesses and takes measures to prevent the opposition from exploiting them. Successful international batsmen also have plenty of strengths which the bowling team, for their part, have to combat.

Technology can confirm your hunches and enable you to test your ideas. A large part of any cricket match is spent waiting for the bowler to deliver the next ball; so the video editing machines allow you to watch a lot of cricket in a short space of time and from every conceivable angle. The most valuable attribute of the technology can be summed up in the phrase 'seeing is believing'. The first time I saw myself bat in a TV highlights package I felt like retiring on the spot. I looked awkward and unnatural, a far cry from the poetry in motion I yearned to be. You can watch yourself when you're in peak form and when you're in a trough, and compare the two. What's changed? What's missing? A coach can sit down with a player and help him find the solution to his problem (although the good ones tend to do it on their own). It might be glaringly obvious or it might be subtle, or there might be nothing whatsoever wrong with the batsman's technique and his lack of runs might be a result of what's going on — or not going on — in his head.

To sustain improvement you have to measure performance, and we measured various performance targets and factors in bowling, batting and fielding. Fielders were assessed individually in terms of runs saved and runs conceded. Mohammad Kaif and Yuvraj Singh were nearly always in credit. These assessments often met with protests from those who didn't emerge in a good light, and the more experienced the player, the louder the protest. But seeing is believing, and if the rest of the team is seeing and believing, you haven't got a leg to stand on.

The danger of technology-driven analysis is that you can slip into the mindset of focusing on the opposition and what they do, rather than on what you have to do. To win you have to have your own house in order. The legendary American college basketball coach John Wooden didn't bother scouting the opposition. He concentrated on preparing his own team so meticulously that it didn't matter what the opposition came up with. I certainly embraced the new technology, but if I coach again, I'll reassess how, and how much, I should use it.

Whenever a journalist asked me for a self-evaluation, I told them to judge me on the results. I always coached to win and expected my players to play to win. My ears prick up whenever I hear a captain or a coach saying something along the lines of, 'It's going to take time and we may have to lose a few before we win a lot'. Of course you have to look at the bigger picture, but I dislike that approach and the diminished expectations that it's trying to create. At international level, you're representing your people and your country, and they're entitled to expect you to be doing your utmost to win every game. After one defeat an Indian fan said, 'Coach, you can't lose the next match — my little boy cried for three hours last night.' After we'd won in Pakistan, I was the best coach in the world, according to the Indian newspapers. (I kept those issues.) A year later when we drew the test series and lost the ODIs, I was back in the pack.

A young Pakistani net bowler said to me: 'Coach, winning doesn't matter, it's the struggle that counts.' He was right in the sense that the struggle teaches some of life's most valuable lessons and forces us to confront our fears, doubts and insecurities. But why do you embark on the struggle in the first place? Because you want to succeed; you want to win. If the result doesn't matter, then why bother struggling? To say that winning isn't important is to diminish the effort and heartache that goes into getting there. Your toughest opponent is always yourself, and a large part of the struggle involves fighting internal battles which, if won, can provide some of the sweetest victories of all.

The paradox of sport is that your chances of getting the desired result increase when you stop focusing on the outcome. Winning is a process. If you worry about the result while you're in the contest, it will impact on your performance. Again, this is easier said than done. The key is to focus your attention and effort on what you can control, starting with the way you live, prepare and practise. Attitudes are habits of thought; creating successful habits as individuals and as a team is a big step towards achieving a successful outcome, whether that's a century, or a five-wicket bag, or an innings victory.

As Sandy Gordon says, the main reason why climbers fail to reach the summit is that they start thinking about reaching the summit, which takes their mind off the pressing matter of where their hands and feet need to go next. To make a big score you have to negotiate ball after ball for over after over and session after session. You have to stay in the present and stick with your method and plan and mindset. After you've passed a few road signs pointing the way to your destination, confidence and self-assurance increase and your performance takes on a momentum and rhythm of its own.

What applies to the individual, applies to the team. As a group you're trying to establish a culture of success, which begins with establishing good habits of behaviour and good attitudes towards everything you do as a team, whether that's practice, punctuality, fitness, or going to one of those functions that no one wants to go to but are part of the deal. Creating that sense of being a team often requires individuals to do things they'd prefer not to do, but being prepared to sacrifice for the larger cause is the essence of team spirit.

In this context, team discipline is critical. You're on the slippery slope when players start to do what they like whenever they feel like it, with no regard to the team's situation and requirements. I had no time for players with those attitudes, and even less for selectors who couldn't or wouldn't understand how those players compromised the team and harmed performance. I wanted a say in selection solely to be able to hammer home the message when a poor performance on the park was clearly the consequence of bad attitudes and sloppy behaviour off it.

If you take a short cut or the easy track, it will show — and sooner rather than later. If a team is dropping catches, you can bet your life they're not doing enough catching at practice. If individuals are lazy in the field, team spirit may be the issue. Good fielding requires selflessness, because it seldom gets the recognition it deserves. Who gets the credit when a fieldsman turns four into three through lung-busting effort and the batsman who shouldn't have been facing is dismissed next ball? It's rarely the fielder. When you see fielders consistently choosing not to make that extra effort, you have to wonder about their commitment to the team.

Cricket is unusual, if not unique, in that it's a team game made up of many individual performances. The fact that each individual's contribution is precisely measured reinforces the dichotomy. This can create tension, in that players need to be self-focused and motivated by individual goals in order to excel in their individual roles but also have to be able to put individual aspirations aside, pull their heads in and become good team men. It's what makes cricket coaching so challenging — like herding cats, as someone once described it. Your most valuable performers are sometimes the most difficult personalities because of their relentless drive to excel. Managing the needs and demands of the individual performer within the wider team context is the coach's constant challenge; it can be a rewarding process, but it can be a pain in the neck.

I had my non-negotiables: punctuality, honesty, intensity at practice. The rules were simple and clear; they applied to everyone from the global superstar to the teenaged debutant, and could be understood and adhered to by a graduate or a dropout. What inhibited performance and stopped us from being as good as we were capable of being were off-field issues of behaviour and attitude. It was no coincidence that the true champions were never the source of the problem. Tendulkar was never late onto the bus. He was once a bit slow out for warm-ups and I pointed that out to him in front of the team. He wouldn't have enjoyed that, but he would have expected it because, as a leader within the group, he understood that the minute you step back from universal application of your team rules and protocols, you're just paying lip service to them.

Leadership derives from performance and example. If you don't deliver those things, people will stop listening. You can make as many fine speeches as you like, but you'll be operating on the law of diminishing returns. Ganguly and I were fortunate to have a group of outstanding leaders — Dravid, Tendulkar, Kumble, Javagal Srinath and V.V.S. Laxman — who set an example of honesty, integrity and commitment. There were many times when I marvelled at their qualities and was humbled by their maturity and wisdom.

Among the younger players, Harbhajan grasped what I was trying to bring to the team. If I climbed into someone, he'd tell them not to take it personally, that I'd only 'fired' them because I felt their misdemeanour might harm the team. That's not to say we didn't have our moments. The saying 'if looks could kill' could have been coined to describe Harbhajan's reaction to being demoted in the batting order. When one of his extravagant cameos came to an all-too-predictable end, I met him at the changing room door and told him that after a shot like that, he could stay outside.

During my last season Sehwag said to me, 'John, you can say things to us that one of us cannot. If you speak your mind and upset someone, he can take it to his heart and it can remain with him for a long time. We have strong likes and dislikes.'

The team and I had to get used to each other. Even after a stern chat it was important that you could go and have a cup of tea or a drink with them. It's a fine line, but it should never get personal. Sometimes that can be difficult, particularly for a player who feels hard done by. The key is honesty. Once any member of the team felt there was an inconsistency in your behaviour or honesty, you ran the risk of losing his respect.

A good coach will make a difference to any team, but as a rule good coaches have good players. In terms of what's needed to be successful at international level, I believe that accurate selection is more important than coaching. It starts with choosing the right captain.

The captain is the most important person in the organisation. Captaincy is more significant in cricket than it is in almost any other sport for a host of reasons, the most obvious being the need to react tactically to variations in playing conditions. I've yet to see a great cricket team without an outstanding captain, no matter who the coach is. A team can overcome having a poor coach, because once the game is under way, his ability to influence proceedings is limited. However, if they're saddled with a poor captain, that will be reflected in virtually everything that happens on the field. The coach's role is to teach and mentor the skipper, and provide him with the information he needs to do his job, which is to lead the side. The coach can do so much and no more, because the captain must feel free to do it his way, to trust his knowledge and back his hunches.

Obviously, tactical nous is critical. It's not hard to spot a good tactician: they're the captains who are always ahead of the game, who see situations developing and anticipate opportunities. A minor adjustment to the field can win a game. The coach might think mid-on should be three metres wider rather than five metres deeper, but the captain's making the call in the heat of battle rather than in a team meeting or on a computer screen.

Even though I sometimes disagreed with Ganguly's choices, I respected the captain's right to choose. I figured that if I couldn't talk him around to my point of view, then either my communication skills weren't up to it or my case wasn't strong enough. If it turns out that the captain's decision to ignore your advice costs you the match, then you can only hope that he listens to you a little more carefully next time.

The players take a keen interest in the captain-coach relationship because it's critical for them that their leaders form a compatible, rather than a combustible, combination. But no matter how well they get on, there will be times when they disagree, when their thinking is poles apart, and when they question each other's judgement or lack of it.

When a team underperforms over a period of time and there's little basis for believing that their fortunes are going to improve, they've reached the point in the sporting cycle at which someone's got to go. Whether it's the captain or the coach often depends on who's been in the job longer. However, the one who survives does so in the shadow of the axe, because if results don't improve, his neck will be next on the block.

Captains and coaches feel defeats and victories more intensely than players because they carry more responsibility and the result goes down on their records. When the team wins, they're like best mates from way back, but losses test the relationship and their resolve to support each other through thick and thin.

My relationship with Ganguly was the subject of as much media speculation and gossip as a Bollywood marriage. And like any marriage there was a honeymoon period, then reality set in and we settled down for the long haul. We had our moments, and sometimes we saw cricket from totally different perspectives, but we stayed the course. I hope when Sourav looks back on our partnership, he feels he had the freedom to captain the team his way.

Coaches have different methods and criteria for evaluating players. I looked for two characteristics: firstly, hunger, or what I call 'want', and secondly, presence. It's difficult to coach want, and presence is almost indefinable. When I met a player I asked myself, 'Would this guy win you a game? Would he get you home when the cause seems lost?' If the answer's 'yes', that's presence.

Obviously these qualities aren't always evident at first sight. The old method of looking them straight in the eye can be useful, as can observing their reaction to a couple of provocative questions. I liked to watch how they trained, how busy they were at practice, how quickly they packed up their gear after a loss. These little things add up, but none are definitive and sometimes they can deceive. The only unqualified evidence is how they respond when the pressure comes on out in the middle.

When I met Irfan Pathan, he was just a kid; young, keen, still developing and underrated by his peers. But there was something about him that told you he'd find a way to get you home. I wouldn't pick a fight with him. It annoyed me when pundits questioned whether Dravid was aggressive enough or tough enough to lead, as if his perfect manners off the field reflected the qualities he brought to the contest. Toughness is on the inside; it's what you're made of, not what you display. Anyone can walk with a swagger or turn their collar up.

When I was looking for an overseas player for Kent, I rang old Aussie mates like Allan Border, David Boon, Geoff Marsh and Bob Simpson, and ran the candidates by them. They said the same thing about all of them: 'He's a good player.' I'd tell them I could read averages too; I wanted to know what he was really like. I was waiting for one of two answers: soft or hard. Having pretty much settled on Andrew Symonds, I rang him and asked, 'How much do you want to play for Australia?' 'I'd give my left bollock,' he replied. I told him that if he came to Kent, he mightn't have to do that. Neither Dravid nor Symonds came to Kent for the money, which wasn't spectacular. They came because they were hungry for success and wanted to become better cricketers.

The first time I played against Ian Healy, he didn't look too flash. When I said that to his coach, Bob Simpson, he admitted that Healy had a bit to learn, but added, 'I'll tell you one thing about Ian Healy: if you were in a bar and a fight broke out, you'd want him right next to you'. When we lost a series in the West Indies that we should've drawn, I had some private conversations with individual players to try to get a handle on why we couldn't seem to win outside India. 'We don't fight enough,' one player said. 'Who doesn't?'

I asked. He named names; they were exactly the same names as I had on my list.

Talent and skill are obviously hugely important as well, but a player who lacks that fighting quality will struggle to do justice to his talent and skill at the top level. The champions have both in abundance, as well as the ability to get it all out when it counts. The guys you could never write off are the ones who have technical flaws or less ability, but possess a very sound temperament. You never know how far they might go. The other side of the fence — talent without character — is a crowded place. I've seen plenty of net practice hotshots who thrashed it like Viv Richards or whizzed it past some poor sod's nose from 19 yards but who went missing in action come game time. I signed a few of them at Kent: 'A poor investment for no return,' as the club treasurer used to say. These were the guys who'd hurt their little fingers in warm-ups half an hour before the game and declare themselves unfit to play, or who'd turn greener than the wicket they'd just inspected, scurry back to their hotel rooms and not be sighted for five days.

As coach I tried to give the players direction and quiet leadership in a supportive environment and let them get on with it. Sometimes you have to be out front, for instance, when the players need reminding of the principles and goals they've committed to, or after a heavy defeat when they need time and space to lick their wounds but the fans and media are demanding answers. But ideally coaching is done in the background. Where I live, the warm nor'wester is the bonfire wind. You light a few little fires at the back and the wind does the rest. I saw my job as starting the fire. When my players caught fire together and blazed in the same direction, they could burn anyone down.

One of my favourite passages in cricket literature comes from *Matters of Choice* by John Benaud, an account of Ian Chappell's 1972/73 Australian team that toured the West Indies undefeated. Ian Redpath described them as 'a team of desperates' for whom the only thing better than having a good time was winning. In an after-dinner speech following the tour, the leg spinner Kerry

O'Keeffe tried to put his finger on what made them such a successful team:

'I just don't know how we won. We got liquored up at the pool every day. We slogged their medium pacers every game. I bowled them out, which was a total shock to everybody. We had a captain who thought P and R were two letters late in the alphabet.

'We had two openers who looked like Laurel and Hardy, and played like them. Two weeks into the tour Greg Chappell could have played for either side, with his golliwog hair. We had a middle-order player in [Doug] Walters who was nicotine-riddled and alcoholic. We had a poofy middle-order player in [Ross] Edwards who strummed a guitar and wrote sort of gay songs. We had a wicketkeeper [Rod Marsh] who was eight hamburgers over par. Jeff Hammond was called 'Crayfish' because he was all arms and legs, and had shit for brains. Dennis Lillee was touted as a sex symbol — he's bald, with false teeth and an IQ around his bowling average. Bob Massie was in hospital with food poisoning. He was discharged and found by a keg two hours later. And we won. I can't believe it.'

This was legendary broadcaster Alan McGilvray's slightly more sedate take: 'I travelled with teams from Bradman on and never saw a team that had more discipline, more unity, more desire. They were real Australians, those fellows.'

And as salty old Ian Chappell would be very quick to point out, there wasn't a coach in sight.

Don't Dream It's Over

My trolley was laden with four practice kit bags, a suitcase and a guitar case. When I got to the baggage compartment at Ashford station, a conductor looked me and my load over. 'Rolling Stones, are we?' he said.

Well, there was the guitar case, and Mick Jagger had been knighted the previous weekend. And perhaps he thought I wouldn't have looked out of place in the Strolling Bones.

I explained who I was. 'Used to play a bit then?' he asked. I nodded. 'So what's your name?' I told him; it didn't ring a bell. 'Who'd you play with?'

'Hadlee, Howarth, that lot.'

'Oh yeah, I've heard of them.' That was enough about me. 'I used to love cricket,' he said. 'I wrote to Nottinghamshire for a trial once. They invited me up but I didn't go. I thought, what am I going to do for a job?' After a pause, he added, 'I wish I'd gone — just for the experience'.

With India, I'm glad I went. Coaching India was the most challenging and exciting experience of my life and I wouldn't have missed it for the world.

No one thought having a foreign coach would work. There would be too much culture shock: the language barrier, the seniority system within the team, the regional rivalries and jealousies, the politics . . . The list went on and on. In the beginning I thought about learning Hindi, but it hardly seemed worthwhile when the conventional wisdom was that I wouldn't last three months. In fact, language was more of an issue with taxi drivers than the team. When the boys got excited, team meetings would suddenly switch to Hindi; I'd let it run because I wanted to encourage discussion and, when they'd had a decent go at it, ask them what the hell that was all about. And having a bit of a knack for languages, I picked it up as I went along. By the time I finished, my Hindi vocabulary consisted of *chalo* (let's go) *jaldi* (quickly) and *A.C. bund* (air conditioning off). But my pronunciation was impeccable.

When I went to India, I didn't see the barriers; all I saw was a bunch of talented cricketers and all I thought about was trying to help them win cricket matches. If there's such a thing as caring too much, I was probably guilty of that. I shared the players' joy and I bled for them. Matthew Hayden once asked me, 'Have they driven you mad yet?' 'No,' I said, 'but they're winning.'

After a bad day, I'd watch baseball from the US. There'd be a winner and a loser, and I'd think, well, I'm not the only coach who's taken a beating today. Someone else had the same set of problems and the same range of emotions. It helped me to put it in perspective and get up and go again the next morning.

All teams are works in progress, although not necessarily in the right direction. I'd like to think I helped India to go forward. There were a lot of things I wanted done differently, but I didn't have the clout to make it happen so I had to live with them. I suppose I had the confidence — or naiveté — to believe that I'd find a way to get around whatever obstacles were in my path.

The players emerged from the shadow of match fixing and took some very big strides. They competed with the best and began to win away from home. They became a true team. They lived up to their themes to 'be the first' and 'change the trend'. When I started, I was told that changing things in Indian cricket would be very difficult. This team disproved that view and the consequences of their ability to change may be far-reaching and momentous.

One of the keys to our progress was the fact that there were two distinct generations within the team. The older generation led; the younger generation sparked. The older guys were great role models, but the experience they had as young players in the Indian team was very different from that of the guys who came in after the 1999 World Cup. From the outset, Sourav Ganguly, Rahul Dravid, Sachin Tendulkar, Anil Kumble and Javagal Srinath supported me and my push for change, and they backed me and Andrew Leipus when there were moves to get rid of us.

Ganguly and I were lucky to have a cadre of senior players who were leaders, and one of my last jobs was to start the process of replicating that leadership group in Generation Next. When one or two of the younger guys were having prima donna moments in Bangladesh in 2004, I gathered that group together and challenged them to match the example set by the team leaders of the older generation. There are definitely leaders-in-waiting amongst them. As we were drifting towards the rocks at the 2004 Asia Cup, Mohammad Kaif sent me a lucid and thoughtful six-page letter outlining where we were going wrong. And the coach didn't get off scot-free either.

The big difference between the generations is that the younger guys, the likes of Harbhajan Singh, Virender Sehwag, Yuvraj Singh, Kaif, Mahendra Singh Dhoni, Parthiv Patel and Irfan Pathan, are worldlier, more confident, more savvy and much more assertive of their national identity. They were proud of who they were and where they came from and didn't mind showing it. Sometimes they could almost be too arrogant, but better to err on the side of pride than diffidence. They wanted to be themselves and express themselves. They were the new-aged kids who'd travelled the world. Went to the Under-19 World Cup and won it. That meant more discipline issues, but I loved their attitude. They were happy to mix it and didn't take shit from anyone. They embody the confidence of the new India, a superpower in the making.

V.V.S. Laxman was the bridge between the generations. He had a foot in both camps and the youngsters loved and respected him.

No one ever had to pull them up for their public, off-field behaviour — they were wonderful ambassadors — but on the field they had mongrel. In some way, that's part of Ganguly's legacy, in that he gave the younger guys licence to bite and snarl and set a maverick and defiant tone. He didn't give a stuff about convention, other people's expectations, niceties or officialdom — especially match referees. He got heavily criticised and called all sorts of names, but it was water off a duck's back: he didn't stop being himself, for good or ill. I got irritated with him being constantly late for the toss against Australia in 2001 — but not half as irritated as Steve Waugh.

He and I were something new in Indian cricket: a foreign coach and a captain who wore his heart on his sleeve. On the face of it, we weren't a natural fit: I grew up on a Canterbury farm and, as a player, had a method based on doggedness and stickability; he's from a wealthy family, the Prince of Kolkata, and as they say in his hometown, only God could play the cover drive like Ganguly. It was never going to be all sweetness and light, but in the end the issues that divided us — and there were a few — were insubstantial compared to the cause in which we were united: to create a new team culture and give the most passionate cricket nation in the world the team they deserved.

I'll miss many things about India. Its everyday surprises, the smiles and the colours on the street. Despite my bad back, I'll miss the long bus journeys that enabled me to see more of the country. My favourite bus trip was from Kanpur to Lucknow late at night, through villages lined with people who'd waited in the dark for who knows how long to wave to their team as they swept past. If we'd won, the chatter would be loud and incessant; if we'd lost, the atmosphere would be subdued. Either way, there was a sense of togetherness as we rolled through the night, sealed off from the outside world. For a few hours, the stars were out over India and the team bus was a place of peace and warmth.

I'll miss the boys winding me up: 'So, coach, have you changed rooms yet?' I was single-minded in my need for an absolutely quiet hotel room and drove many a hotel manager to gibbering distraction. I didn't want to stay on a floor below the opposition because I believed we should always be above them and, besides, batsmen can practise their footwork and play shots in front of a mirror at any hour of the night. Other no-nos were being close to elevators, or the physio's room with the constant traffic in and out. And before we got there, I dreaded hearing the players saying that this hotel was noisy; they could sleep anywhere, at any time, so if they reckoned it was noisy, it was obviously utter bedlam.

The Landmark in Kanpur was unique among the hotels I've stayed at. The room had no windows, but did have red velvet curtains. You were provided with a torch in case the lights went out and, along with the Bible and the Bhagavad Gita, the bedside cabinet contained a cornucopia of pharmaceutical products: Disprins, Vicks Action 500, Ibuprofen, bronchospasmic tablets and digesic tablets. If you're ever going to wake up feeling off colour, the Landmark in Kanpur is the place to do it.

I'll miss the little reminders that I was the Indian coach: being greeted effusively by an Indian family while wandering anonymously around Singapore Airport; having a taxi driver tell me who deserved to be dropped; stepping into the corridor of an English hotel to find it stacked with mattresses because the players didn't like soft beds and would replace their mattresses with bed boards.

Touring India as a player was an amazing experience, but being part of the Indian team was almost like being an honorary citizen. I was very fortunate to be granted the privilege of coaching the team with the biggest following in world cricket and one of the biggest in team sport worldwide.

India hits you the moment you set foot there. It engages all your senses, but behind the clamour and bustle and colour and crush of humanity, there's a peace and serenity I haven't encountered elsewhere. India taught me many things. As a child I was often told that patience is a virtue, but I didn't really understand the meaning of that saying until I went to India.

I saw grace under pressure from people for whom everyday life is a struggle, if not an exercise in survival. The great Australian all-rounder Keith Miller put cricket in perspective by comparing it to his war-time experiences. 'I'll tell you what pressure is,' he said. 'Pressure is a Messerschmitt up your arse. Playing cricket is not.' What you see every day in India reminds you of how extraordinarily fortunate you are to be earning a handsome living from being involved in the game you love. However, you also see much that is admirable and uplifting: the emphasis on family, the humility, the spirituality, the grace and dignity in the face of hardship. These were people you wanted to do well for and who deserved a team which shed blood, sweat and tears.

Going to India is like coming home. It touches something in you, leaves a mark and you forget what it is until you go back. Then in an instant, suddenly that part of you comes alive again. Wherever I am and whatever I do, it will be reaching out to me, drawing me back.